Our Huckleberry Friend

JOHNNY MERCER

The Life, Times and Song Lyrics of

Our Huckleberry Friend

Collected and Edited by BOB BACH
and GINGER MERCER

Designed by Christopher Simon

*The three sections listing Johnny Mercer's songs and his song
contributions to movies and theatrical productions were
reviewed, updated and expanded by Dianne S. Thurman
with assistance from Lee Maltenfort.*

Cherokee Publishing Company
Atlanta, Georgia

Library of Congress Cataloging in Publication Data from the Original Publication

Mercer, Johnny, 1909–
    Johnny Mercer, the life, times and song lyrics of our huckleberry friend

    1. Music, Popular (Songs, etc.)–United States–
Texts   2. Mercer, Johnny, 1909–
3. Librettists–United States–Biography.
I. Bach, Bob   II. Mercer, Ginger.   III. Title
ML54.6.M4509   1982   784.5´05   82-10503

PHOTOS COURTESY OF:

Down Beat Magazine
Charlie Mann
Jules Davis
Frederick C. Baldwin
Bud Selzer
Capitol Records
NBC
Gjon Mili
Bill Durrence
Garrett-Howard Inc.
Seymour Rudolph
The Memory Shop, New York
The Archives Department, Georgia State University
and The Mercer family

Cartoon page 63 courtesy of *Playboy* Magazine
Cartoon page 123 courtesy of *Esquire* Magazine

This book is printed on acid-free paper which conforms to the American National Standard Z39.48-1984 *Permanence of Paper for Printed Library Materials*. Paper that conforms to this standard's requirements for pH, alkaline reserve and freedom from groundwood is anticipated to last several hundred years without significant deterioration under normal library use and storage conditions.

Published with permission from the children of Johnny and Ginger Mercer and the Johnny Mercer Foundation for the benefit of The Friends of Johnny Mercer.

Manufactured in the United States of America

ISBN: 978-0-87797-375-1

Index by Alexa Selph

Originally published by Citadel Press, a division of Lyle Stuart, Inc.
Additional material in this edition Copyright © 2009 by Cherokee Publishing Company.

Cherokee Publishing Company
P O Box 1730, Marietta, GA 30061

For Jean

Acknowledgements

Special thanks for help and guidance in the preparation of this book to Jean Bach, Marc Cramer, Walter Rivers, Marshall Robbins, Jim Mahar, Margaret Whiting, Maurice Levine, Dr. William Suttle, Dr. Leslie Hough, Geoff Parker, Bob Dinwiddie, the Department of Archives at Georgia State University, the American Society of Composers, Authors and Publishers, the American Guild of Authors and Composers, and our editor, Arthur Smith.

♪ ♪ ♪

A number of people have been very helpful in bringing this new edition to life. Among them are Dianne S. Thurman, Nancy Gerard, Lee Maltenfort, David Oppenheim, Steve Taksler, John Marshall, Laura Botts, Bill Hardesty, Peter Roberts, Caroline Hopkinson, Andy Norwood and Pamela Haury.

Contents

Contents

Savannah's Huckleberry Friend

John Herndon Mercer was born in Savannah, Georgia on November 18, 1909. At an early age Johnny exhibited a love of music—often slipping away to nearby parks to listen to local bands. He and his cousin, Walter Rivers, spent many hours at music stores on West Broad Street (now Martin Luther King, Jr. Blvd.) listening to gospel, jazz, and African-American folk music. His summers were spent at the Mercer summer home at Vernon View. Johnny and Walter would go down to the Pin Point Oyster and Crab Packing Factory to listen to the ladies singing gospel and folk tunes in their Geechee dialect as they worked.

After the family business failed in the late 1920's, Johnny and Walter stowed away on a boat to New York. Johnny wanted to become an actor. He worked as a Wall Street runner, wrote poetry, drew cartoons, and eventually wrote lyrics for *The Garrick Gaieties,* a popular music and comedy revue. It was here that he met his wife, Ginger.

Throughout his career, Johnny returned to his native Savannah to visit family and friends. His love for Savannah was evident throughout his life in his contributions to local charities and his willingness to offer his services to the city. In 1962 the Chatham County Commission renamed the Back River to Moon River in his honor.

Johnny enjoyed success as a lyricist, vocalist, and businessman. His lyrics are still loved today. He said to be a good lyrist, you should read, read, read. He included everything from comics to the classics. The works of Johnny Mercer are certainly classics. They have withstood the test of time. Many future generations will be able to enjoy the lyrics and music of Savannah's Huckleberry Friend.

Johnny Mercer died on June 25, 1976 and is buried in Savannah's famous Bonaventure Cemetery.

Jan-3-1926

JOHNNY MERCER *Capitol* RECORDS

Photos from the Mercer Family Collection,
Courtesy of Armstrong Atlantic State University

Top: Johnny Mercer, age 17, on the porch of his home at 236 East Gwinnett Street in Savannah, Georgia on January 3, 1926.
Bottom: Capitol Records Promo Picture

The Friends of Johnny Mercer

Chartered in 1994, The Friends of Johnny Mercer (FJM) is a group of Savannah area residents dedicated to perpetuating the lyrics, music, life, and memory of Savannah's native son, John Herndon Mercer. Johnny is our own cultural icon and treasure. Mercer enriched the annals of Tin Pin Alley for almost five decades and brightened the lives of millions. Mercer was a folk poet who eloquently told his "stories" in song—feeding the hearts and souls of those whose listened.

The mission of Friends of Johnny Mercer is multi-faceted. Currently underway is a program called "Accentuate the Positive" which involves taking the message to students in public and private schools by exposing them to the timeless lyrics and vocalizing of Johnny Mercer.

FJM organized a "Johnny Mercer Music Scholastic Award." We raise funds as an ongoing project for this yearly event, which benefits music students in the local school system. The individuals chosen by a special music committee can use the awarded monies towards their college expenses. A scholastic award of $1,000 is presented to a graduating high school student pursuing a career in music. Donations from individuals and corporations are encouraged for this project. Friends of Johnny Mercer received their 501 C-3 tax status as a non-profit organization in 2004. Donations to our scholastic award are now tax deductible.

Another goal of our organization is to establish a permanent exhibit in Savannah of Johnny Mercer's photographs, letters, personal memorabilia, sound recordings, radio performances, and television appearances for local residents, visitors and students to enjoy and study.

The Friends of Johnny Mercer also perpetuate the memory of Johnny's great songwriting talents by observing his November birthday each year with a Mercer musical program held at different locations in the Savannah area. *Please join our efforts.*

1909-1976

MOON RIVER STATION
Johnny Mercer Theater
November 18, 1996
Savannah, GA 31401

32 USA

JOHNNY MERCER

MOON RIV - ER

Legends of American Music Songwriters

Photo from the Mercer Family Collection, Courtesy of Armstrong Atlantic State University

Envelope from first day of issue of Johnny Mercer stamp

Membership Level

❏ Single $25.00   ❏ Family $30.00

Sponsorship Levels

*All sponsorship levels receive a complimentary
(one year) Family Membership.*

❏ *Laura*	$50-$99
❏ *Huckleberry Friend*	$100-$250
❏ *Skylark*	$251-$499
❏ *Charade*	$500-$999
❏ *Moon River*	$1,000-$4,999
❏ *Tangerine*	$5,000-$9,999
❏ *Dream* (Underwriter)	$10,000 and above

Title: _____ Last Name: _____

First Name: _____

Spouse's Name (for Family Membership): _____

Street Address: _____

City: _____ State: _____ Zip: _____

Home Phone: _____ Mobile/Business: _____

e-Mail Address: _____

The information provided above will only be used by our organization.

Friends of Johnny Mercer

www.friendsofjohnnymercer.com • 501 C-3 Organization

1 Oglethorpe Professional Boulevard, Suite 102 • Savannah, GA 31406

telephone 912-354-2262 • fax 912-354-3561

The Johnny Mercer Statue Fund

Reproduce Statue Form as Desired

Savannah's magnificent collection of statues honoring a wide range of famous people will be enhanced with the addition of a life-sized bronze of Mercer to be placed in a prominent location downtown.

The very talented local sculptor, Susie Chisholm, has been commissioned to execute the statute. She has completed the maquette and readied it for molding and casting at the foundry. Her award winning work is in numerous public and private collections and can be seen in galleries throughout the U. S. She currently has a studio in the Art Center in Historic Savannah's City Market where she can be seen working on her latest projects.

Your help is needed for Johnny to be memoralized by more than his lyrics and music. Contributions to this project are tax-deductible.

To donate, please make your check payable to: **FJM Statue Fund**. Mail to: 1 Oglethorpe Professional Blvd, Suite 102, Savannah, GA 31406. For more information, write to the address above, or email: dsthurman@bellsouth.net.

Sponsorship Levels for the FJM Statue Fund (501 C-3 Tax Deductible)

All sponsorship levels receive a complimentary (one year) Family Membership.

❏ **Laura**	$50-$99
❏ **Huckleberry Friend**	$100-$250
❏ **Skylark**	$251-$499
❏ **Charade**	$500-$999
❏ **Moon River**	$1,000-$4,999
❏ **Tangerine**	$5,000-$9,999
❏ **Dream** (*Underwriter*)	$10,000 and above

Name: _____

Address: _____

Address: _____

Phone Number: _____

e-Mail Address: _____

Donation Amount (if less than $50): _____

The information provided above will only be used by our organization.

FJM Statue Fund

1 Oglethorpe Professional Boulevard, Suite 102, Savannah, GA 31406

Georgia State University Library Popular Music Collection

Following Johnny Mercer's death, Ginger Mercer donated his personal papers to Georgia State University in Atlanta. The papers and other Mercer collections, which include manuscripts, photographs, draft music and lyrics, sheet music, sound recordings, oral histories, and awards, form the core of the Popular Music Collection in the Special Collections and Archives Department at Georgia State University Library. Any member of the public with identification may visit the Special Collections' Johnny Mercer Room for Research and Study during research hours to view the material (see **www.library.gsu.edu/spcoll** for hours and more information). Select items from the collection are on permanent display in the interactive exhibit, "Johnny Mercer: The Bard from Savannah," located in the Library's Information Commons and open during regular library hours (see **www.library.gsu.edu** for hours and directions).

404-413-2820 • 100 Decatur Street SE • Atlanta, GA 30303-3202

The Johnny Mercer Educational Archives

Please join over 1 million people from around the world who have discovered a website dedicated to the legacy of Johnny Mercer. A fitting tribute to America's greatest lyricist. **www.JohnnyMercer.com** features sheet music, audio samples, and personal anecdotes about Johnny from the people who knew him best. The site is maintained by Stephen Taksler, a big Johnny Mercer fan!

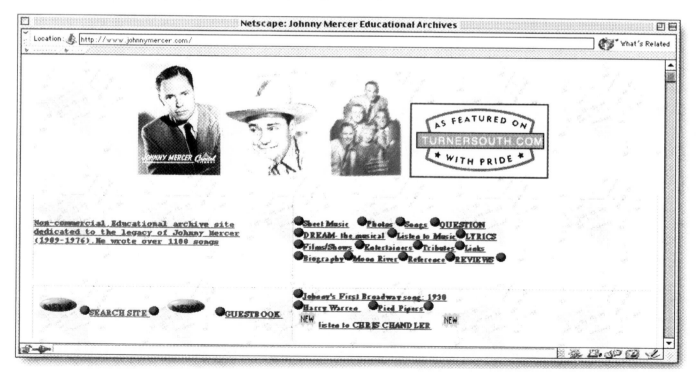

Non-commercial educational archive website dedicated to the legacy of Johnny Mercer (1909–1976)
www.JohnnyMercer.com

Georgia Music Hall of Fame

The mission of the Georgia Music Hall of Fame is to operate and maintain a music museum for the general public, Georgia music lovers, music scholars, and musical artists that celebrates our state's musical genius by: preserving Georgia's musical heritage; providing innovative museum exhibits and educational programs; becoming a public-private partnership for cultural preservation; and promoting a heritage tourism destination with growing economic benefits.

Johnny Mercer was inducted into the Georgia Music Hall of Fame in 1980. Among the permanent exhibits is the Jazz and Swing Club. The Jazz and Swing Club is reminiscent of a Savannah music club. The ragtime music of Tom Turpin and Nellie CoCroft, the jazz sounds of Fletcher Henderson, and the unforgettable songs of Johnny Mercer, Harry James, Lena Horne and Joe Williams are all found in this storefront building. Included in the archives are sound recordings, sheet music and personal correspondence of Johnny Mercer.

478-751-3334 • 200 Martin Luther King, Jr. Blvd. • Macon, GA 31201

www.georgiamusic.com

Armstrong Atlantic State University

The Mercer Family Collection is part of the Special Collection of Lane Library, Armstrong Atlantic State University and located in Savannah, Georgia. Nancy Mercer Keith Gerard, Johnny Mercer's niece, donated the core of the Collection to the University in 2006. Members of Friends of Johnny Mercer helped found the collection and have contributed to it, along with other members of the Mercer family. The Collection consists of photographs, letters and memorabilia of the Mercer family. At the heart of the collection is a small set of affectionate letters from Johnny to his parents, George Anderson Mercer and Lillian Cieucevich Mercer, dating from the 1930's-1950's. The letters have been used in Gene Lees' published biography of Mercer, *Portrait of Johnny*. The Collection also includes record albums and sheet music that recall popular music and the music industry from the 1920's through the 1970's.

912-344-3019 • 11935 Abercorn Street • Savannah, GA 31419-1997 • www.armstrong.edu

The Johnny Mercer Foundation

The Johnny Mercer Foundation and the preservation of American Popular Song is vital to the future of our children and our nation, our sense of pride in ourselves, and our understanding of one another. Our goal is to reflect Johnny's lifetime of generosity and to support, through his royalties and through private donations many of the causes he cared so deeply about where he realized a need for "accentuating the positive."

Our foundation's most passionate goal is to initiate a series of dynamic new fun, hands-on educational programs designed to introduce the songs of Mercer, and Berlin, and Gershwin, and Ellington and all our great American songwriters to our children. We are determined to convey to our kids that these songs belong to them. They're not their grandparents' songs. They are our musical heritage, and we are dedicated to helping children embrace them as their own. To that end we are proudly launching a series of special children's educational programs providing the study of American Popular Song to our elementary school system.

Our American Popular Song
Why is it so important?

Why is it so important to preserve our Great American Songbook? Because our songs – our music and lyrics are who we are! American popular songs reflect our passions, our diversities, our ideals. The American Popular song is our musical legacy. Our American dream is in the energy and the romance and the ethnic diversity of our music and lyrics. It's our songs that brought us together as a nation. From folk and country, to ragtime, jazz, and blues, to musical theatre—our songwriters, who came here from all over the world—brought with them the sounds and rhythms of their own roots, imbued them with the wonder and excitement of this new free world, and combined them with the sounds of their neighbors to ultimately create a multi-textured quilt that is uniquely ours; our tunes, our vocabulary, our Great American Songbook!

And yet today, our children are growing up having never heard the legacy of Stephen Foster, Jerome Kern, Irving Berlin, Duke Ellington, George Gershwin, Cole Porter, Johnny Mercer, Hoagy Carmichael, Richard Rogers, Lorenz Hart—children today know nothing of their musical heritage, and without it they can't know who they are as individuals and as a special part of a culturally rich tapestry.

If we lose these songs we lose our musical history, and our musical history is our collective soul.

The Johnny Mercer Foundation, through musical performances, media pressure, entertaining educational programs, and financial support, seeks to put the Great American Songbook back on the airwaves, in the schools, and in concert halls and theatres throughout the United States, and celebrated throughout the world.

Help us preserve your musical heritage by supporting the Foundation.

www.johnnymercerfoundation.com

Songwriters Hall of Fame

Songwriters Hall of Fame's ongoing mission is to celebrate and honor the contributions of our great popular music songwriters who have written the soundtrack for our nation's history, while developing new writing talent through workshops, showcases, scholarships and digital initiatives.

Established in 1969, the Songwriters Hall of Fame honors those whose work represents a spectrum of the most beloved songs from the world's popular music songbook. Songwriter Johnny Mercer and publishers Abe Olman and Howie Richmond who founded the organization wanted to shine the spotlight on the accomplishments of songwriters who have provided us with the words and music that form the soundtrack of our lives. Each year the Hall of Fame inducts a slate of songwriters voted on by the membership at an awards gala that has been recognized by the music industry and the media as the most important of the year. In this digital age, the Hall of Fame has put together an award-winning online museum to honor songwriters who have been inducted. This has become a leading destination for music industry professionals and researchers, along with popular music fans.

There are well over 300 inductees who make up the impressive roster inhabiting the Hall of Fame. Some include:

John Fogerty
Isaac Hayes and David Porter
Steve Cropper
Richard and Robert Sherman
Bill Withers
Carole King
Paul Simon
Bob Dylan
Billy Joel
Sir Elton John
Bernie Taupin
Brian Wilson
James Taylor
James Brown
Bruce Springsteen
Curtis Mayfield
Hal David and Burt Bacharach
Jim Croce
Phil Collins
Alan and Marilyn Bergman
Jimmy Webb
Van Morrison
Kris Kristofferson
Dolly Parton and
Cy Coleman
among many, many others.

For the last several years, the music industry focus every June has been on the "Songwriters Hall of Fame Week." During this special week culminating with the Annual Awards gala, the Hall of Fame sponsors other activities, one being the latest in the series of acclaimed "Master Class" events, in which songwriters the likes of Hal David and Jimmy Webb talk about their craft and answer questions posed by the audience. During the course of each year, the Hall of Fame hosts many special series, including the groundbreaking "Words About Music." This is part of an offering of conversations and music, providing a unique look at some of America's most admired songwriters, lyricists and composers.

The Hall of Fame not only celebrates these established songwriters, but is also devoted to the development of new songwriting talent through workshops, showcases and scholarships. There is an array of programs designed to teach up-and-coming songwriters the craft and business, while then giving them a platform upon which to shine. We host groups of seminars designed to offer our members an opportunity to interact with working songwriters about their experiences in the industry and their process of songwriting, thus providing new perspectives.

The Hall of Fame has specifically concentrated on digital initiatives, developing two distinct sides to our songhall.org website; both serving to combine an array of innovative features and a wealth of informational content. Those who go to the Virtual Museum will find it provides a much needed and comprehensive research tool. A full list of our esteemed inductees with over 250,000 records of

data and over 10,000 pages of content that include biographies, discographies, audio clips, photo galleries, timelines and recommended materials profiling their lives and their works can be accessed there. The other side of songhall.org is geared toward our membership and enhancing communications with the songwriting community. The Hall of Fame has taken great pride in laying the groundwork for the process of building a community with resources to assist our members in all aspects of the art and business of songwriting. This has become the premier go-to songwriter organization, whether it's to research history or plan the future.

Join us! Our mission is to remember and honor our great songwriters while building our musical future, and as Chairman/CEO and legendary lyricist Hal David has said, "Over the past four decades, the Songwriters Hall of Fame has come to represent the legacy of great popular songs in all of their richness and variety. They break down barriers and bring people from every walk of life and all corners of our world together, as one."

www.songwritershalloffame.org

Front and back of envelope from first day of issue of Johnny Mercer stamp

Academy Award Nominations for Johnny Mercer

Unless otherwise noted (**), a song written by Johnny Mercer was nominated for an Academy Award.

1938 (11th)	"Jeepers Creepers" from *Going Places*	**Music by** Harry Warren	**Lyrics by** Johnny Mercer
1940 (13th)	"I'd Know You Anywhere" from *You'll Find Out*	**Music by** Jimmy McHugh	**Lyrics by** Johnny Mercer
	"Love of My Life" *from Second Chorus*	**Music by** Artie Shaw	**Lyrics by** Johnny Mercer
1941 (14th)	"Blues in the Night" from *Blues in the Night*	**Music by** Harold Arlen	**Lyrics by** Johnny Mercer
1942 (15th)	"Dearly Beloved" from *You Were Never Lovelier*	**Music by** Jerome Kern	**Lyrics by** Johnny Mercer
1943 (16th)	"My Shining Hour" from *The Sky's the Limit*	**Music by** Harold Arlen	**Lyrics by** Johnny Mercer
	"That Old Black Magic" from *Star Spangled Rhythm*	**Music by** Harold Arlen	**Lyrics by** Johnny Mercer

NOTE: This song was nominated under the title 'Black Magic,' as it was submitted by Paramount's Music Department. Academy records have been changed to show the more common form of the title.

1945 (18th)	"Accentuate the Positive" from *Here Come the Waves*	**Music by** Harold Arlen	**Lyrics by** Johnny Mercer
1946 (19th)*	"On the Atchison, Topeka and the Santa Fe" from *The Harvey Girls* [**statuette**]	**Music by** Harry Warren	**Lyrics by** Johnny Mercer
1951 (24th)*	"In the Cool, Cool, Cool of the Evening" from *Here Comes the Groom* [**statuette**]	**Music by** Hoagy Carmichael	**Lyrics by** Johnny Mercer
1955 (28th)	"Something's Gotta Give" from *Daddy Long Legs*	**Music and Lyrics by** Johnny Mercer	
1960 (33rd)	"The Facts of Life" from *The Facts of Life*	**Music and Lyrics by** Johnny Mercer	
1961 (34th)*	"Moon River" from *Breakfast at Tiffany's* [**statuette**]	**Music by** Henry Mancini	**Lyrics by** Johnny Mercer
1962 (35th)*	"Days of Wine and Roses" from *Days of Wine and Roses* [**statuette**]	**Music by** Henry Mancini	**Lyrics by** Johnny Mercer
1963 (36th)	"Charade" from *Charade*	**Music by** Henry Mancini	**Lyrics by** Johnny Mercer
1965 (38th)	"The Sweetheart Tree" from *The Great Race*	**Music by** Henry Mancini	**Lyrics by** Johnny Mercer
1970 (43rd)	*Darling Lili* (Original Song Score)	**Music by** Henry Mancini	**Lyrics by** Johnny Mercer
	"Whistling Away the Dark" from *Darling Lili* ** Song – Original for the Picture	**Music by** Henry Mancini	**Lyrics by** Johnny Mercer
1971 (44th)	"Life Is What You Make It" from *Kotch* ** Song – Original for the Picture	**Music by** Marvin Hamlisch	**Lyrics by** Johnny Mercer

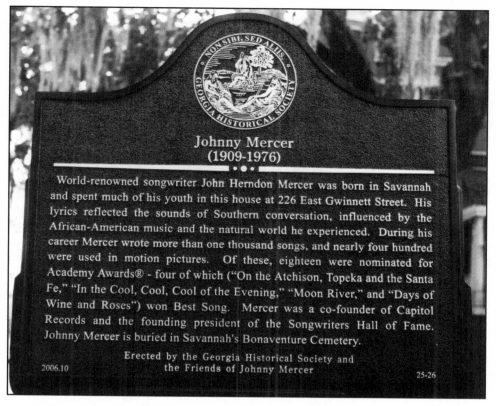

Georgia Historical Marker in Savannah, Georgia commemorating Johnny Mercer

The Mercer Home on Gwinnett Street in Savannah

Photos

Johnny Mercer's Grave Stone (Born November 18, 1909 – Died June 25, 1976)

Front of Memorial Bench near Johnny Mercer's Grave

Back of Memorial Bench near Johnny Mercer's Grave

Photos

The road to Mercer's Summer Home

Mercer Summer Home near the Pin Point Oyster Factory

The A. S. Varn & Son Company, packer of the famous Pin Point brand Oysters, where Johnny Mercer–as a young man– would go to listen to the songs of the women packers.

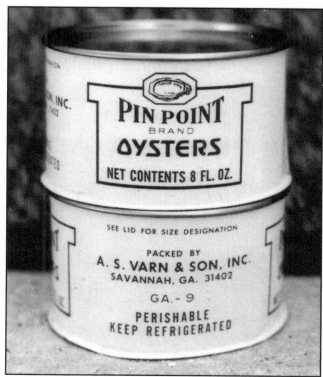

Stories from Pin Point

Johnny Mercer, as a youngster, spend his summers at the family home at Vernon View near Pin Point. The following are stories written and illustrated by Johnny and several friends of the time.

Published with permission from the Papers of Johnny Mercer, Popular Music Collection, Special Collections & Archives Department, Georgia State University Library.

The Shark and The Fisherman.

Once upon a time it was a man, and this man was a poor fisherman. And one time he was out fishing and a storm arose. And such a storm that the boat just got flooded.

And this man, being a good swimmer, swam until it was over,

And while he was swimming he was nearly to the shore in shallow water. And he saw the white belly of a shark underneath the water.

But before the boat got wrecked he had taken the fish knife, used to kill the cat-fishes and the fishes he didn't want, and put it in his pocket.

And, as the shark came towards him, he dived, with the knife in his hand, and just as the shark came towards him to cut him with his fin, he stuck the knife in him, and killed him.

John Herndon Mercer, aged 9.

KILLING THE SHARK

Illustration by the Author

Stories from Pin Point

<u>George and Jack's Daring Adventure.</u>

Once there was a boy who had the name of George who lived at the sea-side.

One day as he was in swimming he went out a little too far. There was plenty of men and women on the beach but they did not see him.

And as he was out there a big wave came and puched him under. He was under there at least ten seconds, and was straggling for breath. He came to the top after all and hollered out "Help! Help!"

A man came out there that was a life saver, and got him and brought him in, and when he had got on the beach he went home and told his father all that had happened.

And so they moved from the sea-shore and went to the country where it was plenty of rabbits and minks and possums to shoot.

And one day as he was out hunting with his friend Jack, who lived in the country too, they saw a robin. Jack took good aim, but just as he began to fire, another robin sang out, and the other robin want to where the sound came from. George and Jack followed him, and George had a gun too. And then they saw both robins on a tree. George aimed at one and Jack aimed at the other. They both fired at the same time, and killed the robins. And soon, as they were going home with their prey, along the path, what should they see in their way, but a monstrous rattle-snake!

Now both of them lived down in the South, and have hearing people tell how to kill rattle-snakes except to shoot them. They did something else. They were two big stones lying at the other side of the road. Both boys made a rush for the stones, each picking up one. The reason they did this was because they didn't have any more shot in their guns. They could have killed him with their guns right off, but as not having any more shot, they picked up two stones.

Jack threw and missed him. The rattle-snake was rattling his rattle fiercely now, and George took good aim with his brick, but somehow just seemed to hurt him and glance off.

The reason the boys hit him was this, because if you hit a rattle-snake they will bite themselves if you do not kill them the first blow. The boys knew this and that is why they did it.

The rattle-snake immediately rattled one more loud rattle, and immediately bit itself, and when the boys took it home, the boys' father said it was a monstrous rattle-snake they killed, because it was four and a half feet long, and as big around as Jack's leg.

And when his father saw what a narrow escape George made, he said he would have to live in the mountains, cause that was the only safe place.

And while they were in the mountains, (George's father had taken Jack too to the mountains) as I told you before; one day "Let us take a hike" said Jack to George.

George agreed, and so they got their father to fix up lunch for them, and then started out. While they were up about the mountains a mile above their house, just as they got past one part of the path, it caved in and there was no way to get home. There was only one way, and that was to jump or climb.

These boys were very plucky, as you must know, and so they started to climb. Down, down, down! It was going to be a hard climb, but they were going to do it. They were more brave than scared. As this was going to be a mile climb, it must be a hard one, also running the risk of your life to fall a mile.

They were down almost to the ledge. About ten feet below them they could see their house, when Jack gave a whoop and a yell, because the rock was crumbling fast beneath his hands that he was holding on.

George and Jack's Daving Adventure.   #2.

     As Jack being the lowest down to the house, and George, being the highest, hollered "Hold fast Jack! Hold fast!"   and George climbed down and put one foot right in Jack's reach, so he could hold on to it. He never thought of his own life, how if he dropped it would cause the life of both of them.

     And just below them Jack looked down and saw George's father with a rope in his hand. He lassoed a point of rock, jutting right out above George's head, and George, to see that it was securely fastened, held on with one hand and pushed it farther on with the other.   He put both hands on the rock that he was holding, and took one off, and caught hold of the rope with it that was hanging to the ground.

     George told Jack to hurry up and slide down the rope, because it was slipping off the rock very fast. Jack did so, and was very glad to get down to solid ground once more.

     George was sliding down, and was about a half a foot from the ground, and the rope slipped off, but did not hurt him because he was so low.

     George said he was very lucky because he got saved from drowning, saved from being killed by a rattle-snake, and saved from falling off the mountain and crushing him to death.

     But who had done all this? It was only he himself.

     And for saving the life of Jack, George's father gave him a pony and a wheel, and Jack a bicycle too, but not a pony. Jack was not jealous, but stayed with George all his life, because his father and mother were dead.

     But they have moved to the city, where nothing can hurt them except being run over, and Jack and George are very careful about that.

     But they never had any more adventures like that last one.

     George is very happy with his bicycle and pony, and so is Jack.
The End.

John Herndon Mercer, aged 9.

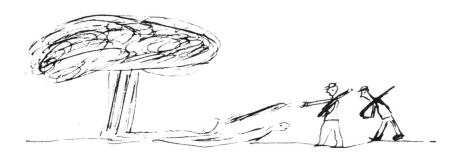

makeing the rattlesnake bite him
self

Illustration by the Author.   From George and Jack's Daving Adventure.

Jimmy's Adventure.

Once upon a time there was a boy that lived in a forest. His mother was dead. His father was the only one living in the family.

One day as he came out of the forest with his dog, whose name was Top, a big wind came up. It blew over trees, and it started raining. He found a cave to stay in though, and his dog was with him all the time.

At night he heard horses approaching. He looked out of the cave and there were twelve robbers with a bag of gold that they had stolen.

Now as this boy was very poor, he wished he was the one who had the gold.

The robbers came in the cave. He hid his dog and himself behind a big old stone that was in the cave. The robbers came in and they had supper. And this boy, before the robbers had had supper, put something in their wine to make them sleep. And after awhile the robbers were asleep and snoring.

The boy came out and looked all round for the bag of gold, but it was nowhere to be seen. He heard footsteps approachibg. He jumped behind the rock, and just as he had done so, he saw a man come in with a bag across his shoulders that was bigger than the bag of gold. He saw something fall through the bag. It was silver. He saw the man press a little button on the wall. A little square stone door opened. The man put the bag inside of it, and shut it, and pressed another button and the door closed.

Now at the other end of the cave were two empty sacks, just the size of the two that had the gold and silver in them.

This man soon drank the wine, and was soon asleep and snoring also like the others.

The boy filled the empty sacks with sand, and took the others out, and found some planks nearby, and some nails and a hammer, and made a little wagon.

He called Top. He called and called, but Top did not come. He put the bags in the wagon. He called Top again.

He was walking along home, when he heard something coming like the sound of a man, and he hid behind a tree. But to his surprise it was only his father and Top. And he toom him home, and he built the new house, and was made a very rich man. And he married again, and has lived very happily.

John Herndon Mercer, aged 9.

JohnHerndon
mercer

JIMPulling HOMETHEGold
and silver.

illustration by the Author

From Jimmy's Adventures.

Sukey.

--

Once upon a time I had a little chicken named Sukey. I loved the chicken
so. I call it an feed it. The preacher man come, and the chicken had
to die. The Precher Man so loved chicken, till Mother had to kill the
chicken for the Preacher.

--

Anna Sands (Colored) Aged 7.

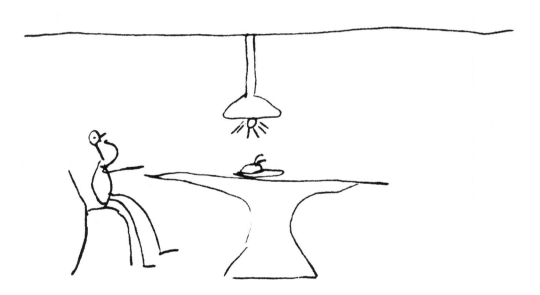

and sukey had to die

Drawn by John Herndon Mercer aged 9-   From Sukey.

The Bear and The Hunter.

Once upon a time it was a man, an he went out to hunt, and he had two dog.
An so he stopped underneath a tree one night, an it was cole, an
he made a fire under the tree. An it was a big bear up the tree, and the
bear tell him he was cole. So he tell him to come down and warm.
An so the bear tole him he would come down ef he would carry his dog
away and his gun. And so he did what the bear tole him, an he take his dog
and chain em.
So the bear came down and start runnin after him. An he holler out
for he dog, and the dog was chain. So the dog start biting his chain but he
couldn't git a-loose.
An was a crow come down the chinmey and set on the mantel-peice, an
the buzzard come down the chimney. An the man wife was sleeping, an the buzzard
went to the bed, and shat beating the woman. Take his wing and beat her. An the
woman wake, an he get up. The tub was full of blood, an the basin.
An she loosed the dog. And the dog killed the bear. An the man came home.

Ceaser Dilbert (Colored) I2

* Probably a folk story.

The bear running the Man

Drawn by John Herndon Mercer aged 9.   The Bear + the Man

Jack and Jinks.

There was once a boy named Jack. He lived in the West, and had a pony nemed Jinks.

His father told him to go to town and take a letter for him. He had to go through a desert full of cactus. It was a pit in the desert.

He was riding along pretty fast, and his pony saw the hole and stopped, and Jack fell over the pony's neck into the pit. When Jack sxxx hit in the bottom of the pit he heard a rattle -snake rattling.

The rattle-snake would not harm him, until he tried to climb up the side, but he could not climb up.

He looked up and saw his pony. He then took his lasso, and threw it over the saddle. Then he said "Go home Jinks".

Jinks, the little pony statted off and pulled Jack out of the pit. And them Jack went on with the letter.

Walter Rivers, aged 12.

N. Rivers.   PULLING JACK OUT.

Illustration by The Author   From Jack and Jinks.

Ben's Daring Adventure.

Ben lived with his father out in the West by the Rocky Mountings. Ben had a pony and a gun, and was very fond of hunting.

One day as he was in the mountings he had been riding for about an hour, riding along the mounting path, and as he had turned a short turn, a low growl greeted him some distance away.

It was a bear, but he did not know where he was. This bear was a grissly bear, a very fierce kind.

Ben was a plucky boy and a good shot, and as having his rifle with him he held it in a more handy grip, and while he was turning another turn, a turn right to the side of a canyon, and a mounting on the other side, and no way to turn back except to go around the front trail and go back to his house.

And right in front of him was a big grissly bear, of which he could not cross the path. And about ten feet below them was a big ledge, a ledge that almost reached to the other side of the canyon. Ben fired at the bear, but missed. He had only one more shot left in his gun. He said,

"Jump, Bessie, old girl, Jump!"

The horse jumped, and was none too late, for the bear had sprung, and landed right on the spot where the boy had been.

Ben had fallen and broken an arm, but saved his life. And there was a tunnel going through the mounting to a trail which lead to his home. And he looked up and saw the bear leaning over the cliff, and he went through the tunnel.

As he was just beginning to see day-light on the other side, right in his path there was the same bear! He had only one shot, as you must remember. As the bear was rushing forward, he put his rifle to his shoulder and shot him behind the ear. Over fell the bear dead.

Ben hurridly rushed home, and told his father, which got on his horse and brought the bear home, and made a coat for Jack out of his skin.

And that was Ben's daring adventure.

John Herndon Mercer, aged 9.

AND WENT HOME as fast as he could bust it.

Drawn by
John Herndon Mercer aged 9.

From The Deer Hunt.

Saving The Cattle.

Tom lived out in the West. His father owned a cattle ranch. Tom was about to go to
his father's ranch, when Harry, his friend, rode up on his pony.
Tom said "Ihave to go to my father's ranch."
And Harry said "Well, I'll go with you."
Soon they were riding along the trail. When they reached the ranch, Jim,
one of the cattle men, said that 50 head of cattle had been stolen, and their father
had gone out in search of them.
Tom and Harry started back home. They proceeded to take a short cut
through the woods. They had ridden about a mile, when Harry stopped and looked at the
ground. He said,
"Tom, here are some tracks of cattle. Maybe they are your father's."
They followed the tracts closely, and they went through deep canyons.
They had gone about two miles when they heard voices, and coming around the bend,
they saw five rough looking men. One of them called out "Halt" Then they rode up to
the boys and told them to dismount.
Then one of the men started to grab the bridle rein. Tom said "stop"
That's my pony. What are you going to do with him?"
One of the men said "That's enough. Just come on."
They led the boys into the forest, and under a tree they saw some
rope. One of the men picked it up, and began to tie Tom and Harry with their hands
behind their backs. They came to a tall rock, and going around it they went into a
deep dark tunnel. After walking awhile they came into a valley.
Tom immediately saw they must be rustlers, for there were lots
of cattle there.
The men took Tom and Harry into a cabin and lovked the door. Tom
sat down and began to think of some way of getting out. As his hands were still tied
behind his back, he called to Harry and said "Try to unfasten this rope with your
mouth."
In about five minutes Harry had the rope off, Tom untied Harry's
bonds. Then they began to try to break down the door, but could not, for the door
was heavily barred on the outside. Tom looked around the room and saw a high window.
He could not reach it, so he got up on Harry's shoulders. When he was in the window
he pulled Harry up. Then they both dropped to the ground outside.
Looking around he saw that all the men must have gone somewhere.
They went around to the front of the cabin and saw a man with a big black mustache
sitting down in front of the door. Moving up behind him, they pulled his revolver
out of his holster, and held him up. Harry took some twine out of his pocket. Then
they tied the man securely.
A little distance away they saw their ponies. Mounting on them
they rode away as fast back to their father's ranch.
Tom's father was there. They told him where the place was,
and, going there with a few cow boys, they soon overpowered the outlaws.
That Christmas Tom and Harry both had a rifle and a new pony,
and they certainly are proud of them.
The End.

Walter Rivers. aged 12 yrs.

Then they both dropped to the ground outside.

Illustration by the author.   Saving the Cattle

The Duck and The Guinea.
————————

Once it was a duck and a Guinea.

An de firs one fine day was to marry de King's Wife.

An de Guinea wake up firs. An de Guinea holler,

"Bro Duck' Bro Duck:"

And de Duck wake up and holler,

"Day Day".

An so de Duck marry de King's Wife.

THOMAS BARNEY (COLORED) aged I2.

From One Singer to Another—A Tribute

Johnny Mercer is a great, great songwriter—and I use that word "great" advisedly because it's thrown around so much. You see, Johnny Mercer—and I go way back with him, when he first came out to R.K.O. and a publishing firm I was associated with published some of his songs—he's not just a lyricist, he's a songwriter, and there's a big difference. He was a singer to begin with (and so was I) and so he knows where words should fall and when to use an open vowel instead of a closed vowel. He has a great feel for words. He had a good education and so he's literate enough to know all those six- and seven-syllable words—but, and this is important, he's smart enough to know when not to use them. He feels things very deeply—as a matter of fact, he's very sentimental and knows how to use tender corn; there's nothing wrong with good corn, believe me.

My favorite Mercer song? Oh my goodness, he's written so many. . . . But I know that all songwriters like their latest hit the best. "Moon River"? Well, that's a great song—I don't know whether the melody came first or what, but it's the perfect combination of words and music; he always knows where to put the right words—sort of like a minister or priest or rabbi who's going to perform the marriage ceremony. Yes, he's a great songwriter and a wonderful person too.

IRVING BERLIN

JOHNNY MERCER

Introduction

"Just Too Very Very"

It was not exactly contrived imagery that for so many years labeled the center of popular music production Tin Pan Alley. The upright, timeworn pianos on which the songs were first banged out *were* tinny, and the side streets surrounding Broadway rarely saw sunshine, thus putting them in the category of what might be called alleys. At the same lengthy period of time—that is, the better part of this century, up until the calamitous arrival of rock 'n' roll and the Beatles—the writers of the nation's song hits were mainly the products of these same citified surroundings. In fact many of the leaders of the Tin Pan Alley fraternity had been born and raised within a subway ride of that musical center. To be even more precise, the overwhelming majority of songwriters and their patrons, the publishers, were not only born and bred New Yorkers but Jewish into the bargain. The oddity, of course, was that these city-born musicians and lyricists wrote lovingly and longingly about country lanes and waterfalls rather than the hustle and bustle of Times Square (the song "Forty-second Street" was the exception rather than the rule) and the song-plugging gang that gathered around Al Jolson, the Elvis of the twenties, knew as much about Jolie's often-sung Dixie as they did about Labrador. The authenticity of regional songwriting had to wait until the arrival in the late twenties of two young men from different rural parts of the country: Hoagy Carmichael from Indiana and Johnny Mercer from Georgia.

Their similarities were quite remarkable: they both sang in a most distinctive, down-home, nasal-tinged style; they both had a great affection for jazz; they both operated from a marvelously sly sense of humor. Where their spiritual predecessor Willard Robison, had been equally authentic and brilliant in a down-home musical way, Carmichael and Mercer were more commercial, and that opened doors. They were a peach of a pair together, sparkling individually, Hoagy slim and saturnine, Johnny "a perfect butterball of a Southerner" as Carmichael describes him in his autobiography. Above all they were twin gusts of fresh air in the troubled days of the early thirties. Together they wrote a whole string of thoroughly distinctive songs, beginning with "Lazybones" in 1933 and ending up with the Academy Award winner of 1951, "In

George Anderson Mercer, grandfather of John Herndon Mercer, our Huckleberry Friend.

the Cool, Cool, Cool of the Evening." Through those years one had an awful time trying to remember which was which in the songs they wrote together and separately: "Small Fry," which Johnny sang many times, sounds as if he wrote it, but it was a solo job by Hoagy; Johnny's famous "Moon River" sounds as if it were written with Hoagy (who wrote "Moon Country") instead of Mancini, and "Jamboree Jones," which Johnny wrote by himself, is somewhat like "The Old Music Master," which he wrote with Hoagy some years before they collaborated on "Skylark," which was written a few years before Hoagy wrote "Baltimore Oriole" without Johnny but several years after Johnny wrote "Mister Meadowlark" without Hoagy. There was a great song they wrote together, "How Little We Know," and a piece of esoterica that probably only Mel Tormé knows, "The Rumba Jumps." There was "Washboard Blues" (Carmichael) and "Blues in the Night" (Mercer), "Stardust" (Carmichael) and "Midnight Sun" (Mercer), "Georgia on My Mind" (Carmichael) and "Pardon My Southern Accent" (Mercer). Between them it seems as if they have contributed the greatest hunk of musical Americana since Stephen Foster and that they may also have laid down the tracks for the current rush of country-flavored blues and ballads.

Luck smiled on Johnny Mercer in other ways than just bringing him to New York at the same time as Hoagy Carmichael's arrival. Mercer was born in Savannah, undoubtedly one of the most aristocratic and languorous cities of the old South. The family, while not of the wealthy land-owning class, was at least well-off, and so young John Mercer was able to be sent to the select Woodberry Forest School in Virginia. One of his major accomplishments at Woodbury was booking the bands for the school's proms. The luck of the Depression (not smiling in this case) brought about Mercer senior's business trouble in the real estate market, and thus John had to forego college, a situation that brought him to New York. The cherub face, the jazz, collegiate clothes, the soft Southern speech and easy-going manner must certainly have set him apart as he went looking for acting jobs and submitting songs around the Broadway area in those bewildering days of 1929 and 1930. There were the usual ups and downs of show business until the first sizable break came in the person of the sizable Paul Whiteman. It was Mercer the "cute" singer with Whiteman who paved the way for Mercer the singing songwriter. With Whiteman, who understood talent better than most, Mercer was able to sing alongside one of his heroes, the great jazz trombonist Jack Teagarden. As with Hoagy, it was a pairing made in jazz heaven—Mercer with the South in his mouth, Teagarden with the rich blues sound of Texas—and they were commercial too! There is much that can be said about Mercer's singing style, almost as much as about his songwriting. He had, of course, an impeccable sense of how a jazz phrase or a blues nuance should sound; all of that came naturally to a man who had spent some of his boyhood years crossing the tracks to the Negro section of town to buy what were then called "race records" (the result may be seen in the postcard from a Black social club shown later in this book which voted him "our favorite colored singer on radio"). The jazz flavor was inherent in him, but he also had a wonderful way with a ballad—for instance, his recorded versions of "Laura," "Tangerine," and "Little Ingenue." It seemed back then in the Whiteman and mid-thirties period that a lot of listeners who became Mercer fans, particularly when Crosby stepped in, were country club types who thought they both sounded like friendly boozers (ho-ho-ho) and there were others who had fun mimicking that devil-may-care singing style in the shower. Johnny Mercer's early following may have been small but it was select, including in it such knowing and well-connected gentlemen as Irving Berlin and Arthur Schwartz

When one begins to consider what were the main influences that made Johnny Mercer tick, two settings come into view: there was the sophisticated East represented by Broadway—still not too far removed by overnight train from the man's true heartland, Savannah; and there was the widespread California arena that stretched from homes in Palm Springs and Newport Beach to the studio of Warner's, Paramount and 20th Century-Fox. Weaving these widely separated and dissimilar influ-

ences together was Mercer's triple strand of talent: the professional singing that came so naturally and contributed so helpfully, as Irving Berlin noted, to his understanding of where the words should fall; the acclaimed songwriting that was often cleverly topical, sometimes universal, and generally touched, as his British show collaborator, Ronnie Harwood, put it, with "the genius of simplicity"; and there was a surprising interest in organization that founded, first, a record company of size (Capitol) in California and then a trade group (the Songwriters Hall of Fame) in New York. On top of all this was a boyish enthusiasm, not necessarily the rah-rah kind of thing, more self-contained, for material and talent he liked. His range of perception was as illuminating and wide ranging as radar. He still liked some Victor Herbert and Rudolf Friml, but he was aware of newcomers and singled out Jimmy Webb, Marvin Hamlisch and Jobim. Whether it was a funny phrase noted in *Time* magazine or a singer heard on the car radio, Mercer picked it up, used the information some way or other, became a booster. He had, as the saying goes, his pores open. Mercer was, particularly in the hectic war years of the forties, a workaholic, an on-top-of-everything guy. But even with such an assembly-line output of jazzy topicality Mercer never strayed too far from

(Here and facing page) Scenes of Savannah during the first two decades of the century.

Scenes from the Mercer family scrapbook, circa 1910.
Pose number seven—"any place I hang my hat."

14

his deep South, down-home feelings: birds, meadows, sky, rivers, trains (particularly trains)—these references were with him throughout his life, they were the things he was most comfortable with. The composer and musical guru Alec Wilder put it very well when he said, "Larry Hart was an indoor writer and Johnny was an outdoor writer." One can almost see Mercer sitting on a front porch, watching the fading sunlight—a tall drink (or better still a short one) not far from his side.

While on the subject of drink, it is still somewhat surprising that this true son of the South, while neither a Good Ole Boy nor an out-and-out Bible-smacker, was quite moralistic, even among the heathens of show biz. He did read the Bible often, he never used directly erotic lyrics, and he was openly angered by Tennessee Williams' preoccupation with depravity in bayou country. Johnny Mercer was basically an Ivy Leaguer, much more in the Walker Percy image than Capote, Williams or the current playwrights of off-off-Broadway. He was for progress but not too much of it—and better leave the things at home alone. In California he took on some of the colorations of that sybaritic paradise: golf (briefly), painting (pretty good watercolors), cooking (with a distinctly Southern flavor)—these were a few of the outside interests; that is, after the first fling of cronyism and partying with Bing's crowd wore off. There was also a time for the Mercers with the writing crowd—Nunally Johnson, the Hacketts, etc—where Johnny was a sort of celebrity because he was the only one of his kind in that heady world. In short, he was, to use Duke Ellington's marvelous phrase, Beyond Category.

To take Johnny Mercer through all the ups and downs of his career would consume more space than this volume allows—a full-scale biography is in the works—and so it is best for the moment to let his many wonderful lyrics, such telling visions of time, place and listener as for example, "hear that lonesome whistle blowing cross the trestle" sketch out the portrait. Another song contains a similar hauntingly autobiographically picture:

> *Cross the river,*
> *Round the bend,*
> *Howdy, stranger,*
> *So long, friend.*

To Bob Bach
From Walter Rivers

Bob, as discussed with you on the phone, re "Huckleberry Friend" - John and I and three black boys, Ceasar, Eli and Tommie, in early summer, June or July, went picking these berries. We each had a quart measure, - a small pail from which the hucksters sold a quart of okra, peas, beans, or whatever. John looked forward to these safaris with great pleasure. The black boys knew mainly the best places for finding the berries, and I think now of the brambles, briers and snakes which we encountered. I wouldn't dare go into some of the places now!

We would spend several hours to fill our pails and trudge homeward on the oyster shell roads of Vernon View.

I remember vividly that Walter Mercer, Johns half brother making ice cream for Sunday dinner - Huckleberry Ice Cream - It turned out pretty bad and no one would eat it - I think Huckleberries the same as blue berries - look and taste the same but grew wild in our area.

Shortly after Moon River became a hit, I called Johnny and told him I loved the line "my Huckleberry friend". He laughed, and said "Hell! you ought to - you were there!"

Another memory was West Broad Street in Savannah. This was totally Black.

Johnny Mercer's cousin, long-time pal, and one-time executive of Capitol Records, Walter Rivers, is now living in retirement in Birmingham, Alabama. He recently wrote this letter when asked for an explanation of the expression "huckleberry friend."

Stores, houses, R.R. Station, Churches, everything for blacks. Just like old time Harlem! John and I frequently slipped off from our families and went over to a record shop, called Mary's Records, or Mamie's Records. There we would listen for hours to Bessie Smith, Armstrong, Joe Pal Sullivan, and many people I can't recall - you would know of many musicians of that era - John loved to imitate Bessie Smith's Record of "Go Back Where You Stayed Last Night" We were good customers so we were allowed to listen for hours. A real Victrola, with a horn on top! His Master's Voice - This, I believe, is where Mercer picked up his beat and phrasing.

I must digress for a moment: The Easter Parade on West Broad St. in Savannah. Black ladies dressed in evening gowns, triple high heels and big flowered hats. Men in everything tuxedos, tails morning formal wear, most with orange shoes, strolling musicians(?) - it seemed that every man in the crowd had a trumpet, banjo, or clarinet.

On this day, Easter, the curb was lined with white people with ancient cars, buggies and wagons, watching the spectacle and it was almost Madi Gras. I didn't miss one for years and usually went with my mother and some disapproving Aunts - John was there with his father

(Bob. Hope this is what you ...)

16

We lived in the country in the summer. The roads were still unpaved, made of crushed oyster shell, and as they wound their way under the trees covered with Spanish moss, it was a sweet, indolent background for a boy to grow up in. Savannah was smaller then and sleepy, full of trees and azaleas that filled the parks which make it so beautiful and as we drove out to our "place in the country" at Vernon View there was hardly a scene without vistas of marsh grass and long stretches of salt water.

Punctured tires on the Model T made the trips longer at times, but when the family arrived finally to spend the summer there were many things to be done around our summer home. We had to get sawdust to pack the ground bin where we kept the ice, fill the lamps with kerosene, put up the mosquito netting on the beds and have "Man'well" walk the cow out from the commercial dairy farm so we'd have our own milk all summer long.

JOHNNY MERCER

17

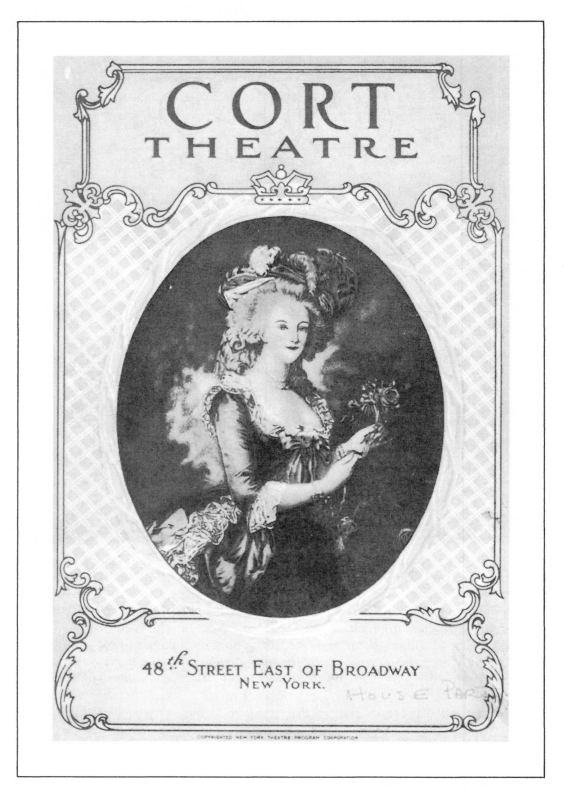

CORT THEATRE

48th STREET EAST OF BROADWAY
NEW YORK.

HOUSE PAR

COPYRIGHTED NEW YORK THEATRE PROGRAM CORPORATION

Program cover for *Houseparty*

The Twenties

For a young man, such as Johnny Mercer, whose life centered on music the decade of the 1920s—a breezy time that has since been rather overly-dubbed the Jazz Age—was a period rich in musical delights. The wind-up Victrola and crystal-set radio evolved during that time to the orthophonic phonograph and the three-dial superheterodyne made by Atwater Kent, Zenith or Stromberg Carlson, and these wonders of the communications industry brought with them—certainly reaching all the way to Georgia—such musical novelties as a crazy song called "Yes, We Have No Bananas," a man named Wendell Hall singing "It Ain't Gonna Rain No More No More," and a nimble-fingered pianist named Zez Confrey playing "Kitten on the Keys." There were also the comedy records by Billy Jones and Ernie Hare ("The Happiness Boys"), and The Two Black Crows, Moran and Mack ("Has you ever felt goofer feathers? . . . they is soooooo soft"), "race" records that were rumored to be very naughty, sung by Ma Rainey and Bessie Smith, and records by fellows named Ukelele Ike (Cliff Edwards) and Fuzzy Knight that featured a new way of presenting a song—not so much singing but a sort of gargling sound that seemed "hot," that popular 1920s word appropriated from the colored (no Negro or Black yet) community.

There were also in this flourishing decade, in addition to the passive forms of musical enjoyment, the more active art forms: the banjo, beloved of minstrel shows and dockside revels, now spawned the sprightly ukelele (the uke), which proved so easy to manipulate in a rumble seat or a canoe, and every parlor of any consequence could boast of a piano on whose music rack would be sheet music copies of the latest rage—"Dardanella," "When Day Is Done," "Whispering," "California Here I Come." If all of this remarkable cornucopia didn't prove enough to satisfy the appetite of a music-minded teenager in 1924-25-or-26, there was also a new dance called "The Charleston" to practice in private or in front of the phonograph. At least once a week he could go to a movie in town with a local fellow seated at the upright piano down front, helping the plot along with sentimental surges and agitated rumblings in moments of high passion and peril. And that's how it was in most middle class

American homes during that decade, though a Southern boy had the added advantage of hearing—if even at a distance—the exotic and compelling sounds coming from an occasional tent show or gospel meeting for the colored folk across town. Music was *everywhere*, in the air, for America was beginning to stretch and feel its oats after the heady business of winning a war for those people "over there."

Then there was the most intoxicating discovery of all—jazz—and Johnny Mercer in Savannah of the mid-twenties plunged into it head over heels. There were two giants of jazz (both of whom would appear in Johnny's later life) that were worth hanging around the local record store and waiting for: Louis Armstrong (and his Hot Five) and Paul Whiteman. Though Paul was mistakenly labelled "King of Jazz," he did nonetheless feature the brilliant jazz cornettist Bix Beiderbecke, and that was enough to pacify the purists of the jazz community. There were countless other recording jazzmen on whom an affluent young man could spend his weekly allowance: Red Nichols and his Five Pennies, McKinney's Cotton Pickers, Miff Mole's Molers, Venuti and Lang, Fletcher Henderson, the California Ramblers, the Wolverines, the Mound City Blue Blowers—the amazingly colorful names ran on and on at the local record store or 5-and-10.

But if young John Mercer knew the names and numbers of all the players in jazz, that was only a part of his ever-growing, knowledgeable attention to the entire world of pop culture in that period: there were the stage plays by Ibsen, O'Neill, Molnar, Golden, and that new fellow Nöel Coward; books by Sherwood Anderson, Irvin S. Cobb, Sinclair Lewis; and various small literary magazines. But mainly there was the element that struck the most responsive chord—the great outpouring of popular songs from a place up north recently named Tin Pan Alley.

His heroes became Victor Herbert, Irving Berlin, George Gershwin, Walter Donaldson, Gus Kahn, Isham Jones.* There were two other songwriters he appreciated perhaps more than that illustrious list, two who came along a few years later and represented the down-home country flavor so dear to Mercer's heart. They were Willard Robison and Hoagy Carmichael.

Johnny Mercer was bursting with the spirit of the age, and so it was inevitable that he come to challenge the tough guys and wise dolls of New York in 1927.

---

* These were added to his early and continuing passion for the rhymes of W. S. Gilbert.

Houseparty was not quite the disaster that took place farther downtown in Manhattan that October but it might have turned John Mercer's sights in other directions a little.

THE CORT THEATRE

Forty-Eighth Street
Just East of Broadway

BERNARD KLAWANS
Manager

FIRE NOTICE: Look around now and choose the nearest exit to your seat. In case of fire, walk (not run) to that exit. Do not try to beat your neighbor to the street.
JOHN J. DORMAN, Fire Commissioner.

WEEK BEGINNING MONDAY EVENING, OCTOBER 14, 1929
MATINEES WEDNESDAY AND SATURDAY

"HOUSEPARTY"

With ROY HARGRAVE

A NEW PLAY

By KENNETH PHILLIPS BRITTON and ROY HARGRAVE

STAGED BY HARRY WAGSTAFF GRIBBLE
DIRECTION A. L. ERLANGER AND GEORGE C. TYLER

CAST

ALAN BRADFORD, a Sophomore.................ROY HARGRAVE
RONALD EVANS, a Sophomore...................EDWARD WOODS

PROGRAM CONTINUED ON FOURTH PAGE FOLLOWING

[7]

PROGRAM CONTINUED

SALLY ANDREWS, Ronnie's girl.............PENELOPE HUBBARD
FLORENCE, of Williamstown...................HARRIET MacGIBBON
HORTENSE PFEIFFER, a houseparty girl..........BETTY LAWRENCE
MRS. MILLIGAN, Florence's mother.............ANNE SUTHERLAND
MRS. WHITE, a chaperone.............................JULIA HAY
MRS. RUTHERFORD, a chaperone............LOUISE MACKINTOSH
EDWARD CANBY, a Freshman.................CHARLES CROMER
DARROW JENCKES, a Senior, House President......MATTHEW SMITH
DORIS CALLANDER, Darrow's girl...................HELEN DODGE
MALCOLM F. R. WHITE, M. A., Phd, a Professor..EDWARD J. LeSAINT
BILL WARREN, a Sophomore.....................WALDO EDWARDS
CHICK SMYTH, a Sophomore........................CHARLES DILL
MARIANNE GUION, Chick's girl.................EDITH HARGRAVE
BOB DAVIS, a Junior..............................BILLY QUINN
BETTY CREELING, Bob's girl...................CYNTHIA ROGERS
JAMES, the steward.........................LAWRENCE BOLTON
STUDENTS—Richard Ewell, John Mercer, Wm. C. Haskell, Edwin Whitner and Everett Miller.
HOUSEPARTY GUESTS—Helen Oursler, Beatrice Holtby, Dorothy Harris, Jane Dewey and Betty Stoddart.

PROGRAM CONTINUED ON SECOND PAGE FOLLOWING

[11]

The newlywed Johnny and Ginger heading down the Atlantic City boardwalk to hear Archie Bleyer's band.

The Thirties

Consider for a moment the following list of popular songs:

April in Paris
Brother Can You Spare a Dime
Night and Day
How Deep Is the Ocean
Forty-second Street
I Gotta Right to Sing the Blues
Mimi
Isn't It Romantic
I'm Getting Sentimental Over You
Dancing on the Ceiling

Say It Isn't So
It Don't Mean a Thing if It Ain't Got That Swing
Mad About the Boy
Of Thee I Sing
A Shine on Your Shoes
Shuffle Off to Buffalo
The Song Is You
You're an Old Smoothie
Drums in My Heart
My Silent Love

They were *all* published and became popular within the space of one year—1932. And if the public wanted more of such quality, 1933 wasn't a bad year either, having produced the all-time hit songs "Easter Parade," "Stormy Weather," "Lover," "The Carioca," "Yesterdays" and "Sophisticated Lady." No question about it that, although the Depression had set in grimly, bringing with it the closing of banks, the foreclosing of mortgages, and men selling apples on street corners, the great majority of us who had the good fortune to own radios or phonographs were being offered a banquet of rich musical dishes to brighten up the times. And though "Brother Can You Spare a Dime?" caught the public's imagination in the busy year of 1932, Franklin D. Roosevelt, cigarette holder airily tilted to the sky, had ridden into the White House that same year with a theme song from 1930 titled "Happy Days Are Here Again." There was a lot of good and functional music around.

Movie musicals were also inexplicably thriving in the early thirties: If the rather dull ones of '30-'31, with squares such as Lawrence Tibbett, John Boles and Janet

Gaynor, were hardly lighting up the screens, at least by 1933 there was *Flying Down to Rio* with the beginning of the Astaire-Rogers magic (music by Vincent Youmans); the blockbuster *Forty-Second Street;* Al Jolson, of all people, in a very avant-garde musical by Rodgers and Hart, *Hallelujah I'm a Bum;* Joan Crawford, Clark Gable and Fred Astaire (briefly) in an M-G-M extravaganza called *Dancing Lady;* two jazzy Bing Crosby musicals with the wonderful Jack Oakie in support; and, finally, the successful continuation of the great Maurice Chevalier's Hollywood career which had begun to soar in 1931 with *The Smiling Lieutenant* and in 1932 with *Love Me Tonight.* There were plenty of movies, and many of them were featuring performers lifted from the East, from Broadway and vaudeville: Mae West, W. C. Fields, Burns and Allen, Eddie Cantor, Eddie Foy, Jr., Texas Guinan, Jimmy Durante—even Paul Robeson performing his classic role in *The Emperor Jones.* The music for all these great movies was being written for the most part by other refugees from Broadway, and they constituted the first wave of East to West show tune know-how. There was Ralph Rainger, who had started out as one half of a two-piano team in the pit of several Broadway shows; Dorothy Fields, the brilliant offspring of a distinguished theatrical family; (Weber & Fields) a former dance band pianist, Jimmy McHugh; a chunky ex-Broadwayite named Mack Gordon, who could sell his own lyrics better than most professional crooners; Richard Whiting, a marvelous music man from the Middle West; and—probably without question kings of the heap—the great team of Harry Warren (music) and Al Dubin (words), who were responsible for the success of both *Forty-second Street* and *Gold Diggers of 1933.*

The fun-filled musical movies helped us stave off the Depression-time blues but there was also Broadway, where if you got to Gray's cut-rate ticket office in the basement just off Times Square, you might be lucky enough to pick up a ticket for one of the great musical shows for $1.50—certainly for well under any astronomical five dollars. Between 1932 and 1933 there were many gems to choose from: *Flying Colors* (Schwartz & Dietz) with Clifton Webb and Imogene Coca; *Gay Divorce* (Cole Porter) starring Fred Astaire; the Gershwins' Pulitzer prize-winner *Of Thee I Sing; Music in the Air* (Jerome Kern); *Through the Years* (Vincent Youmans); *As Thousands Cheer* (Irving Berlin) starring Marilyn Miller; *Roberta* (Kern) with Bob Hope and Sydney Greenstreet; *Blackbirds of 1933* with Bill Robinson; *Take a Chance* starring Ethel Merman and Jack Haley; and—who knows?—you might even have wanted to take in *Earl Carroll's Vanities* (Arlen & Koehler) starring Milton Berle. Broadway was swinging then, and it's a safe bet that Johnny Mercer, still in the early thirties a fairly recent arrival on the scene, took in all the shows. One we know he saw—and many times obviously—was 1932's revue *Americana,* for which he collaborated on lyrics with the man he later named "my guru," E. Y. "Yip" Harburg. (Harold Arlen wrote the melodies, and they were called "Whistling for a Kiss" and "Satan's Little Lamb".)

In addition to the "hot" bands that young guys like Johnny Mercer collected in their "frat" houses down south or out west, New York City in 1932-33 was alive with

25

The skinny kid from Savannah strikes a Joe E. Brown/Martha Raye publicity pose for his first boss "Pops" Whiteman. Johnny's stepping-stone gig with Whiteman's vast Hotel Biltmore band placed him alongside such talented veterans as Ramona, Roy Bargy, Jack Fulton, Peggy Healey and, best of all, Jack Teagarden.

"sweet" or just plain dance bands. They played mainly in the grill rooms and dining places of the town's leading hotels. There was George Olsen (vocals by wife Ethel Shutta) at the Pennsylvania, Vincent Lopez forever at the Taft, Don Bestor at the McAlpin, Guy Lombardo packing them in at the Roosevelt, and a hot new band from Canada via the Midwest, Casa Loma, at the Essex House. Rudy Vallee was no longer at his own Villa Vallee on east Sixtieth Street, but one could still hear him weekly on radio thanks to the Fleischman's Yeast Program. Ben Bernie ("yowsah yowsah"), Horace Heidt and Kay Kyser could all be heard on dance band "remotes" from various places around the country. But still the top man of them all—the King of Jazz, the man who brought you "Rhapsody in Blue" (his theme song too)—was Paul Whiteman, holding court in the Bowman Room of the Hotel Biltmore, in the summer months at The Cascades atop the hotel. Here's how Johnny Mercer describes his meeting with Whiteman, the man most responsible for launching the Mercer career:

"I got to New York in the first place by winning a little theatre contest at the New Amsterdam Roof. Then the next contest was the Pontiac Youth of America contest, which Paul Whiteman held in every city. [Singing a couple of songs] I won the one in New York. Archie Bleyer (later Arthur Godfrey's orchestra leader) was playing piano for me and Paul came out and said, 'Who's that piano player?' I said, 'That's Archie Bleyer, the jazz arranger.' Then he said, 'No wonder.' That's probably why I won the contest. (Mister Modesty.) Anyway, the three songs that sort of constitute my Whiteman career were 'Fare Thee Well to Harlem,' 'Pardon My Southern Accent,' and 'Here Come the British With a Bang Bang.' "

26

Johnny Mercer's film acting career begins and ends with RKO's *Old Man Rhythm*; Joy Hodges and Evelyn Poe show that girls wore sweaters before Lana Turner.

Every college boy had to play a ukelele.

Out of Breath

1930

Music by EVERETT MILLER

When tasks superhuman demand such
    acumen
That only a few men possess,
I never have fear to volunteer.
But though others fear me,
Still when you are near me
And willing to hear me express
Such childish delight,
I'm filled with fright.

Mine's a hopeless case,
But there's one saving grace,
Anyone would feel as I do;
Out of breath and scared to death of you.
Love was first divined,
Then explored and defined,
Still the old sensation is new;
Out of breath and scared to death of you.
It takes all the strength that I can call to my
    command,
To hold your hand.
I would speak at length
About the love that should be made,
But I'm afraid.

Hercules and such
Never bothered me much,
All you have to do is say "Boo!"
Out of breath and scared to death of you.

Since you must propose,
Then I'll have to disclose
Secrets that I've hidden from view;
Out of breath and scared to death of you.
When we met, my heart
Gave a queer little start
And the feeling's growing in to
Out of breath and scared to death of you.
Always I've been used
To having my affections spurned
And not returned;
Once my passion's loosed,
Then that's the time to be concerned,
You may be burned.
Think I could be made,
But I'm still so afraid,
Hurry and change my point of view!
Out of breath and scared to death of you.

"Out of Breath" was written for the Theatre Guild's bright young musical revue *Garrick Gaieties* and sung in that show by Sterling Holloway. It was the first really professional song by John Mercer (as he was billed) and an attention-getter in the show. One of the dancers in *Garrick Gaieties* was a lady named Ginger Meehan, who a few years later changed her second name to Mercer.

Words by
JOHN MERCER

OUT OF BREATH
(and Scared To Death Of You)

Music by
EVERETT MILLER

THE THEATRE GUILD PRESENTS

THE GARRICK GAIETIES

PRODUCTION DIRECTED BY
PHILIP LOEB
SETTINGS DESIGNED BY
KATE DRAIN LAWSON
COSTUMES DESIGNED BY
KATE DRAIN LAWSON
AND LOUIS M. SIMON
DANCES ARRANGED BY
OLIN HOLLAND
ASSISTED BY STELLA BLOCK

MADE IN U.S.A.

I Am Only Human After All
You Lost Your Opportunity
Put It Away Till Spring
Too, Too Divine
Out Of Breath
Ankle Up The Altar With Me
Love Is Like That
I've Got It Again

HARMS
INCORPORATED
62-64 WEST 45TH STREET
NEW YORK
CHAPPELL & CO LTD
LONDON   SYDNEY

Would'ja for a Big Red Apple?

1932

By HENRY SOUVAINE   EVERETT MILLER
JOHN MERCER

Greater men than I have sought your favor,
But you merely glance at them and grin,
You spurn the vermin,
Who offer ermine and just a bit of sin.

Even though these propositions bore you,
Even though you're weary of the chase,
Let me put a plan before you,
Maybe it will help my case.

Would'ja for a big red apple,
Would'ja for my peace of mind,
Could'ja for a big red apple
Give me what I'm trying to find.

Just imagine you're my teacher,
Teaching me the Golden Rule,
If I had a big red apple,
Would'ja keep me after school?

Cakes and sweets and sugar beets,
May be what a girl deserves,
Choc'late drops and lollipops are sweet on
    the taste
But "H" on the curves.

Would'ja do it just for instance,
Would'ja for my fam'ly tree,
If I had a big red apple,
Would'ja fall in love with me?

The author of "Lazybones" doing what comes naturally.

Buddy Rogers was the star of *Old Man Rhythm* but there was also at far right Lucille Ball (2), under Buddy's left foot Johnny Mercer (4) and under Buddy's right arm Betty Grable (5).

Spring Is in My Heart Again

1932

Music by WILLIAM WOODIN

You've been away so long,
And all the world was wrong
Each little meeting place
Has missed your smiling face;
But now the world is gay
Because you've come to stay,
Those lonely hours
Have passed away.

Spring is in my heart for you are here;
Spring is in my heart and skies are clear.
Life will be the way it used to be
Now that you are back with me.

Ev'ry place I wandered to,
Ev'ry winding street we knew
Brought me memories of you,
Dreaming of the night you said you loved
   me.

In our little moonlit rendezvous
I've so many things to say to you;
We will never be apart again.
Spring is in my heart again.

Mercer's co-writer was an interesting partner to have in those Depression days. Banker William Woodin became Franklin Roosevelt's Secretary of the Treasury—which helped not a bit to make this early ballad a money-maker. Fame was still only on its way.

Four music masters: Hoagy Carmichael, Jack Teagarden, Wingy Mannone and J.M.

Mr. Mercer and Mr. Teagarden—they paired off ideally in the Paul Whiteman days and later.

Lazybones

1933

Music by HOAGY CARMICHAEL

Long as there is chicken gravy on your rice,
Ev'rything is nice.
Long as there's watermelon on the vine,
Ev'rything is fine.
You got no time to work,
You got no time to play,
Busy doin' nothin' all the live long day.
You won't ever change no matter what I say,
You're just made that way.

Lazybones, Sleepin' in the sun,
How you 'spec' to get your day's work
    done?
Never get your day's work done,
Sleepin' in the noonday sun.

Lazybones, sleepin' in the shade,

How you 'spec' to get your corn meal
    made?
Never get your corn meal made
Sleepin' in the evenin' shade.

When 'taters need sprayin',
I bet you keep prayin'
The bugs fall off of the vine
And when you go fishin'
I bet you keep wishin'
The fish won't grab at your line.

Lazybones, loafin' thru the day,
How you 'spec' to make a dime that way?
Never make a dime that way
(Well looky here,)
He never heared a word I say!

The first real hit for the now newly first-named Johnny Mercer (out with that inappropri-
ately square monicker, John!) It also marks the beginning of a two-peas-in-a-pod musical
partnership and a song that was like home cooking to these relatively new boys in town.
Lazybones took the big city and then the whole country by storm. Mercer and
Carmichael had arrived.

34

Hamilton

Lazybones

WORDS & MUSIC BY

JOHNNY MERCER

AND

HOAGY CARMICHAEL

Featured by
DO-RE-MI TRIO

WITH GUITAR
AND UKELELE
CHORDS

SOUTHERN MUSIC PUB. CO., INC.
1619 BROADWAY, NEW YORK

The Old Music Master

1933

Music by HOAGY CARMICHAEL

One night long ago by the light of the moon,
An old music master sat composing a tune,
His spirit was soaring and his heart full of
    joy,
When right out of nowhere stepped a little
    colored boy.
You gotta jump it, music master,
You gotta play that rhythm faster,
You're never gonna get it played
On the Happy Cat Hit Parade.
You better tell your friend Beethoven,
And Mister Reginald De Koven
They better do the same as you,
Or they're gonna be corny too.
Long about nineteen seventeen
Jazz'll come upon the scene,
Then about nineteen thirty-five,
You'll begin to hear swing,
Boogie Woogie and Jive,

You gotta show that big broadcaster,
That you're a solid music master,
And you'll achieve posterity,
That's a bit of advice from me.
The old music master simply sat there
    amazed,
As wide-eyed and open-mouthed he gazed,
And he gazed.
How can you be certain, little boy,
Tell me how?
Because I was born, my friend,
A hundred years from now.
He hit a chord that rocked the spinet
And disappeared in "the infinite,"
And up until the present day,
You can take it from me
He's as right as can be,
Ev'rything has happened that-a way.

The team's second outing, but not quite the hit of their first product—(what could be?). Both Hoagy and Johnny enjoyed writing about jazz, for, after all, the former had been around Bix and the latter was a dyed-in-the-wool fan who had booked the bands for his prep school's proms. The words "jive" and "corny" were somewhat avant-garde in 1933, and not many Broadwayites were hip to—who?—"Mister Reginald DeKoven." But at least "the Happy Cat Hit Parade" could draw a chuckle.

THE OLD MUSIC MASTER

Words by JOHNNY MERCER · Music by HOAGY CARMICHAEL

When a Woman Loves a Man

1934   Music by BERNARD HANIGHEN

Love to a man is just a thing apart,
To take or leave, according to his whim,
Love to a woman means her very heart,
She only wants to live her life for him.

Maybe he's not much,
Just another man,
Doing what he can,
But what does she care,
When a woman loves a man.

She'll just string along,
All thru' thick and thin,
Till his ship comes in,
It's always that way,
When a woman loves a man.

She'll be the first one to praise him
When he's going strong,
The last one to blame him
When ev'rything's wrong,
It's such a one-sided game that they play,
But women are funny that way.

Tell her she's a fool,
She'll say "Yes, I know,
But I love him so,"
And that's how it goes,
When a woman loves a man.

A great standard among torch songs, recorded by such knowing singers as Billie Holiday, Kay Starr and Jane Harvey. It also marked the beginning of another fruitful alliance, this one with Bernard (soon to be Bernie) Hanighen, a Harvard graduate of *simpatico* musical tastes. Gordon Jenkins went on to achieve great fame for the popular *Manhattan Towers Suite* and Benny Goodman's haunting theme, "Goodbye."

Good songs are like street cars . . . there'll be another one along in a minute.

Fare-Thee-Well to Harlem

1934

Music by BERNIE HANIGHEN

Mister Jackson, you sho' look cute,
You must have on your trav'lin' suit.
It looks as if you're really gonna go
    somewhere,
Mister Budley, you spoke a book
You just got time for one more look,
'Cause Mister Jackson is leaving you for fair,
For fair, for:

Fare-thee-well to Harlem!
Fare-thee-well to night life!
Goin' back where I can lead the right life
Fare-thee-well to Harlem!

Things is tight in Harlem,
I know how to fix it.

Step aside, I'm gonna Mason Dix it
Fare-thee-well to Harlem!

Lately here my soul is reachin'
For the Bible's kindly teachin'.
Want's to hear the Rev'rund preachin'
"Love each other."
Wants to hear the organ playin'
Wants to hear the folks a prayin'
There's a voice within me sayin'
"Ease off, brother."
So, fare-thee-well to Harlem!
All this sin is "frighteous."
Goin' back where evrybody's righteous.
Fare-thee-well to Harlem!

Mercer had by now found a ready market for his unique and hip (but not too hip) style of song; what was soon added was his stylish way of presenting these songs vocally. This witty and most original specialty number wowed the customers who gathered around the bandstand of New York's Hotel Biltmore when Paul Whiteman (then very popular) presented Mercer and Jack Teagarden as a sort of novelty act. Calling a big, burly jazzman like Teagarden "cute" was way ahead of its time, and the word "frighteous" may be a made-up word but it seems okay for an allowably ethnic song of that time.

FARE-THEE-WELL TO HARLEM

LYRIC BY
JOHNNY MERCER
BY ARRANGEMENT WITH MILLER MUSIC, INC.

MUSIC BY
BERNIE HANIGHEN

Featured by
LEON
BELASCO

SOUTHERN MUSIC PUB. CO. INC. 1619 BROADWAY, N.Y.

Here Come the British

1934

Music by BERNIE HANIGHEN

Children, open up your history,
Turn to lesson twenty-three.
Take a look,
Then close the book,
And I will review it rapidly.

Paul Revere—he took a ride,
Just to look around the countryside.
All at once his horse got skittish;
Here come the British,
Bang! Bang!
Washington—at Valley Forge
Tried to cross the river.
Look out, George!

All at once his boat got skittish;
Here come the British,
Bang! Bang!
Just look around,
No matter where—whoa!
You'll find that
The British are there.
Napoleon at Waterloo
Writin' Josephine a billet doux.
Josie, I've got to close it,
Close this epistle,
There goes the whistle;
Here come the British with a Bang! Bang!

A perfect example of the Mercer wit and originality that caused a stir in professional circles in New York during 1934-35. Broadcasts from the Biltmore spread the Mercer magic, and among those who recognized this new talent on the scene was Irving Berlin. Mr. B's interest led to a working agreement with his major music publishing firm, an important step along the way. Songwriter Arthur Schwartz (& Dietz), big on Broadway in the thirties, also hopped aboard the Mercer bandwagon when he heard Johnny sing this and other originals on the Whiteman broadcasts.

42

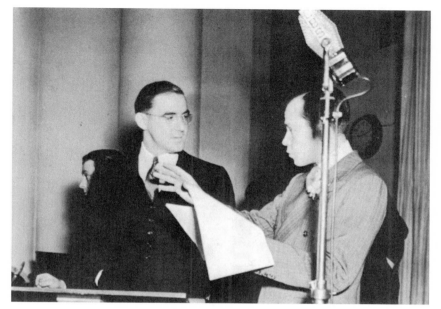

Is the King of Swing giving Johnny his infamous "ray"? J.M. made the Benny Goodman program Camel Caravan a popular tune-in with his very topical "newsy bluesies"

Affable but not yet balding Mercer is shown here obviously song-plugging Benny Goodman's first and best singer, Helen Ward.

Pardon My Southern Accent

1934   Music by MATTY MALNECK

It's a universal moon above you,
Ask the Irish, ask the Greek.
They can always understand "I love you,"
No matter how they speak.

Pardon my Southern accent,
Pardon my Southern drawl;
It may sound funny,
Ah, but honey! I love y'all.

If you don't like my accent,
If you don't like my drawl,
Then just don't listen,
Let's start kissin', bet you'll fall.

Come on, now,
Let me hear you steal my stuff.
When I say,
"Do you love me"
All you gotta say is "Sho'nuff."

Pardon my Southern accent,
Didn't I hear you drawl,
Were you just sighin',
Or replyin'
I love y'all.

Matty Malneck, a violinist in the huge, star-studded Whiteman organization, was another good early partner for Mercer's wonderful way with words. How could anyone from out of Savannah miss with a natural like this? By now even Hollywood was aware of that fresh spring of talent.

Pardon My Southern Accent

Words by
JOHNNY MERCER

Music by
MATT MALNECK

STANDARD EDITION

PRICE
60¢
IN U.S.A.

BOURNE INC.
Music Publishers
799 SEVENTH AVENUE · NEW YORK 19, N. Y.

The Dixieland Band

1935   Music by BERNIE HANIGHEN

Dj'ever hear the story of the Dixieland
   Band?
Let me tell you, brother,
That the music was grand.
They had piano and a clarinet,
Only think they needed was a second
   cornet;
And that's what lead to the ruin;
Ruin of the Dixieland Band.

When the folks would holler for the "Maple
   Leaf Rag,"
They would get to swinging,
But the trumpet would drag.
They had to keep him 'cause he played so
   sweet,
But they needed someone who could give
   them the beat;
Someone who swung with the rhythm,
Rhythm of the Dixieland Band.

He'd play so sweetly.
'Stead of playin' [*musical riff*]
He'd play so sweetly.
They'd be sayin' [*musical riff*]

Sure enough, he got 'em so they couldn't
   play right;
Finally he fixed 'em on a Saturday night.
He hit a figure that was off the chord,
Apoplexy got 'em and they went to the
   Lord;
And that's the pitiful story,
Story of the Dixieland Band.

Now they're up in heaven and they're
   happy at last;
'Cause they found a trumpet man who
   really can blast.
The way he swings 'em is an awful shame,
He can really do it, Gabriel is his name.
And now, folks, here is a sample,
Listen to the Dixieland Band.

If you hear a trumpet start to play,
Don't you be afraid, it's the judgment day!
'Cause it's just Mister Gabriel soundin' his
   "A."
And the Dixieland Band is fixin' to play.

From Whiteman to Goodman and Mercer is swinging all the way: this is another of the period's hip numbers that not only must have pleased the author's taste but also found a fairly good commercial audience to boot. This one was one of Benny Goodman's first big record hits on the Victor label, helped tremendously by Helen Ward's throbbing vocal. Mercer as usual writes from inside the jazz fraternity with such references as "The Maple Leaf Rag" and a figure that was off the chord. In addition, the song neatly tells a complete little story.

On the Nodaway Road

1935

Music by CHARLES BATES

Ploddin,' ploddin,' ol' Betsy's head keeps a
    noddin' noddin'
Ol' Betsy's hoofs are a kickin' up the dust
    along the road,
Haulin' a load down the Nodaway road.
Creakin' creakin'
Ol' wagon wheels keeps a squeakin'
    squeakin'
Groanin' a tune while the crickets sing their
    song,
Go 'long, go 'long
Haulin' a load down the Nodaway road.

Got to get a load o' hay to town,
Hurry back before the sun goes down.
Smoke in the chimney as we climb the hill
'Round evenin' time,

'Round evenin' time.
Ol' Besty hurries goin' past the mill
'Round evenin' time,
'Round evenin' time.
I can hear the dogs bark as I open up the
    gate,
Ain't missed meetin' me yet,
And the lights thru the dark say,
"You'd better not be late, supper table is
    set."
Night is creepin' creepin'
I'll bet ol' Betsy is sleepin' sleepin'
Dreamin' away of another dusty day
To toil away,
Haulin' a load down the Nodaway road,
Haulin' a load down the Nodaway road.

Near the top of the list for thoroughly regional Mercer writing, "Nodaway Road" is a gem of a song, unfortunately known mainly to the true believers. It is a vignette of heartbreaking simplicity that Mercer seems to have recreated in the lovely little watercolor that appears in the front of this book.

48

1937, and another college musical, *Varsity Show*, with Johnnie "Scat" Davis and Fred Waring's Pennsylvanians performing most of the Mercer-Whiting score ("Have You Got Any Castles, Baby?," "Love Is on the Air," "Moonlight on the Campus").

I'm Building Up to an Awful Let-Down

1935   Music by FRED ASTAIRE

I'm like Humpty Dumpty,
Upon the garden wall.
I'm riding high and who can deny,
That whatever goes up must fall.
Poor old Humpty Dumpty,
He got the toughest break,
And yet his fall was nothing at all,
Like the tumble I'm gonna take.

I'm building up to an awful let-down,
By playing around with you.
You're breaking down my terrific buildup,
By treating me as you do.

My castles in the air,
My smile so debonair,
My one big love affair.

Is it just a flash
Will it all go smash,
Like the nineteen twenty-nine market crash?

I'm building up to an awful let-down
By falling in love with you.

As with so many songwriters and lyricists, the opportunity to have the classy Fred Astaire involved with a song of his was pure joy to Mercer, still new to Hollywood in 1935. Benny Green's book on Astaire quotes Mercer as saying that they met at a recording session that he (Mercer) was doing with Ginger Rogers. They sang "Eeny Meeny Miney Mo," one of Johnny's less illustrious efforts. The idea of their collaborating on a song came about in the casual manner that both men featured so well. The word "debonair" certainly fit at least one of the authors and the reference to the "nineteen twenty-nine market crash" was still a bit of nonchalant bravado in those belt-tightening days.

Jamboree Jones

1936

Words and Music by JOHNNY MERCER

I begin my story out in West Virginia
In a little college.
All the student body only cared for football,
Never mind the knowledge.
Never mind the sheepskin,
They preferred the pigskin.
Seemed to have it in their bones.
They knew all about it,
Couldn't live without it,
All except a certain Mister Jamboree Jones.

He played the clarinet with all his might,
He studied night and day,
He practiced day and night;
No running up the field for Mister Jones,
He'd rather run up the scale, what tones.

Even though his buddies
Always cut their studies
To attend a rally,
While they all were rootin'
You could hear him tootin'
"What became of Sally."
How they used to hate him,
Co-eds wouldn't date him,
Thought he was an awful bore.
But he liked his rhythm
More than bein' with 'em,
So he only grinned and went to practice
    some more.

Meanwhile, the team marched on to greater
    fame
Till they were asked to play
The famous Rose Bowl Game;
And on that day of days the students
    beamed,

What did they do when the team marched
    on the field,
They screamed.

Startin' from the kick off
They pulled ev'ry trick off,
But they couldn't win it.
'Stead of goin' forward
They were goin' backward
'Bout a mile a minute.
Seein' their position
They called intermission,
And they heard the ref'ree say,
Seventeen to nothin' ain't exactly nothin'
And you've only got about a minute to play.

Then from the stands there came a distant
    wail
And it was Jamboree
A-swingin' "Hold 'em Yale,"
And then the students all began to yell,
The players marched up the field and down
    the field,
Pell mell.

Rah Rah Rah Rah
Sis Boom Bah Bah
Bop De Oddle-da
Yea Bo Watch'em go.

Now, on a certain West Virginia hill
There stands that college still,
Just as it always will,
And there's a picture in its Hall of Fame.
You'll see the boy in the frame
Who won the game.
Jamboree Jones is the gentleman's name.

the search for
JAMBOREE JONES

How come Johnny Mercer to write "Jamboree Jones," that quintessential celebration of the fuzzy-cheeked man in the college band? What pixyish muse shunted aside the vibes that were to create "That Ol' Black Magic" and stirred instead the distant wail of Jamboree?

Ask a probing question and get a surprising answer. "I went to a ball game at Yankee Stadium in 1934," said Mercer from his Manhattan apartment. "Fordham was playing some team from Texas, and the Texans had the first college band I ever heard play Dixieland. And they had a kid trumpet player take a solo break — another first. He played 'Peanut Vendor.'"

The breakout of show biz onto the sports field so turned on Mercer that he hurried home to immortalize the moment. "It's a satire on narrative folk ballads," Mercer says. "I wrote it for Benny Goodman," (which explains Jamboree's transfer to the clarinet) "because I was joining his outfit as a singer, but Benny never would play it. It was Dixieland, and he wanted to swing. It never was a big hit, but it has lots of fans. It's Hugh Hefner's favorite song, he tells me. I heard Michele Lee do it the other night, and Mel Torme has it in his act . . ."

Mercer stretched his memory a bit more and said, "I think the Texas team was SMU." Sure enough, SMU met Fordham in New York in '34 and, to the tune of "Peanut Vendor," won 26-14. The problem then came to tracking down the original Jamboree Jones: Who was the soloist? The Reverend Robert Goodrich, an unlikely director of a Dixieland band, remembered that it had to be either Garner Clark, Jim Cullum or Ed Green. A fourth band member, Layton Bailey Jr., solved the mystery.

"Garner never did a solo," Bailey said, "and Jim Cullum played the clarinet. Eddie Green had to be Jamboree Jones." The handsome young swinger you see in the photo above died in 1965. But Mercer's classic tune and its sis-boom-bah will live on. Turn the page and try it out on your old upright.

Here's the way Johnny spoke about this collegiate caper: "I wrote it for Benny Goodman. . . . just a kind of admiration for the way he played. But he didn't play it much, because I don't think he liked it. It's kind of a put-on of 'Casey Jones' and 'Steamboat Bill,' don't you think?"

Mel Tormé, a Mercer buff of the top echelon, does this story-telling novelty often and, of course, is perfect for the performance.

Goody Goody

Music by MATTY MALNECK

You told me that there wasn't a lesson in
   lovin'
You hadn't learned
Oh yeah?
Oh yeah?
You told me that you keep playin' with fire
Without getting burned.
Oh yeah?
Oh yeah?

So you met someone
Who set you back on your heels,
Goody goody!
So you met someone
And now you know how it feels,

Goody Goody!
So you gave her your heart too
Just as I gave mine to you
And you broke it in little pieces,
Now how do you do?
So you lie awake
Just singing the blues all night,
Goody Goody!
So you think that love's
A barrel of dynamite.
Hooray and hallelujah!
You had it comin' to ya.
Goody Goody for him,
Goody Goody for me,
And I hope you're satisfied, you rascal you.

© Malneck Mercer
20th Century

Somebody told us (Malneck?) that Mercer got the idea for this double-word title from the menu of a Chinese restaurant and then stashed it away with other notes in a bureau drawer under some shirts. Several years later he rediscovered it—and *voilà!* Or, ah-so! Helen Ward remembers that she pleaded with Benny Goodman, "Please don't make me sing that damn song." BG knew—it became one of Helen Ward's biggest hits with the Goodman band.

BY AIR MAIL
PAR AVION

BERMUDA 6d POSTAGE

BERMUDA 3d POSTAGE

Mr. John Mercer
Warners Brothers Studio
Burbank, California
U.S.A. —

Air ½ 1.

very pleasant and make good servants.
This is sort of between seasons here
now, so we're getting plenty peace
and quiet. We're way out on a point
with fine beach, surf etc —

I spoke to the boys about your
going on the Kraft show, and hope
something definite has been done about
it. Present plans indicate I will
be in Hollywood on the 17th of
October —

Best regards to Ginger. Saw
Bennie in N.Y. He was working slightly.
Jack White a riot —

regards
Bing —

I'm an Old Cowhand

(From the Rio Grande)

1936   Words and music by JOHNNY MERCER

Step aside you ornery Tenderfeet
Let a big bad buckeroo past
I'm the toughest hombre you'll ever meet
Tho' I may be the last.
Yessirree we're a vanishing race,
Nosirree can't last long.
Step aside you ornery Tenderfeet
While I sing my song.

I'm an old cowhand
From the Rio Grande,
But my legs ain't bowed
And my cheeks ain't tanned,
I'm a cowboy who never saw a cow,
Never roped a steer 'cause I don't know
    how,
And I sho' ain't fixin' to start in now.
Yippy I O Ki Ay,
Yippy I O Ki Ay.

I'm an old cowhand
From the Rio Grande,
And I learned to ride
'Fore I learned to stand,
I'm a ridin' fool who is up to date,

I know ev'ry trail in the Lone Star State,
'Cause I ride the range in a Ford V-Eight.
Yippy I O Ki Ay,
Yippy I O Ki Ay.

I'm an old cowhand
From the Rio Grande,
And I come to town
Just to hear the band,
I know all the songs that the cowboys know,
'Bout the big corral where the doagies go,
'Cause I learned them all on the radio.
Yippy I O Ki Ay,
Yippy I O Ki Ay.

I'm an old cowhand
From the Rio Grande
Where the West is wild
'Round the Border land,
Where the buffalo roam around the Zoo,
And the Indians make you a rug or two,
And the old Bar X is a Bar B Q.
Yippy I O Ki Ay,
Yippy I O Ki Ay.

©John H. Mercer

Mercer told us: "Between movie assignments Ginger and I took a trip down to Savannah in a little car. We took three days out of six just to cross Texas, and I saw all those guys down there in those spurs and ten-gallon hats driving cars around. That struck me as kind of funny and so I thought maybe I should put it all into a song. Bing put the song into a picture, and I really think he saved my Hollywood career, because I began to get more offers after that."

   Modest Mercer there. But it was the first of many tie-ups between these two, who had more than just the Hollywood clubbiness in common. Ex-Whiteman vocalist Crosby must certainly have been listening once or twice when Johnny sang later on with that band, and Ginger had had a few dates with Bing before she became Mrs. Mercer.

Skinny Johnny and the old pro, Richard Whiting, who seems to be striking not only a serious chord but a serious pose as well. They made a peach of a productive pair, but who would have thought then that some day the composer of such great hits as "Japanese Sandman" and "Sleepy Time Gal" would be known to millions as the father of little Maggie Whiting.

Too Marvelous for Words

1937

Music by RICHARD A. WHITING

I search for phrases,
To sing your praises,
But there aren't any magic adjectives
To tell you all you are.

You're just too marvelous,
Too marvelous for words,
Like glorious, glamourous
And that old standby, amorous,

It's all too wonderful,
I'll never find the words,
That say enough,
Tell enough,
I mean, they just aren't swell enough,

You're much too much,
And just too very very!
To ever be in Webster's Dictionary,

And so I'm borrowing
A love song from the birds,
To tell you that you're marvelous,
Too marvelous for words.

A solid Mercer standard and a natural song idea for the word-minded author. "Very-very" is a nice idiomatic trick and the brilliant fall-into-place of "Webster's dictionary" adds fun that anyone can dig. The super-chic Bobby Short uses this song as a vehicle for community singing in the best cafés and supper clubs.

1937, and one of Hollywood's classic production numbers. Ruby Keeler and Lee Dixon dance on the keys to the tune of "Too Marvelous for Words," making typists all over the world green with envy. The movie was *Ready, Willing and Able.*

Bob White

(Whatcha Gonna Swing Tonight?)

1937

Music by BERNIE HANIGHEN

Mister Bob, don't you know things have
  changed?
You're behind time with the melody you
  always sing,
All the birds have their songs rearranged,
Better get smart,
Whatcha gotta do today is swing;

I was talkin' to the whippoorwill,
He says you got a corny trill,
Bob White!
Whatcha gonna swing tonight?
I was talkin' to the mocking bird,
He says you are the worst he's heard,
Bob White!
Whatcha gonna swing tonight?

Even the owl
Tells me you're foul,
Singin' those lullaby notes,
Don't be a bring-down
If you can swing down,
Gimme those high notes!
There's a lotta talk about you, Bob,
And they're sayin' you're "off the cob,"
Fake it,
Mister B.
Take it,
Follow me,
Bob White!
(whistle)
We're gonna break it up tonight!

A Crosby-Mercer record classic in the tradition of Gallagher & Shean. Mercer always had
an affinity for the fine feathered friends, and so putting this one onto paper (probably on
assignment for the record date) must have been a breeze. If you can find the record,
you'll hear two pros having a ball.

Hooray for Hollywood

1938

Music by RICHARD A. WHITING

Hooray for Hollywood!
That screwy bally hooey Hollywood,
Where any office boy or young mechanic
Can be a panic,
With just a good looking pan,
And any bar maid
Can be a star maid,
If she dances with or without a fan,

Hooray for Hollywood!
Where you're terrific if you're even good,
Where anyone at all from Shirley Temple
To Aimee Semple
Is equally understood,
Go out and try your luck,
You might be Donald Duck!
Hooray for Hollywood!

Hooray for Hollywood!
That phony super Coney Hollywood,
They come from Chilicothes and Paducahs
With their bazookas
To get their names up in lights,
All armed with photos from local rotos,
With their hair in ribbons and legs in tights,

Hooray for Hollywood!
You may be homely in your neighborhood,
But if you think that you can be an actor,
See Mister Factor,
He'd make a monkey look good.
Within a half an hour,
You'll look like Tyrone Power!
Hooray for Hollywood!

Is there a television special coming from the West Coast that *doesn't* use this song for a theme?
  1938 was a big year in the studios for Mercer. It was the year that found him teamed up with no one, but two, of the very best melody men in Hollywood—Richard Whiting and Harry Warren. This collaboration with Whiting was sung in the movie *Hollywood Hotel* by an effervescent musician, Johnnie "Scat" Davis. Davis seems to have fallen by the wayside, but the song has grown and grown through the years.

You Must Have Been a Beautiful Baby

1938   Music by HARRY WARREN

Does your mother realize,
The stork delivered quite a prize,
The day he left you on the fam'ly tree,

Does your dad appreciate,
That you are merely super great,
The miracle of any century,

If they don't, just send them both to me.

You must have been a beautiful baby,
You must have been a wonderful child,

When you were only startin'
To go to kindergarten,
I bet you drove the little boys wild.

And when it came to winning blue ribbons,
You must have shown the other kids how.
I can see the judges' eyes
As they handed you the prize,
I bet you made the cutest bow.

Oh! You must have been a beautiful baby,
'Cause, baby, look at you now.

Harry Warren was already the seasoned pro and Mercer merely the *wunderkind* around the studios when Warner Bros. paired them up in the busy year of 1938.

Here is Harry Warren's impression of that young partner of long ago: "I called him 'Cloud Boy,' and I'll tell you why. A lot of times when I would play a melody for him . . . particularly if it was after a good lunch . . . he'd stretch out on a couch and just lie there with his eyes closed and his hands folded across his stomach. He was way up there some place in the clouds. Of course, what came out later was just great."

As with many a great pop song, once Mercer found the "then–now" gimmick for this song, the rest might have been quite easy for a master lyricist.

62

Jeepers Creepers

1938

Music by HARRY WARREN

I don't care what the weather man says,
When the weather man says it's raining,
You'll never hear me complaining,
I'm certain the sun will shine,
I don't care how the weather vane points,
When the weather vane points to gloomy,
It's gotta be sunny to me,
When your eyes look into mine;

Jeepers Creepers!
Where'd ya get those peepers?
Jeepers Creepers!
Where'd ya get those eyes?

Gosh all git up!
How'd they get so lit up?

Gosh all git up!
How'd they get that size?

Golly gee!
When you turn those heaters on,
Woe is me!
Got to put my cheaters on,

Jeepers Creepers!
Where'd ya get those peepers?
Oh! Those weepers!
How they hypnotize!
Where'd ya get those eyes?

"Jeepers creepers, where'd you get those peepers?"

"Jeepers Creepers" brought Mercer's first Academy Award nomination. And here's what he had to say about the song: "I think I heard Henry Fonda say something like 'Jeepers Creepers' in a movie, and I thought it would be a cute idea for a song. I searched around quite a bit and then found that it fit so well as a title for that melody of Harry's. It was lucky casting that we got Louis Armstrong to sing it, although it wasn't written for him."

The Girl Friend of the Whirling Dervish

1938

Lyric by AL DUBIN and JOHNNY MERCER
Music by HARRY WARREN

One fine day I chanced to stray on a little
   side street in old Bombay
And met a sentimental oriental,
She saw me and I saw she had a manner
   too bold and much too free,
Her eyes were positively detrimental,

When I asked about this gay coquette,
I discovered much to my regret:

She's the girl friend of the whirling dervish,
She's the sweetest one he's found,
But ev'ry night in the mellow moonlight,
When he's out dervishing with all his might,
She gives him the run around.

All the boy friends of the whirling dervish
   are his best friends to his face,

But there's no doubt, when he isn't about,
They all come hurrying to take her out,
She leads him a dizzy pace,
He dreams of a Hindu honeymoon,
He doesn't dream that ev'ry night when he
   goes out to
Make an honest rupee,
She steps out to make a lotta whoopee.

Oh! The love song of the whirling dervish
Has a sweet and tender sound,
But will he burn if he ever should learn,
That while he's doing her a real good turn,
She gives him the run around.

She's got a nervish, throwin' him a curvish,
Which of course, he doesn't deservish,
Poor old whirling dervish!

A good movie novelty song that utilized the inevitable gag, "a real good turn . . . gives him the run around." The three-way collaboration of Dubin, Mercer and Warren produced the song for *Garden of the Moon,* one of the less than memorable movies that came off the Warner assembly line in the thirties. Again it was Johnnie "Scat" Davis who sang it on screen (was he being groomed to be another Jack Oakie or a white Louis Armstrong?).

THE GIRL FRIEND OF THE WHIRLING DERVISH

WARNER BROS.
presents

"GARDEN OF THE MOON"

WITH

PAT O'BRIEN
MARGARET LINDSAY
JOHN PAYNE

JOE VENUTI *and his* SWING CATS
JOHNNIE DAVIS · MELVILLE COOPER
AND
JIMMIE FIDLER

•

DIRECTED BY BUSBY BERKELEY

•

Screen Play by Jerry Wald and Richard
Macaulay · From the Saturday Evening Post ·
Story by H. Bedford-Jones and Barton Browne

•

Music by
HARRY WARREN
Lyrics by
AL DUBIN
JOHNNY MERCER

•

CONFIDENTIALLY
GARDEN OF THE MOON
LOVE IS WHERE YOU FIND IT
THE GIRL FRIEND OF THE
WHIRLING DERVISH
THE LADY ON THE TWO CENT
STAMP

HARMS
INC.
NEW YORK

The Weekend of a Private Secretary

1938

Music by BERNIE HANIGHEN

I went to Havana on one of those cruises,
For forty-nine fifty to spend a few days;
I went to Havana, to look at the natives,
To study their customs, their picturesque
    ways.

In searching for some local color,
I ran across a Cuban gent,
And he was such a big sensation,
I forgot the population;
He showed me the city, he taught me the
    customs;
My trip to Havana was quite a success.

We had Bacardi,
I forgot the clock,
So we were tardy
In returning to the dock.
Tho' I delayed it,
Even dropped my shawl,
The Cuban made it,

As they gave the final call.
Darn it all!

I'm back in the office,
I'm punching the time clock,
But you can bet my mind is not on my
    work;
Instead of Bacardis,
I'm ordering Bromos,
Instead of the Cuban,
I'm stuck with a clerk.

The other girls can go to Europe,
And marry into royalty,
And they can get an Earl or Pasha
Or a gent with lots of casha.

But when I get married
And settle in Brooklyn,
He may be a slicker,
He may be a hick or a Reuben,
But you can bet that he'll be Cuban.

Mercer's handiwork with topicality, a couple of mild jokes, and a neat little story-line paid off for the singer but not too much for the song. It was a natural for the sly, soft-swinging Mildred Bailey, who made it into one of her best records that year.

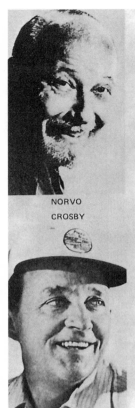

NORVO
CROSBY

MERCER
GOODMAN

The Rocking Chair Lady, Mildred Bailey, another Whiteman alumna, had the sly singing style for Mercer's satirical cruise song.

Bing Crosby
Hollywood

April 13, 1939

Dear "Verseable":

    I thought you would be out this way afore now and was surprised to learn you're not coming for a piece. We all miss your Saturday nite insouciance, but of course you should strike while the iron is hot - and you've got it good and hot right now.

    "Angels," to my way of thinking, is your best lyric to date. You're getting practically poetic. It's a hunk of song. Trouble is, by the time Kapp gets them to me, all the good singers have opened many lengths on me.

    I hope you kept Drinkable out of the clip joints during his Gotham Sabbatical. Doesn't take but two flagons of Trommers' Lager to send him on the town.

    Laughable is a champion now. He's at Palm Springs with his ma, catching a tan and getting well spoiled by all the ladies. He slays the chickadees. Strictly a Crosby, I guess.

    "Eastside of Heaven" was good fun under the expensive aegis of D. Wingate Butler. Never engaged in a more pleasant and, I hope, profitable enterprise. The budget was astonishingly low and, if John Public takes to the picture favorably, we're a cinch to make a meg or two.

    Now, John, we're expecting you here for the racing and the 'surfin' and turfin', so pack up Ginger et al and summer out this way.

                Your friend,

                Bing

Mr. John Mercer
111 E. 60th.
New York, New York

This sheet music cover, included only to illustrate the "jolly darkie" image still afoot in some management offices of 1936, despite the European success of such sophisticates as Josephine Baker, Reginald Foresythe and Leslie Hutcheson during the period. If the songs were not too memorable, at least the art work retains a certain period charm.

And the Angels Sing

1939

Music by ZIGGY ELMAN

We meet, and the angels sing.
The angels sing the sweetest song I ever
   heard.
You speak, and the angels sing,
Or am I breathing music into ev'ry word.

Suddenly the setting is strange,
I can see water and moonlight beaming,
Silver waves that break on some
   undiscovered shore;
Then suddenly I see it all change,
Long winter nights with the candles
   gleaming,
Thru it all your face that I adore.

You smile, and the angels sing,
And tho' it's just a gentle murmur at the
   start,
We kiss, and the angels sing
And leave their music ringing in my heart.

Mercer's association with Benny Goodman continued through the 1930s, when he was selected to co-host a radio show called "Camel Caravan" that featured the King of Swing. (The program would often show off Mercer's ingeniousness with almost on-the-spot satires of the day's news called Newsie Bluesies.) The association led to this classic—sung then by Martha Tilton—which is the result of Mercer's adding lyrics to what had been a Ziggy Elman trumpet specialty called "Frälich in Swing."

I Thought About You

1939

Music by JIMMY VAN HEUSEN

Seems that I read, or somebody said
That out of sight is out of mind,
Maybe that' so but I tried to go
And leave you behind,
What did I find?

I took a trip on the train
And I thought about you,
I passed a shadowy lane
And I thought about you,
Two or three cars parked under the stars,
A winding stream,
Moon shining down on some little town,
And with each beam,
Same old dream,

At ev'ry stop that we made
Oh, I thought about you,
But when I pulled down the shade,
Then I really felt blue,
I peeked thru the crack
And looked at the track,
The one going back to you,
And what did I do?
I thought about you!

One of the rare collaborations with the great veteran Jimmy McHugh, this wonderfully sentimental song is placed in the setting that Mercer loved so much and used so often—the train. The brief pictures evoked ("shadowy lane" "cars parked" "some little town") certainly spell out the feeling of a rural countryside at night, and the triple rhyme of "crack, "track" and "back" is train-like too. The composer-musicologist Alec Wilder singled this song out for special praise—but, then, he was another railroad buff.

You Grow Sweeter as the Years Go By

1939

Words and Music by JOHNNY MERCER

When I look at you
Standing there beside me,
I am filled with pride,
I am happy too,
When the winter lies upon the meadow,
I don't mind if summer time is through,
When I look at you;

You grow sweeter as the years go by,
You grow sweeter as the twilights fly,
I need never dream of our first kiss,
When I know our last one is as sweet as this.

Though September takes the place of June
In September there's a harvest moon,
Let the leaves start falling, darling,
What care I
When you grow sweeter as the years go by.

Although there are several photographs of Mercer seated at the keyboard of a piano, that is only photographic license and a cliché as well. He was not a full-fledged musician, although he could read the notes on a piece of sheet music and could obviously pick out a melody single-finger style. This is one example of a nice but unexceptional little song that Mercer wrote by himself.

Day In—Day Out

1939

Music by RUBE BLOOM

Day in—day out,
The same old hoodoo follows me about.
The same old pounding in my heart
Whenever I think of you
And, darling, I think of you
Day in—and day out
Day out—day in,
I needn't tell you how my days begin.
When I awake I awaken with a tingle,
One possibility in view,
That possibility of maybe seeing you.
Come rain, come shine,
I meet you and to me the day is fine,
Then I kiss your lips
And the pounding becomes
The ocean's roar,
A thousand drums,
Can't you see it's love,
Can there by any doubt,
When there it is
Day in—day out.

Always a blockbuster when sung by the magnificent Lena Horne, this lyric strangely presages the title of another even greater Mercer hit—"Come Rain or Come Shine." The co-writer, Rube Bloom, had played piano for many jazz groups through the years and had written the brilliant piano solo "Soliloquy," so Mercer must have admired him greatly. "The ocean's roar . . . a thousand drums"—great for Las Vegas and big rooms with big bands.

Who can compete with Lena's smile? "Day In, Day Out" has been one of her powerhouse numbers for years.

Two very groovey characters do a typical photographer's switch for the camera. Johnny, hippest of all famous songwriters, was the right one to sing "Happy Birthday" to Satchmo for his 50th at the Newport Jazz Festival.

The Rumba Jumps!

1939

Music by HOAGY CARMICHAEL

There's a Harlem band 'way down in San
   Domingo,
A very talented group,
They kicked 'em off of a sloop,
Even tho' the band can't understand the
   lingo,

They're never down in the dumps,
For when the drummer boy thumps,
The Rumba Jumps!

"Hep, hep!" They hollered the moment
   they landed,
"We've got a rumba the King once
   commanded,"
Then they passed a tin and started in to play
The way they learned to play
Back in the U.S.A.

Now they're on the air and San Domingo's
   lappin' it up,

And I do declare those Harlem boys are
   wrappin' it up;
Folks in ev'ry land tune in on San Domingo,
They're never down in the dumps,
For when the drummer boy thumps,
The Rumba Jumps!

"Hep, hep!" they holler,
"Stay right in your villa,
We're on the air for a brand of vanilla."
If you wanna dance and wanna dance in
   style,
You better turn the dial
To San Domingo Isle,

And when you hear "Aye aye,
Hide aye aye,"
You'll know the reason why
The Rumba Jumps!

Hoagy and Johnny, back together in 1939, wrote a few numbers for the stage show *Three After Three*,
but despite such talented people as Mitzi Green, Frances Williams and Stepin Fetchit the review limped
into New York, where it was re-named *Walk with Music*. This specialty was obviously meant to be the
inspiration and background for lots of hot dancing—"hep hep!" was quite hip then.

THE RUMBA JUMPS!

Lyrics by
JOHNNY MERCER

Music by
HOAGY CARMICHAEL

RUTH SELWYN IN ASSOCIATION WITH
MESSRS. SHUBERT

presents

SIMONE SIMON
MITZI GREEN
and
MARY BRIAN
in
Three After Three
with
FRANCES WILLIAMS
ART JARRETT
STEPIN FETCHIT

★

From the original play by GUY BOLTON
Musical adaptation by
GUY BOLTON, PARKE LEVY and ALAN PRESCOTT
Staged by CLARKE LILLEY
Scenery designed by WATSON BARRAT
Dances by BOOTS McKENNA
Costumes by LUCINDA BALLARD

★

MERCER & MORRIS, INC.
1619 BROADWAY • M•M • NEW YORK, N.Y.

THE RUMBA JUMPS
DARN CLEVER, THESE CHINEE
OOH! WHAT YOU SAID
WAY BACK IN 1939 A.D.
EVERYTHING HAPPENS TO ME
WHAT'LL THEY THINK OF NEXT

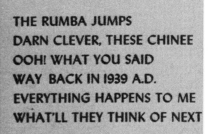

Hooray for Spinach

1939

Music by HARRY WARREN

As a kid, I hated spinach and all its ilk,
I abominated cod liver oil and milk,
That was simply that and I'd leave them flat!
Tho' you stuck a gat at my brow,
But I must admit my opinion's different now;

Hooray for spinach!
Hooray for milk!
They put the roses in your cheek soft as silk,
They helped complete you till I could meet
   you, baby!

Hooray for sunshine!
Hooray for air!
They put the permanent in your curly hair,
They helped to raise you till I could praise
   you, baby!

Bless the summer that freckled your nose,
Those galoshes that sheltered your toes,
Bless the fellow who taught you to kiss,
If he taught you to kiss like this.

Hooray for spinach!
It took you far!
Bless all the nourishment in each candy bar,
They helped you grow up till
I could show up and love you as you are.

©Remick Music Corp.

It has to be tongue in cheek that caused Mercer and Warren to have put in small print on the face of the sheet music "with acknowledgments to Wagner, Lizst, etc." The whole idea of this typically "cute" movie song seems borrowed a bit from the earlier "You Must Have Been a Beautiful Baby," or maybe it was suggested by the tremendously popular *New Yorker* cartoon of that period, "I say it's spinach and I say the hell with it!" At any rate Ronald Reagan might remember it.

Not one of Mercer's greatest efforts but we call your attention to the cast, where even Johnnie (what happened to "Scat"?) Davis takes precedence over the current cowboy from Washington.

Christmas card

BLESSINGS on thee, everyone
Every single mother's son
Blessings, friends of ancient vintage
Blessings, friends of recent mintage
Whomsoever you may be
Merry Christmas unto thee
Old year's gone and we got through it
—though I wouldn't own up to it—
Hope and pray the next one's better
If it ain't we'll make it wetter
Drown our sorrows and our woes
Barkeep, give me one of those!
Let's all drink a toast or toddy
Wishing well to everybody
This is one day hearts have wings
Hark, the Herald Tribune sings!
There is peace in Sunday's chimes
There is—quote—peace in our Times
Brilliant is the Evening Star
Brilliant and somnambular
Let's repeat it once again
Peace on earth—good will to men
Gather neath the mistletoe
A.F.L. and C.I.O.
Wendell Willkie, Gerald Nye
Messers. ASCAP, BMI
With the world hell bent for leather

Now's the time to stick together
Drop the hatchet, stop the fuss
Climb aboard, and come with us
Mr. Kringle drives the sleigh
Don't you hear a reindeer neigh?
Here we go! He cracks his whip
Our imaginary trip
Takes us through the snowy night
—better wrap those blankets tight—
Time for all to go once more
Through the holly-covered door
Down the candle-lighted hall
Merry Christmas to you all!
Things are bad from pole to isthmus
But we still believe in Christmas
Choir, let these guests be carolled!
Annie Arlen, hatless Harold
Johnny Arledge, Fred Astaire
Jane and Squirrel, the Ashcraft pair
Juney Adams, hya, bub?
Ager, Alter, Auto Club
Square and Edith Anderson
Henny Bacchus, Billy Blun
Nora and the kids and Carleton
All of 301 East Charlton
Irving Berlin, Perry Botkin
What's the difference if you're not kin?

For all his sly wit and hip imagery, Johnny Mercer was basically a sentimentalist. Nothing shows this more clearly than the great series of Christmas cards which he began composing and sending to a select list of his friends in the late thirties. He might have been inspired by a similar traditional verse that Frank Sullivan wrote for *The New Yorker* each New Year's, and Johnny's, more California-oriented, were just as eagerly anticipated, as the years went by, for their roll calls of familiar names and their matchless rhymes. Johnny used almost no punctuation in these verses, but so sure was his ear that they read as though carefully copy-edited.

Get together, hug each other
You may be somebody's mother
Berkeley, Bargy, Bleyer, Bloom
This way to the drinking room
Morton Bernstein and his wife
—the first woman in my life—
Gladly did I let her munch on
My first kindergarten luncheon
Johnny Burke, that wine
    should bubble!
Well, poor boy, he's seeing double
I hear Bells—and all the way
From Savannah town, G.A.
Greetings, darling Aunt Nell Blackie
Bless you, and your boys in khaki
Butlers, Burroughs, Mildred Bailey
Try this on your ukelele—
Take this old one off the shelf—
"Love thy neighbor as thyself"
Ronny Burla and his Una
And this summer in Laguna
Henri Blanke, and Miss B
Mr., Mrs., Broccoli
All of A,S,C,A,P
Harry Barris—BVC
Pink and Mary, hey and nonny
Susie, Belle, and killer Johnny
Bing and Dixie and their clan
Barefoot boys with Daddy's pan
And if Daddy's wits are keen
He knows "pan" ain't what I mean
Carol Carol, J. Colonna
All the smudgepots in Pomona
Hattie Clinton, daughter Ann
And the lost Republican
Greetings, Ducky, Bob Carmichael
Hoag and Ruth complete the cycle
Christmas Gift to Chan and Chaplin
Leonard Ross and
    H*Y*M*A*N K*A*P*L*A*N

Bless the Dolans, Mims and Bobby
We the people—Hobby Lobby
Bette Davis, Mary and Mary
And the dwelling of McCarey
Pour the port and fill the chalice
For the Dougalls, Bern and Alice
Tommy Dugan, Buddy Dill
And the folks upon the hill
The DeSylvas—hello, chief!
(When do I go on relief?)
Pass the eggnog, pass the wines
Fill the goblets, fill the steins
William Dozier, Meta Reis
Never let the pouring cease
Drink a cheer to Mr. Dubin
Dorsey brothers, how have you been?
Walter Donaldson, drink hearty
Barney Dean, it's your block party
Jimmy Downey and his mummy
Joseph Dubin and his tummy
E's for Ellfeldt, Emerson
Edelman and everyone
Harry Evans, Eberle
Fill the house with harmony
Skinnay Ennis, have a chair
Everybody, everywhere
Arthur Fishbein, Arthur Franklin
Dwight and Mary, won't you ankl' in?
Shake my writin' hand, Coach Frawley
You still rhyme with Dick MacCauley
Leo Forbstein, start your band
Play for Miss de Havilland
Henry Fonda, Mrs. F
Shout it till the crowd is deaf
O'er the snowy countryside
Happy, happy Xmastide
To the friends too seldom seen
Ira Gershwin, Johnny Green
Close that window—look who blew in
Jack Gordean and Jimmy Gruen

Darling Peggy and their John
Followed by the tribe of Kahn
Benny Goodman, there's Mose Gumble
Won't you help him from the rumble?
Goodwins, get up from the table
Make your bow to Betty Grable
Johnny Galludet and Connie
Looking apple cheeked and bonny
Ring the bells in St. John's steeple
For the Hulls—our favorite people
Here comes Hunter—Christmas calling
Here comes Herzig—ashes falling
Dr. Harris, Byron Harvey
There's the turkey—feeling carvey?
Bob and Peg, and Hanighen
All together once again
Greetings coming—going back
Are you kiddin'?—Murder, Jack!
To the Houstons and the Hitches
And the Hendersons—like Skitch is
Merry Yule and Noel too
Lindsay Howard, Judyroo
Taste the peaches, slice the mutton
For Ray Heindorf, Betty Hutton
—if the madam's glance is wayward
For that dream girl, Susan Hayward
Bob Hope and his bride, Dolores
May I pour a doch-an-dorris?
Footman! Do you hear those klaxons!
Meet the Jenkins and the Jacksons!
Here comes Jarvis and his ballroom
Open up that extra hall room
Irving Kahal and Teddy Koehler
Charlie Chan and Sidney Toler
Hey, toy soldier, hit your cymbals
For Miss Karol down at Gimbels
Hy and Reata, Missy Jill
Holly on your windowsill
I know all you people, but
WHO is Wilhelmina Thutt?

Kaufman, Keyes, and Kuhl and Kress
Everybody—more or less
Even those whom I've forgotten
Jim! My memory is rotten!
And if you think that's a curse
Madam's list is even worse
So if your name is omitted
We both pray to be acquitted
And we love you anyway
If that meets with your okay?
Jimmy Kern, his bairn and mar'm,
Best of luck from madam's arm
Jerry Kern, my circumspect eyes
Say, "Go on and wear those neckties"
Who's that beauty over there?
Gentlemen, meet Annie Lehr
Edgar Leslie, Eddie Lowe
With those cute LaMonts in tow
Jolly, jumping Jerry Lester
John and Mildred Malatester
Lamp Miss Landis' apparel
That's my kind of Christmas Carole
And toujours Lamour toujours
Is my favorite song I'm sure
Who's that in the living room?
Donald Livingston, I presume?
Footman! Bring Priscilla Lane
In out of the frozen rain
Look! We have a pine-cone fire
From the house of McIntire
And some frankincense and myrrh
From the house of Mehlinger
And some old imported vino
Malneck, this is Mannerino
Mayhew, this is Modisett
Have you met the Mitchells yet?
Joseph Wingston (Lawd!) Mannone
Jack, I do not dig your tone!
Miss MacLaughlin . . . Mr. Markey
Always tries that old mullarkey

Here they come—those sailing sharks
Buddy Morris, Albert Marx
Have you met the Mercer tribe?
These cats really can imbibe!
Juliana and Miss Lily
Uncle Robbie—he's a dilly
Hugh and domicile of three
Walter and his family
Mercer, Nancy—best to them
Joseph and Virginia M
Chris and Liz and George and Bess
—Uncle Joe is in distress,
Cousin Mamie's hid the liquor
That just makes a Scotsman sicker—
Uncle Lewis and Uncle Ed
Soiled Aunt Katherine's tablespread!
Pray continue, eat your fill
While we call up Jacksonville
Say hello to Mother there
Ed, and Deborah, and Claire
Goodness how the party grows
Millers, Myers, Monacos
Freddie Martin and Tchaikowsky
Dagmar, I believe, Godowsky
Ray and Eadie Mayer—and Jeanie
Count Oleg and Gene Cassini
Harmon Helson, how's the ham—
Baked and cured by
    Uncle Sam?
Mr. Nobel sound your "A"
Play a simple Christmas lay
To O'Brien, to O'Connell
Out-of-meter John MacDonell
The Orsattis and O'Neills
—Mrs. O's a dream on wheels—
To the Oxnards and the Oakies
O'er the Rockies and the Smokies
Santa brings our heartfelt wish
May your new year be delish!

I could count till I got weary
Playing one, two, three O'Leary
Once again here comes that
    snow man
Fat and smiling faced Phil Ohman
Herb and Midge Polesie, howdy!
Just in time—we're getting rowdy
Hello, Helen Paup and Merle
Whatcha gettin'—boy or girl?
Cheers to Miriam and Jeanette
(If HE calls—I'm on the set)
Really it's too hard to count
All the friends at Paramount
So they'll simply be yclept
Louis Lipstone's Music Dept.
And that goes for Fox and Metro
Warners, R.K.O., etcetro…
And the Pious folk deserve a
Merry Christmas—Hi, Minerva!
Hey, Miss Phillips, talk to Peer
Call him Cuddles—that's a dear
Nina Pape—no teacher's
    topped her
And that goes for Miss Willhopter
Love to Roy and Lucy Potter
Love to all of John Scott Trotter
Dick and Joan, the Powell twain
Walter Rivers—his demesne
We go back in memory
To the old L.B.B.C.
Leo Robin, J.J. Robbins
Park your dog-sleds and your
    dobbins
And that man whose name is spelt
Mr. Franklin Roosevelt
We're 101 percent
With you Mr. President
Mickey Rooney, bring your
    jive in

Greetings to my favorite
   drive-in
Romanoff and Dave and Carl and
David Rose and Judy Garland
Rest your coats and fill your
   glasses
Ere the jolly season passes
—I suppose I'm in a rut
Can't place Wilhelmina Thutt—
Read and Rains, and Smith
   and Shacker
Jimmy Stewart—he's so slacker
Swezey, Schwartz, and Sherwood yet
AND the Navy Blues sextette
Henry Steig bring Artie Shaw in
William Sexton and his squaw in
Silvers, bring both Phil and Sid in
Glad to zee you—we ain't kiddin'!
Footman! Grab that horse's halter
Here's Saroyan—also Salter
Gentlemen, up on your feet
Find Ann Sheridan a seat
(Ha ha, oh boy, that's a hot one—
Just as if she hasn't got one!)
Dave and Libby Shelly, hi!
You're the apple of our eye
Tinturins and Temple too
Gracious, what a varied crew
Square and hip-chick, saint
   and sinner
Lana Turner—"chicken dinner"
Friends and neighbors, love
   you all
Sit thee doon and have a ball
Mighty glad to call your name
Only hope you feel the same

Blessings on you where you are
Glad those wise men saw
   that star
Glad in spite of wars and
   weather
All of us can be together
Rocco Vocco and his cutie
J. Van Heusen, J. Venuti
Jerry Vogel, Rudy Vallee
Come back to our alley, Sally
Come and sit around the tree
Lit without the aid of "tea"
Gangway for the house of Whiting
Still our sweethearts, at this
   writing
Bright red ribbons for Cobina
I mean Juna—also Seena
Brothers Warner, Brothers Barker
Harry Wise and Connie Parker
Sammy Weiss and Vernon Wood
Harry Warren—feeling good
Paul and Margaret Whiteman too
You know what we wish for you!
Double that and add a very
To the "home-folks" at Woodberry
Slicker Warnell, Sambo White
Allie Wrubel—have a bite
Brother, you ain't tasted cakes
Till you've had those mother
   bakes
Choir, sing hello to Young
And your son is almost sung
Now the last guests have been
   kissed
Sam and Maggie Zimbalist
Now the room is really humming

And we thank you all for coming
Eat the food you want to eat
Meet the friends you want
    to meet
This is Christmas—fill your plates
These are these United States
So we won't invent a new toast

We'll propose the tried and true
    toast
We love you and you're our
    friends
And we hope it never ends
So, good neighbors, here's a cheer
Same old

𝕸𝖊𝖗𝖗𝖞 𝕮𝖍𝖗𝖎𝖘𝖙𝖒𝖆𝖘

𝖆𝖓𝖉 𝖆 . . . .

𝕵𝖔𝖍𝖓𝖓𝖞, 𝕲𝖎𝖓𝖌𝖊𝖗 𝖆𝖓𝖉 𝕬𝖒𝖆𝖓𝖉𝖆

P.S. Combed the country over
Under haystacks, deep in clover
Highest snow-cap, lowest cut
Still no Wilhemina Thutt.

From the Desk of
GEORGE A. MERCER, SR.

TO MY FRIENDS AND ALL INTERESTED:

When I visited Johnny at Rumson, New Jersey, in September, 1939 I had some long confidential and wonderful talks with him. I said to him, "John, tell me how it is that a boy of your age can write over 500 songs and does not know music and cannot play an instrument. How do you account for it?" After pondering and thinking a few minutes, John turned to me and said, "Pop, to tell you the truth I simply get to thinking over the song, pondering over it in my mind and all of a sudden, I get in tune with the Infinite." I believe that he then stated the real truth about his inspiration for his song writing. It comes from the Infinite and very high sources That is why I believe that John's talent is from above and that he is a musical genius.

Respectfully, his father,

G. A. Mercer

GAM:R   Age 72.

A couple of cut-ups who both got their start with Pops Whiteman. Johnny must have learned that announcer's ear-shielding pose when they did broadcasts from the Hotel Biltmore.

The whole Mercer family, including faithful dog, in the days when convertibles were popular. The towhead is Jeff and the one in the skimmer far right is Amanda, also known as Mandy.

The Forties

The 1940s were a roller coaster of ups and downs for most Americans, and Johnny Mercer was riding well up in front. The forties were also an interesting time for people in the various branches of the arts and communications.

As the era began, there was some experimentation with the sending of sound *and* pictures through the air, an exciting idea called television that had been shown tentatively to the public at New York's World's Fair in 1939. But with the war in Europe drawing ever closer, the television idea was shelved and the entertainment-hungry public remained true to their radios and phonographs. Popular music—"pop music"—was a common denominator to both. On radio there was "Your Hit Parade," "The Chesterfield Supper Club," "The Camel Caravan" (no anti-smoking campaigns yet!), Kay Kyser's "Kollege of Musical Knowledge," Andre Kostelanetz, Bing Crosby on "The Kraft Music Hall," and dozens of dance band "remotes" later in the evenings, with marvelous musicians and singers performing marvelous songs. Almost any night of the week you might hear Tommy Dorsey's band with Frank Sinatra, Jo Stafford, Connie Haines and the Pied Pipers; or Glenn Miller's band with Tex Beneke and Marion Hutton; Eddy Duchin's piano or Artie Shaw's clarinet; powerhouse jazz by Jimmy Lunceford's band or mickey mouse music from Orrin Tucker. But you had to listen fast, because by 1942, no thanks to Pearl Harbor, most of it was gone.

As for the music that was supposed to go 'round and 'round, 1942 brought an unfortunate and certainly most untimely moratorium on recording because of a contractual dispute between the Petrillo-led musicians' union and the record manufacturers. There followed—necessity (and ingenuity) being the mother of invention—a rather dreary period during which America listened to records made without musical instruments. Singers would sing all right, but the backgrounds were something to boggle the mind. Groups of singers would make up what was intended to sound like sections of horns, reeds or rhythm instruments but sounded instead sappy, syrupy and completely synthetic. Adding to the confusion of the period was the simultaneous flourishing of a mechanical wonder with a tremendous appetite—the jukebox. It was a

89

time for both "Jukebox Saturday Night" *and* "Saturday Night Is the Loneliest Night of the Week" ("Sing it, Frankie!"). There was a crying need for red, white and blue American popular music.

Hollywood, its ear ever to the ground, was particularly sensitive to such a simple demand. So it was full steam ahead for songs and pretty girls. There were Betty Grable, Betty Hutton and Rita Hayworth for starters and plenty more where they came from. There were Hope and Crosby with their put-it-there-pal, regular-guy clowning. Hollywood ground out musicals like clockwork, and so it was a time made to order for Johnny Mercer's wise and sentimental songs. Where Mercer had always had his ear to the streets and country byways, he was now, in the war years of 1942–45, plugged in to the sounds and descriptiveness of wartime gadgetry, to the Jeeps and bombers and blues-seekers of the U.S.A. He was also by this time an accepted member of the Hollywood elite. In 1941 Mercer and his ideal partner, Harold Arlen, wrote what many experts believe to be the greatest blues song of all time, after the classic "St. Louis Blues." It is, of course, "Blues in the Night" with its unbelievably evocative "a-whooooeee da-whooeeeeee" (Irving Berlin was bowled over by that invention) and the great piece of luck (and genius) that prompted Arlen to suggest to Mercer that they move the line "my momma done told me" up from some place farther down and open the song with it. It may be apocryphal, but the story is that when Oscar Hammerstein won his 1941 Academy Award (with Jerome Kern) for "The Last Time I Saw Paris," he told a friend who was returning to the Coast, "If you see Johnny Mercer, just tell him I think he was robbed." Of course the Hammerstein lyric did have the help of that sad period going for it, and Johnny Mercer did get many other Oscars as time went on. But "Blues in the Night" was surely worthy of an award, and its failure to get one was a forerunner of another bitter pill that Mercer and Arlen were to swallow before the forties were over.

But first there was another success for Mercer—this time in a whole new field. With the financial assistance of Buddy DeSylva, onetime member of the Broadway songwriting team of DeSylva, Brown & Henderson, but then producer at Paramount Pictures, Mercer and Glen Wallichs, the owner of a successful Hollywood music store, decided to start their own record company. They named it Capitol Records, based it in the center of things on Vine Street, a short stroll from the famous Brown Derby Restaurant, and proceded to line up an interesting and hip lineup of talent. They had Ella Mae Morse, Freddy Slack, Bobby Sherwood, and Stan Kenton for beginners, and shortly thereafter Peggy Lee and Nat "King" Cole. Capitol also offered its co-founder and part-time guiding light a chance to record too, and he quickly came up with a couple of jukebox winners—"Strip Polka" and "G.I.Jive." Johnny Mercer was now a household name. At one point during this super-productive period Mercer had four of his tunes among the top ten of the weekly radio show "Your Hit Parade." Buoyed by all this success, in 1946 Arlen and Mercer struck out into the more difficult and prestigious field of the Broadway musical theatre; struck out was what they indeed did. Despite a great score ("Come Rain or Come Shine," "Any Place I Hang My Hat," etc.) *St. Louis Woman,* directed by the brilliant Rouben Mamoulian and featuring Pearl Bailey and the Nicholas Brothers, was a resounding flop. Thoroughly disappointed and chastened, the hot songwriting team chugged on back to the warmth of California and the easy life of the movie studios. Mercer was never able to scale the heights of Broadway (a climb he wanted badly), and the 1946 debacle should have warned him of future disappointments. California was where he belonged, and he closed out the forties with a few more good songs and some diminishing attention to the affairs of Capitol Records.

Fellow southerners. Dinah Shore was one of the earliest to do "Blues in the Night," and she's kept it in her books ever since.

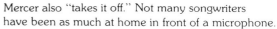

Mercer also "takes it off." Not many songwriters have been as much at home in front of a microphone.

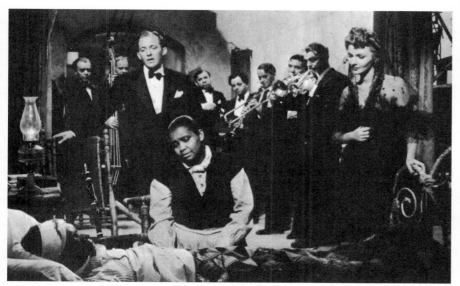

Ruby Elzy and Mary Martin upstage Bing's *Birth of the Blues* combo in this shot, but one can still discover trumpet man Brian Donlevy, trombonist Jack Teagarden and bass player Harry Barris.

On Behalf of the Visiting Firemen

1940

Music by WALTER DONALDSON

Well, blow me down,
Look who's in town,
Pull up a chair,
There's one over there.
How've you been?
How's the next of kin?
Fellas, look who just blew in!

On behalf of the visiting firemen from
  Kansas City,
Let's have a "smile" on me,
On behalf of the gentlemen slicked up and
  lookin' pretty,
Let's make it two or three.
Like the governor of Carolina North,
Told the governor of Carolina South,
On behalf of the firemen from any city,
Let's have a "smile" on me.

[Repeat first 16 bars]

©E. H. Morris Music

We're all gathered here on this auspicious
  day
And we'd . . . Bless my soul there's Elmer
  Whatcha say?

[Repeat last 8 bars]

On behalf of the visiting firemen from
  Minnesota,
Let's have a "smile" on me,
On behalf of the citizen just in from North
  Dakota,
Let's make it two or three.
Just as our forefathers always tried to show
"Give us liberty or give us . . ." well, let it
  go,
On behalf of the visiting firemen who filled
  their quota
Let's have a "smile" on me

By this time it was no longer a case of the mighty King Bing extending a helping hand to a chum on the way up. Mercer had arrived, and this outing was an effort to repeat the unexpected success of "Bob White." It was not quite the hit of the earlier record, but one can hear the fun these two cats (that was the word in 1940) obviously had in the studio. Mercer always enjoyed using place names, not to mention things bibulous.

92

No, he didn't play piano, but of course photographers love to get a little action into their shots. He looks a little like the late actor Myron McCormick in this one.

The dude on the left is obviously glad to see an old pal like Jimmy Dorsey, even though they seem not to be joining the crowd heading for the next hole.

One double-A ASCAP member welcomes another aboard. *(Left to right)* Frank Loesser, Betty Downey, Ginger Mercer, Jimmy Downey, Lynn Loesser and J.M.

93

Mister Meadowlark

1940

Music by WALTER DONALDSON

I'm in the country but I dunno why,
'Cause I am strictly a city lovin' guy,
I'm sittin' there when
A little bird flies my way one day.
I look at him and he's lookin' at me,
Both satisfyin' our curiosity,
Quick like a rabbit,
I get me a thought,
So I up to him and say,
Hey!

Mister Meadowlark,
We've got an awful lot of serenadin' to do,
Mister Meadowlark,
I'm just a city slicker and I'm counting on
   you,
She's got a country guy who whistles,

My whistle is thin,
So when I begin,
[Whistle]
That's where you come in.
[Whistle]

Mister Meadowlark,
If you should cop a gander
When I'm kissin' my chick,
Needless to remark,
I hope you'll have the decency to exit,
But quick!
And if Missus M. thinks you're out steppin',
I'll make it all right,
Mister Meadowlark,
Meet me in the dark
Tonight.

Walter Donaldson was a hero to Mercer. Not only was he an established melody man—good meat-and-potatoes tunes his forte—but he had his name on such successful regional songs as "Georgia," "Carolina in the Morning," "Down South," and (wow!) "How Ya Gonna Keep 'Em Down on the Farm?" The aviary was in use again and Mercer was bringing Donaldson right up to the moment with the line, "If you should cop a gander when I'm kissing my chick." Bing and Johnny relished such tough guy–racetrack lingo mixed with jazz and so they recorded this one too.

Fools Rush In

1940

Music by RUBE BLOOM

"Romance is a game for fools,"
I used to say;
A game I thought I'd never play.
"Romance is a game for fools,"
I said and grinned;
Then you passed by,
And here am I
Throwing caution to the wind.

Fools rush in
Where angels fear to tread,
And so I come to you, my love,
My heart above my head.
Though I see
The danger there,
If there's a chance for me
Then I don't care.
Fools rush in
Where wise men never go,
But wise men never fall in love
So how are they to know?
When we met
I felt my life begin;
So open up your heart,
And let this fool rush in.

"Wise men never fall in love. . . ." An unusually cynical line for the ever-romantic Johnny Mercer. The big record of this ballad was made by Tommy Dorsey's band with an exceptionally silken vocal by Frank Sinatra. The record and many air plays propelled this song onto radio's "Hit Parade," and that was a good change from the Hollywood soundtrack songs of the years before.

Oh, Mr. Crosby,
Oh, Mr. Crosby,
All the orchestras are swinging it today.
And I wanted to find out
What the noise is all about.
Do you really think that swing is here to stay?

Oh, Mr. Mercer,
Oh, Mr. Mercer,
Swing is really much too ancient to condemn.
In the jungles they would play
In that same abandoned way.
On the level, Mr. Crosby?
On the down beat, Mr. "M".

Oh, Mr. Crosby,
Oh, Mr. Crosby,
I've been reading in the latest magazine
That a jivin' jitter bug
Blew his top and cut a rug.
Will you tell me what that language really means?

Oh, Mr. Mercer,
Oh, Mr. Mercer,
As a student of the slang they use pro-tem,
That just means a solid gait
Cut a murderistic plate.
That's amazin', Mr. Crosby,
Elementary, Mr. "M".

Still another go at the back and forth jiving that Gallagher & Shean began and Bing then continued well into the forties with Bob Hope. These are the actual cards that the two guys carried into the studio, since the longish lyric was too busy to commit to memory. "Allegretto—Alligators," "retardo—Lombardo" are Mercer's always successful music-biz jokes.

Oh, Mr. Crosby,
Oh, Mr. Crosby,
Is it true that swing's another name for jazz?
And the first place it was played
Was in New Orleans parade?
And the southern negro gave it all it has?

Oh, Mr. Mercer,
Oh, Mr. Mercer,
I believe that its foundation came from then.
They just slowed the tempo down
And they really went to town.
Allegretto, Mr. Crosby.
Alligators, Mr. "M".

Mr. Mercer,
Well, I trust that I have made the matter clear.
So, when someone plays a thing,
You will understand it's swing,
And appreciate the rhythm that you hear.

Oh, Mr. Crosby,
Oh, Mr. Crosby,
I'm afraid that type of rhythm's not for me.
I prefer my music plain
A la Shubert's Serenade.
Sort of retardo, Mr. Mercer.
Sort of Lombardo, Mr. "C".

The Happiness Boys of 1940 listen to
a playback, but it can't be all that bad.

Blues in the Night

Music by HAROLD ARLEN

My mama done tol' me
When I was in knee pants (knee pants
                                     (pigtails
My mama done tol' me—(son
                                     (hon'
A woman'll sweet talk,
  (man's gonna sweet talk,
And give ya the big eye,
But when the sweet talkin's done
A woman's a two-face
  (man is a two-face
A worrisome thing who'll leave ya t'sing
The blues in the night,

Now the rain's a-fallin',
Hear the train a-callin',
Whooee,
(My mama done tol' me)
Hear that lonesome whistle
Blowin' 'cross the trestle,
Whooee,
(My mama done tol' me)
A whooee-duh-whooee,
Ol' clickety clack's
A-echoin' back
The blues in the night,

The evenin' breeze'll start
The trees to cryin'
And the moon'll hide its light,
When you get the blues in the night.

Take my word, the mocking bird'll
Sing the saddest kind of song,
He knows things are wrong
And he's right. *[whistle]*

From Natchez to Mobile,
From Memphis to St. Jo,
Where ever the four winds blow;
I been in some big towns
An' heard me some big talk,
But there is one thing I know,
A woman's a two-face,
  (man is a two-face,
A worrisome thing
Who'll leave ya t'sing
The blues in the night.
[hum]
My mama was right,
There's blues in the night.

Arthur Schwartz: "Probably the greatest blues song ever written—and that includes 'St. Louis Blues.' "
Robert Emmett Dolan: "I was in New York, and Kern & Hammerstein's "The Last Time I Saw Paris" had just won the Academy Award over "Blues in the Night." Oscar said to me, 'When you get back to Hollywood, tell Johnny he was robbed.' "

Harold Arlen: "It was a jail sequence in the movie, and I wanted to write it as authentic as possible. It took a day and a half to write and I couldn't wait to get over to Johnny's house to play it for him. He's not much of a reactor and so we fussed around with it for quite awhile. I remember he had lots of phrases and lines written down but none of them seemed to fit that opening phrase right. But then I saw those words, 'my momma done tol' me,' way down at the bottom of the pile and I said, 'Why don't we move them up to the top?' It sure worked.

```
Whenever the night comes
I'm heavy in my heart
I'm heavy in my mind - Lawd!
A woman'll sweet talk
A woman'll glad eye
But pretty soon you'll find
A woman's flat two-face
A changeable thing      — a worrisome thing
Who leaves you to sing the blues
In the night
Now the rain's a-fallin'
Hear the train a-callin' --- whoooeee
(whoooeee whoooeee whoooeee)
Hear that lonesome whistle
Blowin' 'cross the trestle --- whoooeee
(I'm heavy in my heart)
A-whoooeee -duh- whoooeee
That clickety-clack
A-echoin' back the blues
In the night
The evenin' breeze'll start the trees to cryin'
And the moon'll hide its light
When you get the blues in the night
Take my word, the mockin'-bird'll sing the saddest kinda song
He knows things are wrong
And he's right
(Whistle)
From Natchez to Mobile
From Memphis to St. Joe
Don' nobody yet know why
A woman'll sweet talk
A woman'll glad eye
Then leave you high an' dry
```

The original work sheet for the classic "Blues in the Night."
Note how the captivating opening line was moved up—
at Arlen's suggestion.

The Waiter and the Porter and the Upstairs Maid

1941   Music and Words by JOHNNY MERCER

As your genial host,
May I offer a toast,
To the wine buying guest on my right.
May his bank account grow,
Heavy laden with dough,
May he spend it in here ev'ry night.
Seeing this night in its glory,
You people so loyal, so true,
Puts me in mind of a story
It might have happened to you.

The people in the ballroom were stuffy and
arty,
So I began to get just a little afraid,
I sneaked into the kitchen and found me a
party;
The waiter and the porter and the second
story maid.

I peeked into the parlor to see what was
hatchin',
In time to hear the hostess suggest a
charade,
But who was in the pantry a-laughin' and
scratchin';
The waiter and the porter and the upstairs
maid.

When they heard the music that the
orchestra played,
The waiter and the porter grabbed ahold of
the maid,
Then they all proceeded to go into a clog,
Hot diggety dog!

If ever I'm invited to some fuddy duddys;
I ain't a gonna watch any harlequinade,

You'll find me in the kitchen
Applaudin' my buddies;
The waiter and the porter and the upstairs
maid.

I went and got a dishpan to use as a cymbal,
The porter found a regular glass that he
played,
The fingers of the waiter were each in a
thimble,
You should of heard the music that the
combination made.

Of course we had to stop for a short
intermission,
When anybody rang for a pink lemonade,
But soon as it was done we were back in
position,
The waiter and the porter and the upstairs
maid.

Marchin' through the kitchen to the party
and back,
Why, man, you should a seen us, we were
ballin' the jack.
Once a half an hour passed without any call,
Jack, we had a ball.

The waltzes and mazurkas, we hate 'em, we
spurn 'em,
We got a lotta rhythms we wanna hear
played,
And we know who to go to if we want to
learn 'em;
The waiter and the porter and the upstairs
maid.

100

The Air-minded Executive

1941

By BERNIE HANIGHEN

Life, Look, Pic, Peek,
Always print a beautiful calf,
And another thing they love
Is a certain photograph.
Over a beer, they agree
The man of the year was

The air-minded executive,
He dearly loved to fly.
He was an up-to-date go getter,
His lady friend was even better,
She went along to take a letter,
Way up in the sky.

The air-minded executive
Would take off on the sly,
He was a most romantic feller,
And oh the things he used to tell her

Above the roar of his propeller.
Somewhere in the sky,
Foggy or fair,
They would be there
Lightin' a flare at the airport.

Fillin' the tanks,
Callin' the banks,
Tellin' 'em,
"Hold up the contract . . . contact!"

The air-minded executive
Became a wealthy guy.
And so he wed his secretary,
They settled down in Waterbury,
And they commute by stratosferry.
My, they love to fly
Even as you and I.

Mercer was a great reader of magazines and newspapers, hence the opening line which may have been the impetus for the rest of this unusual song idea. In retrospect he seems to have been quite prescient about today's glut of executive jets. In this day of space shuttles, the made-up "stratosferry" isn't at all far out. Try and find Mercer's record of this—as always he's the best salesman of his own great material.

(Facing page) Mercer trying his wings solo once again was lucky enough to have the powerhouse trio of Crosby–Mary Martin–Jack Teagarden romping through the lyrics in the movie *Birth of the Blues* (which comes first in chicken and egg style, the song or the spot and the stars?). Good show-stopping lyrics here, the line "I ain't a-gonna watch any harlequinade" pure Mercer.

Skylark

1941

Music by HOAGY CARMICHAEL

Skylark,
Have you anything to say to me?
Won't you tell me where my love can be?
Is there a meadow in the mist,
Where someone's waiting to be kissed?
Skylark,
Have you seen a valley green with Spring
Where my heart can go a-journeying,
Over the shadows and the rain
To a blossom covered lane?
And in your lonely flight,
Haven't you heard the music in the night,
Wonderful music,
Faint as a "will-o-the-wisp,"
Crazy as a loon,
Sad as a gypsy serenading the moon (Oh)
Skylark,
I don't know if you can find these things,
But my heart is riding on your wings,
So if you see them anywhere,
Won't you lead me there?

Move over, Mr. Keats. Mercer's affinity for all the winged creatures of the world served him well, though this complete set of lyrics took him the better part of a year to complete. All the great singers—Sinatra, Ella, Tormé, Tony Bennett—have had a go at this gem.

Christmas Card

THIS modern age we're going through
    has got me in a spin
I ain't too bright to start with—now here's
    the shape I'm in

With everything and anything—there's
    stamps you gotta use
The Bs and Cs are groceries—I think the T's
    are shoes
You have to be a F.B.I. man to figure out all
    the clues
And that's the situation when you get the
    duration blues

The Army and the draft board gets me kinda
    mixed up too
You're in if you are 1A—but if you ain't then
    who are you

The 2As are essential—and the 4F's
    probably have asthma
The 3B gents are in defense—or else they're
    giving plasma
But if you ain't got nothin' then you are
    somebody that nobody at all can use
And that's the situation—when you get those
    duration blues

Now food will win the war they say, and
    that's okay with me
But I went to the corner store—what did I
    see?

There's Spam and wham and deviled ham
    and somepin new called zoom

Just take it home and cook it to the
    temperature of the room
And you can bake it—cake it—flake
    it—make it—take it anyway you choose
And that's the situation—when you got
    those duration blues

And then on top of everything the taxes
    roll around
I went to see the income man and this is
    what I found
You multiplies the profits and incorporates
    the loss
Deducting all expenditures business fees
    you come across
Then if you satisfy the government—it's
    ten to one the little lady sues
And that's the situation when you get the
    duration blues

Howdy do, Mr. Crosby, I would—like
    to say
Happy New Year to you in the—good old
    way

Well, thank you, Mr. Mercer, that is—
    mighty fine
And the same to you from me and mine
And while I'm passin' those—words your
    way
Let's extend 'em to the whole wide—
    U.S.A.

Every city and village and farm and town
And every front door from the—White

House down
To the boys in khaki—and the boys in blue
To the generals and the admirals and the
    company and crew

Let the whistles whistle and the bells all ring
For General Marshall, General Arnold and
    Cominch King

Red, white and blue confetti in a veritable
    shower
For Messrs, MacArthur and Eisenhower

To the fightin' Marines on Guadalcanal
Wherever you are, Happy New Year, pal
To the ship-yard workers and the swing-shift
    crowd
We can't sing good but we sure sing loud

So we send our heartiest felicitations
To all our allies—the United Nations

Get out the brightest-colored paper hats
For Nimitz and Hadley—Doolittle and
    Spaatz

Mr. Nelson, Mr. Jeffers, Mr. Morgenthau
Had the busiest year we ever saw

And an even busier one comin' in
Well, the harder we work—the quicker we'll
    win

Happy New Year, everybody, near and far
From John Q. Public to F.D.R.
To the New New Jersey, and all her crew
To Birmingham Bertha and Suzy Q.

That's our 1943 wish for you
And thanks for all you did in '42
Around this time in forty four
We hope you'll be with us in person once
    more
But till that time be of good cheer
And to everybody—Happy New Year

Strip Polka

1942

By JOHNNY MERCER

There's a burlesque theatre where the gang
  loves to go,
To see Queenie the cutie of the burlesque
  show,
And the thrill of the evening is when out
  Queenie skips,
And the band plays the Polka while she
  strips!

"Take it off," "Take it off" Cries a voice
  from the rear,
"Take it off," "Take it off," soon it's all you
  can hear,
But she's always a lady even in pantomine,
So she stops! And always just in time.

She's as fresh and as wholesome as the
  flowers in May,
And she hopes to retire to the farm some
  day,
But you can't buy a farm until you're up in
  the chips,
So the band plays the Polka while she strips!

"Take it off," "Take it off," all the customers
  shout,
"Down in front" "Down in front," while the
  band beats it out,

But she's always a lady even in pantomine,
So she stops! And always just in time.

Oh! she hates corny waltzes and she hates
  the gavotte,
And there's one big advantage if the
  music's hot,
It's a fast moving exit just in case
  something r-r-rips,
So the band plays the Polka while she strips!

Drop around, take it in, it's the best in the
  west,
Take it off, "Take it off," you can yell like
  the rest,
Take her out when it's over, she's a peach
  when she's dressed,
But she stops! And always just in time.

Queenie, Queen of them all,
Queenie, some day you'll fall,
Some day churchbells will chime,
In Strip Polka Time.

It's the Polka time,
Churchbells will chime,
It's the Polka time.

The war was on, and Mercer was doing his bit in triplicate: He wrote words and music, sang it with the proper amount of humor, and produced it on his new Capitol Records. The song became a solid hit on jukeboxes, particularly those around army bases and GI hangouts. The number was just sexy enough for the guys without being dirty.

Dearly Beloved

1942

Music by JEROME KERN

Tell me that it's true,
Tell me you agree,
I was meant for you,
You were meant for me.

Dearly beloved, how clearly I see,
Somewhere in Heaven you were fashioned
   for me,
Angel eyes knew you,
Angel voices led me to you;

Nothing could save me, Fate gave me a
   sign;
I know that I'll be yours come shower or
   shine;
So I say merely,
Dearly beloved, be mine.

The publisher's subtitle "Suitable For Weddings" is hardly necessary for this fine song, in which Mercer's directness of romantic lyric matches the beauty of Kern's melody. A standard among movie love songs.

DEARLY BELOVED

Song Suitable for Weddings

Words by

JOHNNY MERCER

Music by

JEROME KERN

PRICE 75 CENTS

T. B. HARMS
— COMPANY —
NEW YORK

MADE IN U.S.A.

You Were Never Lovelier

1942   Music by JEROME KERN

I was never able
To recite a fable
That would make the party bright,

Sitting at the table
I was never able
To become the host's delight;

But now you've given me my after dinner
    story,
I'll just describe you as you are in all your
    glory.

You were never lovelier,
You were never so fair;
Dreams were never lovelier,

Pardon me if I stare.

Down the sky the moonbeams fly to light
    your face;
I can only say they chase the proper place.

You were never lovelier,
And to coin a new phrase;
I was never luckier
In my palmiest days.

Make a note, and you can quote me, honor
    bright,
You were never lovelier than you are
    tonight.

A great assignment—writing with the master, Jerome Kern, and for Fred Astaire!
One can imagine the keen sense of pride this musical relationship brought to
Mercer, but at the same time caution, since Kern had a reputation of sometimes
being difficult. Fred sang this dreamy title song to the gorgeous Rita Hayworth,
then did a hip dance number that Mercer titled "The Shorty George" after an
actual dance step of the day and one that was a little removed from the Alt Wien
realm of Kern.

YOU WERE NEVER LOVELIER
Music by JEROME KERN
Lyric by JOHNNY MERCER
FRED ASTAIRE AND RITA HAYWORTH
IN THE NEW COLUMBIA MUSICAL PRODUCTION
"YOU WERE NEVER LOVELIER"
WITH
ADOLPHE MENJOU
AND
XAVIER CUGAT
AND HIS ORCHESTRA
PRICE
75c
T. B. HARMS
COMPANY
NEW YORK

I'm Old Fashioned

1942   Music by JEROME KERN

I am not such a clever one
About the latest fads.
I admit I was never one
Adored by local lads;
Not that I ever try to be saint,
I'm the type that they classify as quaint.

I'm old fashioned,
I love the moonlight,
I love the old fashioned things—
The sound of rain
Upon a window pane,
The starry song that April sings.
This year's fancies
Are passing fancies,
But sighing sighs, holding hands
These my heart understands.
I'm old fashioned,
But I don't mind it,
That's how I want to be,
As long as you agree
To stay old fashioned with me.

More to the Kern taste than "Shorty George." We've been told that when Mercer brought the completed lyric to Kern's home, the composer, generally a rather laconic gentleman, rushed to the staircase and summoned his wife to come hear it—a rare display of enthusiasm. Kern's kudos were warranted, since this is one of Mercer's most sincerely romantic works.

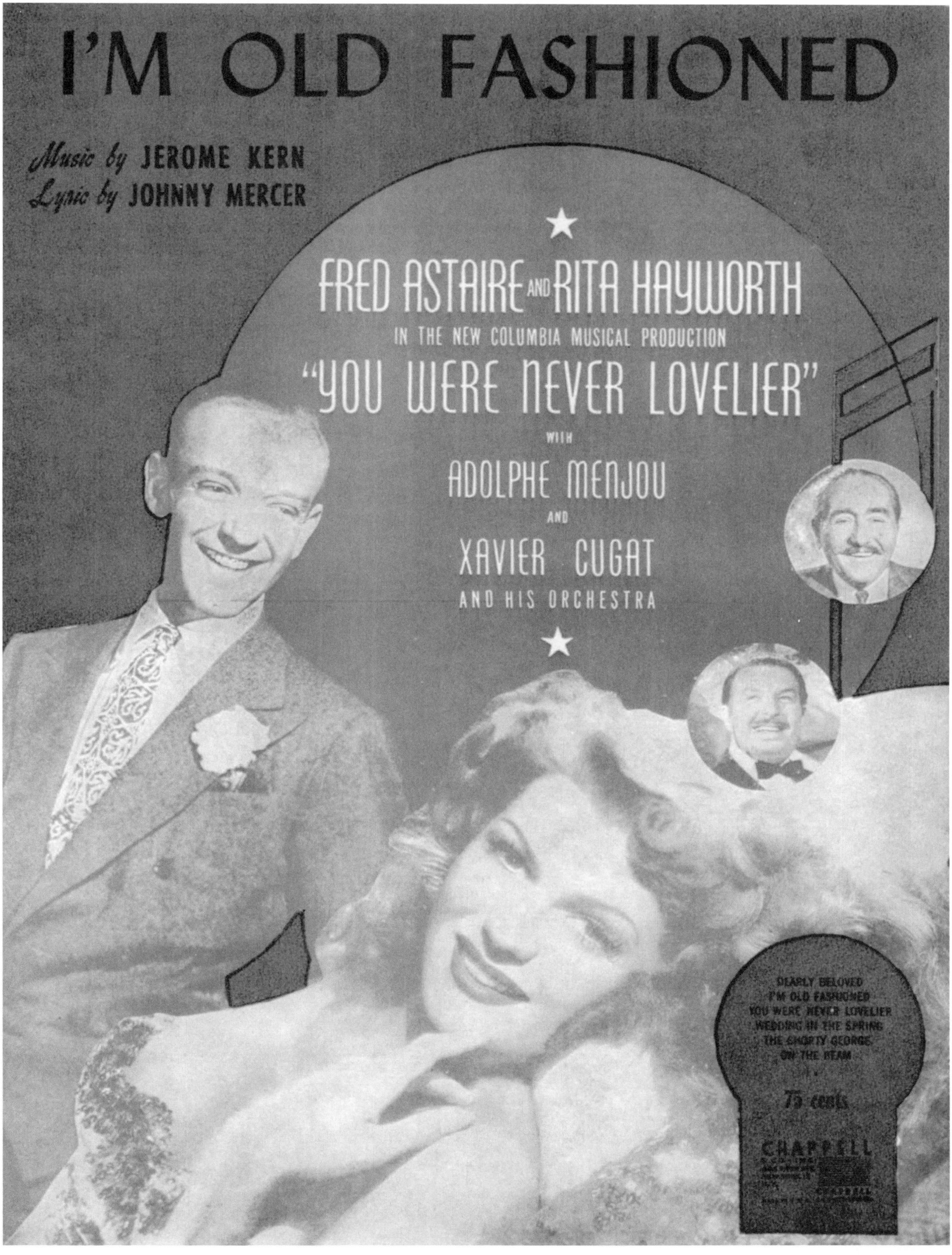

That Old Black Magic

1942

Music by HAROLD ARLEN

That old black magic has me in its spell.
That old back magic that you weave so well.
Those icy fingers up and down my spine.
The same old witchcraft when your eyes
    meet mine.

The same old tingle that I feel inside
And then that elevator starts its ride
And down and down I go,
'Round and 'round I go
Like a leaf that's caught in the tide.

I should stay away,
But what can I do?

I hear your name
And I'm aflame,
Aflame with such a burning desire
That only your kiss
Can put out the fire.

For you're the lover I have waited for.
The mate that fate had me created for,
And ev'ry time your lips meet mine
Darling, down and down I go,
'Round and 'round I go
In a spin,
Loving the spin I'm in
Under that old black magic called love!

©Famous Music Corporation

Another all-time winner from that ideal pair, Arlen and Mercer. (It had been ten years earlier that they first met, during preparations for the Broadway revue *Americana*.) Most people associate this standard with that well known hand-against-ear singer, Billy Daniels. But no, it was a fellow named Johnnie Johnston, who made a bit of a reputation for himself by announcing to the executives of Paramount Pictures, "This lot isn't big enough for him [Bing Crosby] and me—you better get rid of him." That threat must have been made after the movie *Star Spangled Rhythm*, in which Johnston sang this elongated torch song while most of the footage was given over to the dancing of Vera Zorina.

Typical wartime movie plot paired Navy man Eddie Bracken with girl friend Betty Hutton, who showed her loyalty by working in a defense plant. She belted out two good Mercer numbers.

On the Swing Shift

1942

Music by HAROLD ARLEN

Like some old tom cat out like a light
I dream all day of the previous night.
Not that we frequent the same habitat
But in a way I'm a cat.

Life is fine with my baby on the swing shift
On the line with my baby on the swing shift
It's the nuts
There among the nuts and bolts
Plus a hundred thousand volts
Shining from her eyes.
She's a beautiful bomber!
What care I if they put me on the wing shift?
She's near by in the fuselage
Overtime?
Here's why I'm
Doin' it free—
Baby's with me on the swing shift jamboree!

Another bright Arlen-Mercer number from Paramount's all-star wartime musical, *Star Spangled Rhythm*. Betty Hutton, a big movie name in 1942, gave this topical song the required "pizzazz" and also swung another upbeat number called "I'm Doin' It for Defense," in which there was the wonderful couplet, "If you think you're Cary Grant, brother, relax, you're just a rebate on my income tax" Mercer had a ball with all the defense industry and air force verbiage of the day.

Hit the Road to Dreamland

1942

Music by HAROLD ARLEN

Twinkle, twinkle, twinkle goes the star,
Twinkle, twinkle, twinkle, there you are.
Time for all good children to hit the hay.
Cock-a-doodle, doodle, doodle, brother,
It's another day,
We should be on our way!

Bye bye, baby
Time to hit the road to dreamland,
You're my baby
Dig you in the land of Nod.
Hold tight, baby,
We'll be swinging up in dreamland,
All night, baby,
Where the little cherubs trod.
Look at that knocked-out moon,
Been a-blowin' his top in the blue,
Never saw the likes of you;
        (What an angel)

Bye, bye, baby,
Time to hit the road to dreamland,
Don't cry, baby,
It was divine
But the rooster has finally crowed,
Time to hit the road.

Still another interesting song from *Star Spangled Rhythm*. Mercer, with his great attachment to rail rather than air travel, enjoyed the setting of this song in the dining car of an overnight train and it also gave the director an opportunity to introduce the fine Golden Gate Quartet dressed as Pullman porters to sing counterpoint (the NAACP hadn't gained its clout yet). The main lyrics of the song were sung by the always-serviceable Dick Powell in the direction of his tablemate, Mary Martin.

Tangerine

1942

Music by VICTOR SCHERTZINGER

South American stories
Tell of a girl who's quite a dream,
The beauty of her race.

Though you doubt all the stories
And think the tales
Are just a bit extreme,
Wait till you see her face.

Tangerine,
She is all they claim,
With her eyes of night
And lips as bright as flame.

Tangerine,
When she dances by,
Senoritas stare
And caballeros sigh.

And I've seen
Toasts to Tangerine
Raised in ev'ry bar
Across the Argentine,
Yes, she has them all on the run,
But her heart belongs to just one.
Her heart belongs to Tangerine.

An all-time hit song that most people will always associate with Bob Eberle and Helen O'Connell. Their brilliantly conceived two-tempos duet on Jimmy Dorsey's record is a pop classic. Mercer told George Simon that he got the title from Broadway show he had liked way back in the twenties. Mercer's career was really skyrocketing at this point, what with two movie scores, Capitol Records starting to turn out hit records, and the radio "Lucky Strike Hit Parade" often presenting three or four Mercer songs among the honored Top Ten of the week.

Arthur Murray Taught Me Dancing in a Hurry

1942

Music by VICTOR SCHERTZINGER

Life was so peaceful at the drive-in,
Life was so calm and serene,
Life was trés gay
Till that unlucky day
I happened to read that magazine.
Why did I read that advertisement
Where it said . . .
"Since I rhumba, Jim thinks I'm sublime."
Why, oh why,
Did I ever try
When I didn't have the talent,
Didn't have the money,
And teacher did not have the time.

Arthur Murray taught me dancing in a hurry.
I had a week to spare,
He showed me the ground work,
The walkin' around work,

And told me to take it from there.
Arthur Murray then advised me not to
worry.
It'd come out all right.
To my way of thinkin',
It came out stinkin,'
I don't know my left from my right.
The people around me can all sing
A-one and a-two and a-three,
But any resemblance to waltzing
Is just coincidental with me,
'Cause Arthur Murray taught me dancing in
a hurry.
And so I take a chance.
To me it resembles
The nine-day trembles,
But he guarantees
It's a dance.

Rarely does a public figure show up in a popular song title, but this one worked awfully well. It was Helen O'Connell's personal property on the Dorsey record this time. An extra set of lyrics was written for radio performance so that the word "stinkin'" wouldn't offend the dancing master. Ginger tells us that the Mercers had to make peace with Arthur and Kathryn by taking an actual lesson, and, she adds, Arthur was no great shakes on the dance floor (as ex-Broadway hoofer Ginger ought to know).

Helen O'Connell, dressed to the nines, has the mike all to herself, as she did on the great Arthur Murray number.

119

Mandy Is Two

1942

Music by FULTON McGRATH

Look at the ribbon and look at the curl,
Look at the pinafore.
Here's to the beautiful birthday girl,
May she have many more.

Mandy is Two,
You ought to see her eyes of cornflower
    blue;
They really look as if they actually knew
That she's a big girl now.

Mandy is Two,
You ought to see how many things she can
    do,
She knows her alphabet and ties her own
    shoe
And no one showed her how.

If you could see her majesty with braids in
    her hair;
Almost as though her Sunday beau came
    around and
        brought her an orchid to wear.

Mommy is blue
Because her little girl is going on three,
But Miss Amanda's just as proud as can be
That she's a big girl now.

There really is a Mandy (Amanda)—now past forty and a parent herself. Mercer was always a proud father, and this loving lyric certainly tells how he felt in those growing-up years. The music came from a musician pal, Fulton "Fidgey" McGrath.

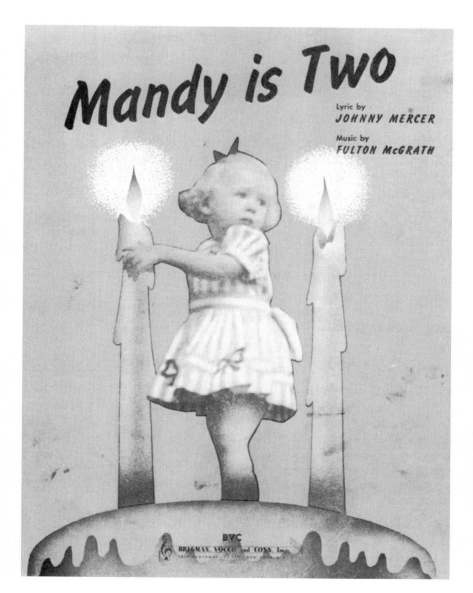

One for My Baby

(And One More for the Road)

1943

Music by HAROLD ARLEN

It's quarter to three,
There's no one in the place except you and
  me,
So, set 'em up, Joe,
I've got a little story you oughta know,
We're drinking, my friend,
To the end of a brief episode,
Make it one for my baby
And one more for the road.

I got the routine,
So drop another nickel in the machine,
I'm feelin' so bad,
I wish you'd make the music dreamy and
  sad,
Could tell you a lot,
But you've got to be true to your code,
Make it one for my baby
And one more for the road.

You'd never know it,
But, buddy, I'm kind of poet
And I've gotta lotta things to say,
And when I'm gloomy,
You simply gotta listen to me,
Until it's talked away.

Well, that's how it goes
And Joe, I know you're anxious to close,
So thanks for the cheer,
I hope you didn't mind my bending your
  ear,
This torch I've found,
Must be drowned or it soon might explode,
Make it one for my baby
And one more for the road.

Another quintessential Arlen-Mercer "late night" song (strong ideas seemed to flow from the two of them in those days). Although the story line was sung with his usual grace, the mood of it doesn't seem to fit Fred Astaire too well in the movie *The Sky's the Limit*. It does suit Sinatra down to his dress shoes and he gives it the full treatment—spoken preamble, spotlight, deep drag of a cigarette—as he so often performs it on concert stages. Mercer knew about bars (uh-huh), and the line, "But, buddy, I'm a kind of poet" is brilliantly on target.

"Make it one for my baby and one more for the road."

Mercer replaced Bob Hope on the Pepsodent radio show for the summer of 1943 ("Poor Miriam . . . forgot to use her irium"), and his hip singing style certainly fooled some people as this postcard plainly shows.

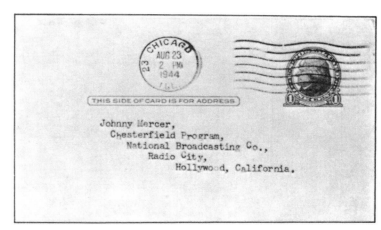

THIS SIDE OF CARD IS FOR ADDRESS

Johnny Mercer,
    Chesterfield Program,
        National Broadcasting Co.,
            Radio City,
                Hollywood, California.

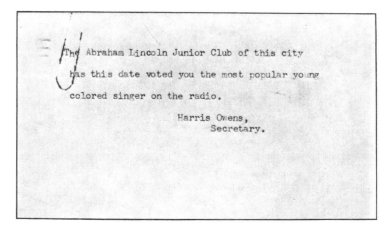

The Abraham Lincoln Junior Club of this city

has this date voted you the most popular young

colored singer on the radio.

                    Harris Owens,
                        Secretary.

My Shining Hour

Music by HAROLD ARLEN

This moment, this minute
And each second in it,
Will leave a glow upon the sky,
And as time goes by,
It will never die.

This will be my shining hour,
Calm and happy and bright,
In my dreams, your face will flower,
Through the darkness of the night.

Like the lights of home before me,
Or an angel watching o'er me,

This will be my shining hour,
Till I'm with you again.

©Edwin H. Morris & Co., Inc.

Fred Astaire was a test pilot (topical theme in 1943) in *The Sky's the Limit* and sang this lofty ballad to Joan Leslie. It is a no-frills, straightaway singer's song and it's therefore not surprising that it appeals to Sinatra, Margaret Whiting, Mel Tormé and other discriminating stars of the music world. As brief as the song appears to be on the page, it packs a wallop when sung thoughtfully.

MY SHINING HOUR

Lyrics by Johnny Mercer

Music by Harold Arlen

Fred ASTAIRE in
THE SKY'S THE LIMIT
with Joan LESLIE

RKO RADIO PICTURES

"MY SHINING HOUR"
"I'VE GOT A LOT IN COMMON WITH YOU"
"ONE FOR MY BABY"
"HARVEY, THE VICTORY GARDEN MAN"

EDWIN H. MORRIS & COMPANY INC.
music publishers
1619 BROADWAY · NEW YORK, N.Y.

BUY
WAR BONDS
AND STAMPS
FOR
VICTORY!

Trav'lin' Light

1943

Music by JIMMY MUNDY and TRUMMY YOUNG

I'm trav'lin' light
Because my man has gone
And from now on
I'm trav'lin' light.

He said "goodbye"
And took my heart away.
So from today
I'm trav'lin' light.

No one to see,
I'm free as the breeze,
No one but me
And my memories.

Some lucky night
He may come back again,
But until then
I'm trav'lin light.

An unusual combination of writers, produced "Trav'lin' Light," and the lyric is not Mercer at his most inspired. Nevertheless, it served as a good vehicle for Billie Holiday and for one of the rare records she made on the Capitol label. It *does* have a good title.

Lady Day with two good saxophonists, Vido Musso and Dave Mathews. No one else could approach her singing of "Trav'lin' Light"

Accentuate the Positive

Music by HAROLD ARLEN

[For verse, sheet music suggests "Slowly . . .
  sermon-like"]

Gather 'round me,
Ev'ry body,
Gather 'round me
While I preach some,
Feel a sermon
Comin' on me.
The topic will be sin
And that's what I'm agin.'
If you wanna
Hear my story,
Then settle back
And just sit tight
While I start reviewin'
The attitude of doin' right.
 You've got to
Accent-tchu-ate the positive,
E-lim-my-nate the negative,
Latch on to the affirmative,

Don't mess with Mister In-between.
You've got to spread joy
Up to the maximum,
Bring gloom down to the minimum,
Have faith, or pandemonium
Li'ble to walk upon the scene.
To illustrate my last remark,
Jonah in the whale, Noah in the Ark,
What did they do
Just when everything looked so dark?
"Man," they said,
"We better
Accent-tchu-ate the positive,
E-lim-my-nate the negative,
Latch on
To the affirmative,
Don't mess with Mister In-between."
No, don't mess with Mister In-between.

The preacher man spirit of this song was ideal for Bing Crosby, who always enjoyed clowning around with a minstrel show dialect. The title came about, according to one story, from a newspaper clipping that quoted the Harlem revivalist preacher Father Divine using the phrase. A friend sent the clipping along to Mercer, who kept it among his many scribbled notes for a long time. It fell into place one day when they were driving in Arlen's car and Harold sang one of his typically provocative strains. It was an Academy Award nominee, but not a winner that year.

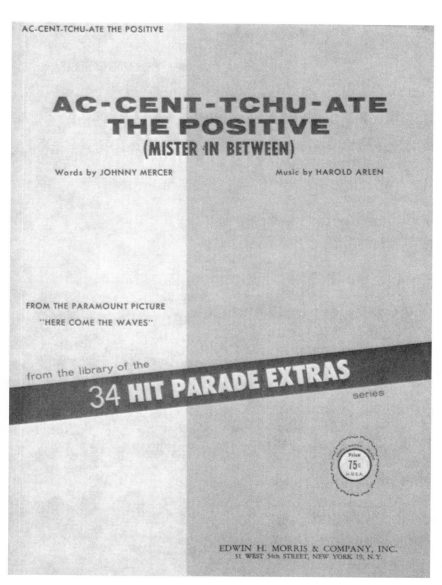

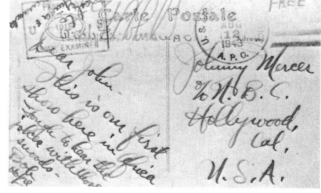

Bob Hope, the perennial gagster, kept in touch with the folks back home from one of his many U.S.O. stops.

How Little We Know

1944

Music by HOAGY CARMICHAEL

Maybe it happens this way,
Maybe we really belong together,
But after all, how little we know.

Maybe it's just for a day,
Love is as changeable as the weather,
And after all, how little we know.

Who knows why an April breeze never
  remains?
Why stars in the trees hide when it rains?
Love comes along casting a spell,
Will it sing you a song,
Will it say a farewell?
Who can tell!
Maybe you're meant to be mine,
Maybe I'm only supposed to stay in your
  arms awhile,
As others have done.
Is that what I've waited for?
Am I the one?
Oh, I hope in my heart that it's so,
In spite of how little we know.

©M. Witmark & Sons

Which is the first team—Arlen & Mercer or Carmichael & Mercer? It's hard to tell when such a marvelously "right" song such as this one comes along to interrupt the flow of the other collaboration. Hoagy Carmichael also appeared on screen in this movie *(To Have and Have Not)* singing "Baltimore Oriole," one of those solo contributions that sounds as if Mercer were looking over his shoulder. This one, however, sounds a little like both of them and therefore has a nice, easygoing feeling to it.

130

G.I. Jive

1944   Words and music by JOHNNY MERCER

This is the G.I. Jive,
Man alive.
It starts with the bugler
Blowin' reveille over your head
When you arrive.
Jack, that's the G.I. Jive
Root-tie-tee toot
Jump in your suit
Make a salute (Voot!)
After you wash and dress,
More or less,
You go get your breakfast
In a beautiful little café they call the mess.
Jack, when you convalesce,
Out of your seat
Into the street,
Make with the feet (Reet!)

If you're a P.V.T. your duty
Is to salute the L.I.E.U.T.;
But if you brush the L.I.E.U.T.,
The M.P. makes you K.P. on the Q.T.
This is the G.I. Jive
Man alive,
They give you a private tank
That features a little device called fluid drive.
Jack, after you revive,
Chuck all your junk,
Back in the trunk
Fall on your bunk (Clunk!)
Soon you're countin' Jeeps,
But before you count to five,
Seems you're right back diggin' that
G. I. Jive!

This breezy wartime favorite was written in practically no time flat, according to Dave Dexter, who was then Capitol Records' publicity director—a & r man—jazz expert—general scout and utility outfielder. Says Dave: "Mercer got the idea for 'G.I. Jive' while waiting for the traffic light at the corner of Sunset and Vine. He noticed all the servicemen on the streets around that busy intersection. So he drove that one block to where our offices were, came upstairs, sat down at the typewriter and dashed the whole thing off in a couple of minutes. It was one of our biggest hits that year."

Dream

1944

Words and music by JOHNNY MERCER

Get in touch with that sundown fellow,
As he tiptoes across the sand.
He's got a million kinds of stardust,
Pick your fav'rite brand, and:

Dream when you're feelin' blue,
Dream, that's the thing to do.

Just watch the smoke rings rise in the air,
You'll find your share
Of memories there.

So dream when the day is thru,
Dream and they might come true,

Things never are as bad as they seem,
So dream, dream, dream.

This proves that Mercer could write a "big" melody. And here's the way he told us about it back in the sixties: "I was just fooling around at the piano and I got a series of chords that attracted me. I played it for Paul Weston and he said, 'Why don't we use it for the theme song on the show?' We were doing the Chesterfield Show on radio—Paul had the band—and I was on it for six months. Then along came Perry Como and did the show for twelve years! I guess that shows something about me as a performer." (Wrong.) And it doesn't show us too much more about the construction of a fine song; we can leave more up to Paul Weston, who added: "Johnny seemed dissatisfied with the sixth note, the one that falls on the word 'blue' but I think that almost 'makes' the song and I convinced him to let it stay."

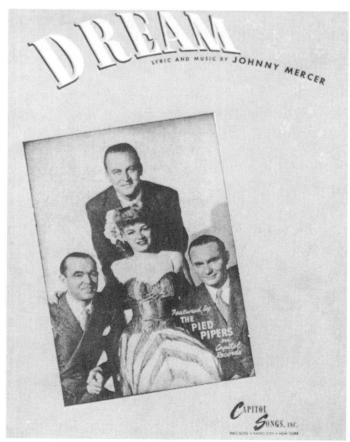

On the Atchison, Topeka and
The Santa Fe

1946

Music by HARRY WARREN

Do yuh hear that whistle down the line?
I figure that it's engine number forty-nine,
She's the only one that'll sound that way.
On the Atchison, Topeka and the Santa Fe.

See the ol' smoke risin' 'round the bend,
I reckon that she knows she's gonna meet a
 friend,
Folks around these parts get the time o' day
From the Atchison, Topeka and the Santa
 Fe.

Here she comes!
Ooh, Ooh, Ooh,
Hey, Jim! yuh better git the rig!
Ooh, Ooh, Ooh,
She's got a list o' passengers that's pretty
 big,

And they'll all want lifts to Brown's Hotel,
'Cause lots 'o them been travelin' for quite a
 spell,
All the way from Philadelphiay,
On the Atchison, Topeka and the Santa Fe.

A blockbuster of a song that helped make Judy Garland's big production number in *The Harvey Girls* a Hollywood classic. It was a natural for Academy Award honors, and win it did for Mercer's first and somewhat overdue Oscar. (Harry Warren once said to Harold Arlen as they went into a party in Palm Springs, "Walk two Oscars behind me.") Once again a favorite subject—this one a daytime train—was running right on time.

"On the Atchison, Topeka and Santa Fe" recently was Johnny Mercer who boarded the Super Chief at Chicago November 2 along with Mrs. Mercer bound for home in Los Angeles via their favorite railroad. President John S. Reed was on hand to wish happy traveling to the well-known couple. This year marks the 25th birthday of that ever-popular song by Johnny Mercer and Harry Warren, which was used in the musical score of "The Harvey Girls." Here, aboard the Super Chief, President Reed appropriately presents an "Award of Appreciation to Johnny Mercer on the 25th Anniversary of the introduction of the song 'On The Atchison, Topeka and Santa Fe' with best wishes."

Judy Garland made any song worth hearing, but "Atchison, Topeka" was a triumph.

Laura

1945

Music by DAVID RAKSIN

You know the feeling
Of something half remembered,
Of something that never happened
Yet you recall it well.

You know the feeling
Of recognizing someone
That you've never met
As far as you could tell; well:

Laura is the face in the misty light
Footsteps that you hear down the hall,
The laugh that floats on a summer night
That you can never quite recall.
And you see Laura
On the train that is passing thru,
Those eyes, how familiar they seem,
She gave your very first kiss to you.
That was Laura,
But she's only a dream.

This song is unquestionably among the top three or four of Mercer's all-time greats, and rightly so: the wispy, mysterious quality that was necessary to match the film holds up well, the haunting "those eyes how familiar they seem," the flash-moment we've all experienced, "Laura on the train [again] that is passing thru" all contribute to this song's universal appeal. Amazingly, Mercer wrote the lyrics some time after the release and subsequent popularity of the movie, thus making it more of a challenge than putting words to a melody usually is.

Out of This World

1945

Music by HAROLD ARLEN

You're clear out of this world.
When I'm looking at you
I hear out of this world
The music that no mortal ever knew.

You're right out of a book.
The fairy tale I read when I was so high.
No armored knight out of a book
Was more enchanted by a Lorelei
Than I

After waiting so long for the right time
After reaching so long for a star,
All at once, from the long and lonely
   nighttime
And despite time
Here you are.

I'd cry out of this world
If you said we were through,
So, let me fly out of this world
And spend the next eternity or two
With you.

The title song of an undistinguished movie that starred Eddie Bracken, Veronica Lake and Diana Lynn and that is remembered, if at all, for the fact that when Eddie Bracken began to sing it was Bing Crosby's voice that one heard. The phrase "out of this world" was somewhat ahead of its time here. T. Dorsey and Bing both had popular records of the tune.

Come Rain or Come Shine

1946

Music by HAROLD ARLEN

I'm gonna love you
Like nobody's loved you,
Come rain or come shine.
High as a mountain
And deep as a river,
Come rain or come shine.
I guess when you met me
It was just one of those things,
But don't ever bet me,
'Cause I'm gonna be true if you let me.
You're gonna love me
Like nobody's loved me,
Come rain or come shine.
Happy together,
Unhappy together
And won't it be fine.
Days may be cloudy or sunny,
We're in or we're out of the money,
But I'm with you always,
I'm with you rain or shine!

A rarity for Mercer because it's probably his only Broadway hit song. "Don't ever bet me" underlines the show's theme, which was the racetrack at the turn of the century and the black jockeys popular at the time. Interestingly, there's no verse to this song.

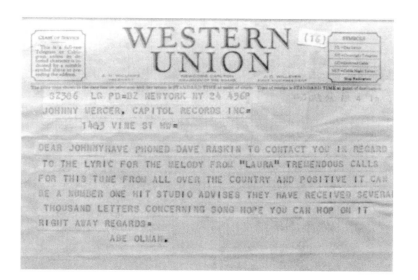

Pearl Bailey was the main show stopper in
St. Louis Woman. She and Mercer were
simpatico souls as the show struggled along.

The original manuscript of one of the lesser songs from Arlen and Mercer's finest score.

The Capitol Records tower on Vine Street. The name Capitol was suggested by the ever-resourceful Ginger M.

Mercer as executive of Capitol Records sits in on a record session with Dave Dexter (left) and co-founder Glenn Wallichs.

The sheet music cover is more interesting than the song, for photogenic reasons alone.

Arlen and Mercer in a marvelously posed shot. They were at their best when this was taken.

I Wonder What Became of Me

1946

Music by HAROLD ARLEN

Lights are bright,
Pianos making music all the night
And they pour champagne just like it was
   rain.

It's a sight to see,
But I wonder what became of me.

Crowds go by,
That merrymaking laughter in their eye
And the laughter's fine,
But I wonder what became of mine.

Life's sweet as honey
And yet it's funny
I get a feeling that I can't analyze,
It's like, well, maybe,

Like when a baby
Sees a bubble burst before its eyes.

Oh, I've had my fling,
I've been around and seen most ev'rything,

Oh, I've had my thrills,
They've lit my cigarettes with dollar bills,

But I can't be gay,
For along the way
Something went astray.

And I can't explain,
It's the same champagne,
It's a sight to see
But I wonder what became of me.

It was a great score, but as so often happens, the music didn't save the show, and *St. Louis Woman* proved a major disappointment to everyone. This song is an unappreciated beauty—like so many others in the score—and could be one of those special favorites, pride of the litter, for the authors. We find the first three lines of this one wonderful.

Any Place I Hang My Hat Is Home

1946

Music by HAROLD ARLEN

Free an' easy, that's my style,
Howdy do me, watch me smile,
Fare thee well me after while
'Cause I gotta roam
An' any place I hang my hat is home!

Sweetnin' water, cherry wine,
Thank you kindly, suits me fine.
Kansas City, Caroline,
That's my honeycomb.
'Cause any place I hang my hat is home.

Birds roostin' in the tree
Pick up an' go,
An' the goin' proves
That's how it ought to be,
I pick up too
When the spirit moves me.

Cross the river, round the bend,
Howdy stranger, so long friend,
There's a voice in the lonesome win'
That keeps whisperin' roam!
I'm goin' where a welcome mat is,
No matter where that is
'Cause any place I hang my hat is home.

Anyone who knew Mercer at all would agree that this is a definitive song of his. In Otis Guernsey's book on *Lyricists and the Broadway Theatre*, writer Jerome Lawrence says, "The line 'Howdy stranger, so long friend' is one that I can't get out of my head." Second the motion. Barbra Streisand has made a fine record of this gem.

It's a Woman's Prerogative

1946   Music by HAROLD ARLEN

I don't know who it was wrote it,
Or by whose pen it was signed
Someone once said, and I quote it,
It's a woman's prerogative to change her
    mind.
He may have you in a halter
Harnessed before and behind,
But till you kneel at that altar
It's a woman's prerogative to change her
    mind.
Promise anything,
Anything at all,
Promise everything,
Everything, honey—don't swerve,
Throw him a curve
String 'em along
Till they show you what they've got in
    reserve.
Though his bank shows a big balance
And he seems heaven designed,
If the boy's short on his talents,
It's a woman's prerogative to change her
    mind.

Any fruit, even a lemon,
Should have a beautiful rind,
But if that lemon's a lemon,
It's a woman's prerogative to change her
    mind.
If he won't bow from the center,
And you're politely inclined,
If he won't rise when you enter,
It's a woman's prerogative to change her
    mind.
They say precedent
Makes a thing a law,
Hooray precedent,
I can say yes
When I mean no.

Hard to believe,
But they tell me that it's legally so.
So don't fret how much you kissed 'em,
If on their couch you're reclined,
Don't forget we've got a system,
It'a a woman's prerogative to change her
    mind.

This was meant to be a show-stopper and succeeded to the extent that it helped Pearl Bailey along on her rise to stardom. Mercer was a great fan of Pearlie-Mae's and so he gave her a lot of good comedy lines here. The theme of female twisting male around her little finger is always surefire, particularly in the theatre.

144

Harlem Butterfly

1948

Words and Music by JOHNNY MERCER

Harlem butterfly, the moon got in your eye
The night you were born.
Harlem butterfly, you listen'd to the cry
Of some lonely horn.
And that combination left you a mark
That you'll never, never lose.
While you chase some will o' the wisp in the
     dark,
Your heart keeps on singin' the blues.

Oh, Harlem butterfly, the writin's in the sky,
You'll come to no good.
But I'm not blamin' you,
I'm certain I would do the same if I could.
For even though a candle burn'd at both
     ends
Can never last out the night
Harlem butterfly, it really makes a lovely
     light.

It was still possible in 1948 to write a lyric with the word Harlem in it, despite the beginnings of postwar race troubles, and Mercer was one of the few major songwriters who had an understanding of what the Black world and its mores were. He often wrote about Blacks, but never in a patronizing way. Though Julie London's picture peps up the sheet music, it was Maxine Sullivan who did (and still does) the song best. Showing his literary interests, the last three lines are a paraphrase of Edna St. Vincent Millay's famous verse.

The lyricist of "Any Place I Hang My Hat," age six.

Though she may always be known as "The Loch Lomond Girl" Maxine Sullivan is closely identified with Mercer's lovely "Harlem Butterfly." This jazzy pose came from the Warner Brothers set of *Going Places*

146

Lazy Mood
(Love's Got Me in a)

1947   Music by EDDIE MILLER

I'll tell you why
The days go by,
Like caterpillars do,
And clouds are cotton blossoms
In a field of blue,
Love's got me in a lazy mood,

I'll tell you why,
Stars in the sky,
Pick ev'ry night to shine.
And why the moon's a watermelon on the
    vine,
Love's got me in a lazy mood.

When a bright and early sun begins to steam
    it up,
You'll find me underneath the nearest tree,
While I dream it up. Pickin' petals off a
    daisy,
Just the absentminded kid, that's me.
I'll tell you why,
I don't reply
    To mail that's overdue.
And why I never answer when I'm spoken
    to,
It isn't that I'm really rude,
Love's got me in a lazy mood.

After the Benny Goodman period, Mercer was hired again to do a weekly radio show that featured commercialized jazz. This time the band was Bob Crosby's Dixieland Band, a happy sounding outfit that was right down Mercer's alley. The tenor saxophonist Eddie Miller played a pretty solo that captured Mercer's ear and the result was this pretty piece.

Early Autumn

1949

Music by RALPH BURNS and WOODY HERMAN

When an early autumn walks the land
And chills the breeze
And touches with her hand
The summer trees,
Perhaps you'll understand
What memories I own.

There's a dance pavilion in the rain
All shuttered down,
A winding country lane all russet brown,
A frosty window pane shows me a town
    grown lonely.

That spring of ours that started
So April hearted
Seemed made for just a boy and girl.
I never dreamed, did you,
Any fall could come in view so early, early?

Darling, if you care,
Please let me know,
I'll meet you anywhere,
I miss you so.
Let's never have to share
Another early autumn.

Who else but Mercer could conjure up such a marvelously nostalgic picture as "a dance pavilion in the rain all shuttered down"? Here are the author's comments on the song: "That's by Ralph Burns—a superior tune—and I've never even met Ralph yet. I think it's one of my best lyrics. [Unusual for him to say] Not a big hit, but you can't tell the public what they like—they usually pick the right ones."

Johnny may be thanking Woody Herman for making possible the great song "Early Autumn." The kid on the right, Woody's grandson, has enough hair for Johnny, Woody, Artie Shaw and George Simon.

Sidney Zion

This, That

BING. When he got away last week, disconnected melodies jumped all over me, and I'll bet over millions of people all over the world. Not only his songs, though of course his songs, but fragments like so: the phone number of a girl I haven't seen in 25 years; my great little red Rambler; the attic where the victrola lived and so did I for hours each day against walls festooned with DiMaggio, Keller, Luckman, Bertelli, Grable and Durante; a sign over a place in Passaic saying Weddings, Banquets, Sandwiches; a high school fraternity dance in *Albany?* where I saw the girl whose number I remembered on Friday afternoon when Bing Crosby . . .

Of course, he changed the whole course of pop singing, and yet in his duos with Jolson and Armstrong, he flowed perfectly, moving the old stuff around like a great control pitcher, and always managing, in that casual way, to take the center and hold it. When he went one-on-one with Sinatra, particularly in the movie "High Society," he simply wiped out Sinatra, took him with the first glance, though Frank was at his peak and Bing supposedly over the hill. Of all the great stars he sang with — it's funny how few of the ladies come to mind — the only one he didn't shade was Johnny Mercer, but then nobody could touch up Johnny Mercer, who broke the mold himself. They did a TV show together years back, and if some tasteful, enterprising producer would only do a replay we'd see the best musical evening television ever made. But is there such an animal as an enterprising producer with taste? There must have been once, but where are they now?

And now, alas, where is Bing and Al and Johnny and Louis?

Christmas Card

Noel

Yule and Christmastide
To everybody—every side
Best of fortune, health, and cheer
In everybody's atmosphere
Let foe kiss friend—and friend kiss foe
Beneath a common mistletoe
Republicans! Be Democratic
Drag the tinsel from the attic
Light the tree and fill the bowl
(You won the Lit'ry Digest poll)
Step right up and love thy neighbor
Capital! Shake hands with Labor
Hurry and unlatch the door
For Santa Claus is here once more
Despite a million annual beatings
Here he is—dispensing greetings
Bringing them from us to you
From who knows, Lord, to Lord
   knows who
To all the people on our list
To everyone we may have missed
To those who'll say to us, "I see—
You didn't send a card to me!"
To those who'll say, "Of all the gall!"
A Merry Christmas to you All!
A Happy Yule to all of you
Who should have sent us something too
Season when the heart has wings
Hark! The Herald Tribune sings!
Have a pretzel, have a beer
Christmas comes but once a year
Greetings Harold, Anya Arlen
Buddy Morris, you too, Carlin
Johnny Arledge, Fred Astaire
Edith Anderson and "Square"

Greetings Ashcrafts, Jane and "Squirrel"
Milton Ager and his girl
Greetings Mr., Mrs. Alter
Billy Blun and Lawrence Salter
All the guys on Bull and Broughton
Messrs. Arco and MacNaughton
Botkin, Borut, Brewster, Blum
Come and make yourselves "to hum"
Drink with Bacchus, ring up Bell
Charles, Ed, Mac and Muriel
Mrs. Baldwin, bring your Earl in
Where's a chair for Irving Berlin
Mr. Bargy, Mr. Bloom
Let's have music in the room
Archie Bleyer, Johnny Burke
Busby Berkeley go to work
Show the Burroughs and the Blowes
How the anvil chorus goes
Merry Christmas—sing it gaily
Ronny Burla, Mildred Bailey
Bacon, Lloyd, and Aunt Nell Blackie
Call time out on "Nagasaki"
Sing a simple Christmas lay
Barris Harry, Bregman J.
So we go from B to C
Greetings Cochran, Charlie B.
Prosit Pink and Mary Cavett
'S only schnapps, but you can have it
Philip Charig, prosit too
Carol Carol—both of you
Greetings Crosbys, Bing and Larry
Dixie, Coop, and Lin and Gary
Philip, Dennis, Everett, Bob
What do you Crosbys hear—from the mob?
Happy New Year—fide bona

Clinton, Clark, and chez Colonna
May the Carmichaels be lucky
Hoagy, Ruth, and Bob and Ducky
Ken Carpenter, Sidney Clare
Everybody—Everywhere
To the Davis clans, hey nonny
Marvin, Mary, Bette, Johnny
Tommy Dugan, Buddy Dill
Buddy (now B. G.) De Syl-
Dorsey J. and Dorsey T.
Dubin Al and Douglas P.
Dubin J. and A. Devine
Hello *Oscar Hammerstein*
Here's a crimson wreath of holly
For Walter Donaldson and Wally
P. De Rose—May Singhi Breen
Jimmy Downey, how've you been?
And Margot de la Falaise
You wear that name—no matter what any
    says
Ere the jolly season pass
Happy, Happy Michaelmas!
Turkey stuffing, hot cross buns
Edelmans and Emersons
William Ellfeldt, Skinnay Ennis
Johnny Faunce (and how's your tennis?)
Fishbeins, Franklins, how you all?
Dave, Dwight, Mary (neé McCall)
Wishes can't be Fonda, Hank
Just like money in the bank
Then there's F for Families
Christmas Gif' to both of these
Mother, Mother, Father too
Walter, Big and Little Hugh
Ed and Deborah and Claire
Polish up the silverware
Lay the snowy tablespread
Uncles Lewis and Rob and Ed
Gather 'round and all get clubby

Meet Elizabeth's new hubby
George and Bess and George the third
Cousin Mamie, cut the bird
Mercer, Adeline, Aunt K.
Polish off the egg frappé
Dorothy and Mary Lou
Joseph and Virginia too
Every oldster—every sprout
Mustn't leave a person out
Uncle Joe will mix the toddy
Happy headaches everybody!
Ira Gershwins, Johnny Greens
Elliott Grennards, Jack Gordeans
Here's a package tied in ribbons
For the Gruens and the Gibbons
While the Goffs and L. Wolfe Gilberts
Get a box of chocolate filberts
And to Goldie, mon chou chou
The remaining nuts to you
Mr. Gumble, Mrs. Geary
Hope your Xmas comes on cheery
While B. Goodman's—Krupa's too
Comes on like Gangbusters do
Farmer or sophisticate
Happy New Year to you, Gate
Galludets and Crooner Frawley
Allie Wrubel, Dick MacCauley
Dr. Joe and Mrs. Harris
Happy, happy plaster paris
Harry Arthur, Harris Jane
Charlotte, Jack, long may you reign
Blessings on your domiciles
Here and in the British Isles
May a goodly batch of manna
Find the Hull home in Savannah
Laughter in the Herzig den
Love to Bernie Hanighen
And may Joe and Mrs. Helbock
Open up a keg of swell bock

To the Harveys—Bob and Peg
Goes the biggest turkey leg
And the Hawkins, Houstons, Herts
May they get their just desserts
Greetings Bob, Dolores Hope
Here's a present—do not ope
Lindsay Howard and Seabiscuit
Here's a fin—or should I risk it?
Sonny Hitch and Margery
Willie Horowitz—how be?
Isaccs, Jarvis, how do you be?
And the Jolsons, Al and Ruby?
Babo Jackson, Poppa Bill
Your socks would be hard to fill
Gordon Jenkins, Georgie Joy
Mrs. Johnston's little boy
Irving Kahal—tap the barrel
Miriam, sing a Christmas Karol
Blessings Margaret Keyes and Zipper
Teddy Koehler—Hi ya, Dipper?
Hiram Kraft and daughter Jill
You too, Reata—now, be still!
I know all you people, but—
Who is *Wilhemina Thutt?*
Lots of Noels, lots of Yules
To the Cal and Mandy Kuhls
Love to Grace and Gus (the Kahns)
"Kosty" Ianetz, Lily Pons
C. and E. Kress—by the way—
Have you ever thought of writing a play?
Harry Kaufman wants to know
Harry, we can't do that show.
Guy Lombardo, Harry Link
Carmen, Leibert, have a drink!
Eddie Lowe and Bonnie Lake,
Have a slice of angel cake!
Hello Fud and hello Don!
In the name of Livingston
Mr. Leslie, Mrs. Lehr

Here's a rather tough affair
How's a guy to rhyme La Mont
Maybe Nash can, but I cawn't
Greetings, greetings, greetings all
Hallelujah! Have a ball!
Have a party and we'll pay
If we get the bank's okay
Put the taper to the fire
In the house of McIntire
Bring the frankincense and myrrh
To the house of Mehlinger
Ralph Malone and Una Merkel
Gather 'round the family circle
Jeeves, get out more firewater
Toast McDonough's wife and daughter
Jeeves, go fetch the old Bacardi
Comes the Malnecks and Mienardi
Comes the Mitchells and Marcels
From the land where King George dwells
Mrs. Mannerino (Mary)
Jno. Mayhew, Leo McCarey
Modisetts and Monacos
Have you tasted some of those?
Have you tried the seven layer?
Have some, Ray and Edith Mayer
Mr. Rothmere, have some too
Really, there's enough for you
I know all you people, but—
Who is *Wilhemina Thutt?*
Greetings Millers—Everett, Charlie
Bless your hearts particularly
Here, you minstrels! Tune your lyres
Sing to Zi and Betty Myers
Mr. Norvo, taste the jam
Mr. Nelson, how's the Ham?
Nolan, Joe and Noble, Ray
Merry, merry Xmas day
Mr. Gordon Oliver
May you get what you prefer

Though the censors find it shocking
May a brunette fill your stocking
Keep the sweets from Oakie, Jack
Or the poundage may come back
To the Tommy Oxnards, hey!
To the Bennys, watcha say?
Greetings, Temple, Dot, not Shirley
Just because her teeth are pearly
Rocco Vocco and his Dolly
Joe Venuti and his Sally
Jerry Vogel's smiling pan
Emmerita Vanneman
Who's that singing in the alley?
Let him in—why, Rudy Vallee!
Hang the geese and stuff the pheasants
Almost time to open presents
Comes the late guest through the yard
To present his calling card
Hang his off'ring on the bough
Jeeves, there goes the doorbell now
In the late arrivals float
Mrs. Whiting, rest your coat?
Margaret, Barbara and Blossom
Cut yourselves a slice o'possum
Look who's here! It's Harry Wise
Christmas spirit in his eyes
Here's the Warner Music Staffs
(Can I have your autographs?)
Kenny, Hazel, Sandy, Sammy

Polished up with soap and chamois
Jack and Ruth and Norman Foley
Harold, Mack, both roly-poly
Love to all the Warner house
Look out, ladies, there's a Mouse
And his brother, Harry Warren
Back with Jo from travels foreign
Hal B. Wallis, J. L. Warner
Sorry I ain't in your corner
But it's nice to have a day off
Knowing that it's not a lay off
Margaret Whiteman! Hello, Paul—
Still the Daddy of them all
Will you say how-do for me
To the Big and Little T?
Vernon Wood, it's time you came!
Mrs. Willingham, the same!
Harold Warnell!—listen, "Slicker"
Don't expect that pre-war liquor
Close the door and lock it tight
Wait a second—something White
All the brothers and their wives
See! the troupe of Young arrives
Youngs from Lincoln St. and Hall
Youngs from N.Y. Enter all!
Everybody's here again
Did I hear a footstep then?
Who's that in the snowy mist?
Sam and Maggie Zimbalist!

Ginger and Johnny at home in Palm Springs (beer or Scotch?).

The Fifties

If phonographs were the big influence on young people in the twenties and radio broadcasting in the thirties and forties, the full-scale arrival of television in the early fifties was equally influential on young and old alike—for awhile. The postwar young would soon become captivated by another phenomenon—a Southern singer with the sex appeal of a Valentino and the unique name of Elvis. As for the rest of the music world, television was not the bonanza that the earlier wonders of American communications had proved: TV producers discovered that pointing their cameras into the bell of a trumpet or into the larynx of, say, Julius LaRosa of "The Arthur Godfrey Show" wasn't nearly as exciting to home viewers as seeing Soupy Sales get a pie pushed into his face or Jackie Robinson sliding safely into second base. The new box in the corner of the living room (not yet called "the boob tube") was causing still another problem for people like Johnny Mercer and other creative fellows: the production of movies—particularly lavish musicals—was being cut back considerably. In the year 1938 Hollywood had produced fifty-nine musical films of one quality or another, but by 1950 the output was reduced to a paltry twenty-one. The sad omens were in the air, particularly with that guitar-playing kid from Tennessee gyrating around so successfully in the middle of the bland Eisenhower years.

The decade of the 1950s was a time of paradox too: there were Dave Garroway and Uncle Miltie, Pat Boone and "Rock 'Round the Clock," *Hellzapoppin* and Rodgers and Hammerstein. For the man we're principally concerned with, however, the time, while not as productive as the previous two decades, saw him now a member of the Hollywood elite. Capitol Records was moving into the big leagues, challenging Victor, Columbia and Decca, Mercer's second Oscar ("In the Cool, Cool, Cool of the Evening"—1951) was resting on the mantel shelf of his Newport Beach home, and the story of an amazing piece of family business had leaked out to make his name known beyond just the music business. The story concerned Mercer's father, a well-known real estate broker in Savannah, who had gone bankrupt in the troublesome times of the late twenties. Johnny Mercer, honorable son of the old, *old* south, decided more than twenty years later to repay his father's debts, and so he tracked down all the original investors or their heirs and sent off a check of $300,000 to a local bank for the complete repayment. This story hit the wire services and, typically of Mercer's quiet, private ways, was a surprise to his wife of so many years, who had to hear about it first from the newspaper reporters. Quiet and private he was, also a bit vague and absentminded at times—the Savannah bank phoned to call to Johnny's attention the fact that he had forgotten to sign the gentlemanly check.

Movie scores were not coming around as often, now that Hollywood was slowing down, and Capitol Records was losing its original flavor as it moved into the world of big sales and big business. "Johnny said, 'There's no fun there any more,' " says Ginger Mercer. "He thought it had become a bit of a bore." Dave Dexter and Margaret Whiting, who were both very much involved with the company, agree that the disenchantment of Capitol's guru was total. "He'd come back from New York, walk in the office and the receptionist wouldn't know who he was," says Margaret. So Johnny Mercer bowed out of the one big business venture he ever became involved with (money and art rarely mix, said some sage) and even though he left Capitol a little resentfully, there was a great deal of financial recompense. It was time to turn his attentions elsewhere.

Undaunted by the total disappointments of both the brilliantly scored *St. Louis Woman* in 1946 and the not-so-brilliant 1949 *Texas, L'il Darlin'*, on which he collaborated with Robert Emmet Dolan, in the fifties Mercer indulged a great deal in one of his favorite sports—riding the trains from coast to coast (and occasionally south to refresh himself in Savannah). Broadway was becoming a tougher mountain to scale, with such strong competition as Frank Loesser's *Guys and Dolls*, Leonard Bernstein's *West Side Story*, and Rodgers and Hammerstein's *Carousel* and *The King and I*, but Mercer kept trying. In the space of ten years that some wits have retrospectfully dubbed the Fabulous Fifties (J. McCarthy fabulous?) he gave the Broadway arena three more tries. In 1951 *Top Banana*, for which he wrote both words and music and which starred Phil Silvers, who, though hot on TV as "Sergeant Bilko," couldn't make it into a real hit; in 1956 *L'il Abner*, based on the Al Capp cartoon strip, with music by a good musician friend from Hollywood, Gene DePaul; and finally, in 1959, *Saratoga*, which had the greatest of ingredients—book by Edna Ferber, costumes and sets by Cecil Beaton, songs by Harold Arlen—and the worst of reviews. But of course the trains could always take him back to California.

And back there where the sun always made it so easy to play a little golf, shoot the breeze on the Vine Street sidewalk outside the Brown Derby, or just laze about in the backyard, Johnny Mercer forgot about the New York rat race. Even though the music he loved so much was changing radically in the late fifties—rock 'n' roll and bebop were never his cup of tea—the Mercer touch continued for awhile, and just ahead were two of his biggest hit songs, bringing in two more Oscars.

Great impromptu shot of two musical greats—J.M. and Nat "King" Cole at a Capitol Records gathering.

The Big Movie Show in the Sky

1950   Music by ROBERT EMMETT DOLAN

A fella can get lonesome when he is all
  alone,
Out there in the Pacific with no friends to
  call his own.
A fella gits to thinkin' if he's gittin'
  anywhere,
A fella gits to wond'rin' how it's gonna
  be up there.

When your final chip is cashed
And the pearly gates swing wide,
And there is old Saint Peter
Askin' you to come inside.
He whispers "Son, go find a seat,
I hope you like the show,"
And then you see a picture of the life you
  led below!

Imagine you are one of that great celestial
  crowd,

A settin' back relaxin' with your feet upon a
  cloud.
You're pourin' buttered sunshine on your
  popcorn
White as fleece
And waitin' for the latest inter-hemisphere
  release.
The stars spell out the title and the cast
Before your eye.
The show commences on the silver screen
They call the sky.
The past begins unfoldin' and you see it
  takin' place,
And pretty soon you're lookin' at your own
  big, ugly face!

Bye and bye, bye and bye,
Can you look your self in the eye,
When you come on the screen "up yonder,"
At the big movie show in the sky?

Mercer's second outing on Broadway was in tandem with a pal, Robert Emmet (Bobby) Dolan, whom Mercer had met on the Paramount lot where Dolan was a conductor/musical director. *Texas L'il Darlin'* never quite got off the ground, which was not surprising considering the competition at the time: *South Pacific, Kiss Me Kate* and *Guys and Dolls*. Dolan and Mercer put together a pleasant but rather undistinguished score which featured a toe-tapper "It's Great to Be Alive" and this hunk of down-home philosophy.

Autumn Leaves

1950

English lyric by JOHNNY MERCER
Music by JOSEPH KOSMA

The falling leaves
Drift by the window,
The Autumn leaves
Of red and gold.

I see your lips,
The summer kisses,
The sunburned hands
I used to hold.

Since you went away
The days grow long,
And soon I'll hear
Old winter's song.

But I miss you most of all, my darling,
When Autumn leaves start to fall.

This, the first of Mercer's three big adaptations of French songs, remains one of the most performed of ballads in nightclubs, piano bars and lounges. It can probably best be categorized as something of a tearjerker and Mel Tormé, a songwriter's best friend, says that the image "old winter's song" knocks him out.

160

Here's to My Lady

1951

Music by RUBE BLOOM

Although it lies outside of my dominion
If you should ask me for my opinion,
When out with good companions and voices
    ring.
There comes a time before the party's
    closing,
Perhaps the old ones have started dozing,
When one toast needs proposing,
I raise my glass and sing:

Here's to my lady,
Here's a toast to my lady
And all that my lady means to me.

Like a hearth in the Winter,
A breeze in the Summer,
A Spring to remember is she.

Though the years may grow colder
As people grow older,
It's shoulder to shoulder we'll be.

But be it sunshine or shady,
Here's my love to my lady.
I pray, may she always love me.

Another collaboration with a pal—they hadn't worked together since "Fools Rush In" in 1940—and, though Rube Bloom was an old jazzman, this song is both musically and lyrically romantic. It was never a big hit, but this song meant a lot to both Mercers, since Johnny announced that it was dedicated to Ginger. "My lady" is a nice way of saying it.

In the Cool, Cool, Cool of the Evening

1951   Music by HOAGY CARMICHAEL

Sue wants a barbecue,
Sam wants to boil a ham,
Grace votes for Bouillabaisse stew.
Jake wants a weeny bake,
Steak and a layer cake,
He'll get a tummy ache too.
We'll rent a tent or teepee.
Let the town crier cry.
And if it's R.S.V.P.
This is what I'll reply:

In the cool, cool, cool of the evenin',
Tell 'em I'll be there.
In the cool, cool, cool of the evenin',
Better save a chair.
When the party's gettin' a glow on,
'N' singin' fills the air,
In the shank o' the night,
When the doin's are right,
You can tell 'em I'll be there.

"Whee!" said the bumblebee,
"Let's have a jubilee!"
"When?" said the prairie hen, "Soon?"
"Shore!" said the dinosaur.
"Where?" said the grizzly bear,
"Under the light of the moon?"
"How 'bout ya, brother jackass?"
Ev'ryone gaily cried,
"You comin' to the fracas?"
Over his specs he sighed;

In the cool, cool, cool of the evenin',
Tell 'em I'll be there.
In the cool, cool, cool of the evenin',
Slickum on my hair.
When the party's gettin' a glow on,
'N' singin' fills the air,
If I ain't in the clink,
And there's sumpin' to drink,
You can tell 'em I'll be there.

The verse is just as swinging and happy as the chorus on this, another Carmichael-Mercer all-timer and the second Mercer Academy Award winner. The movie, *Here Comes the Groom*, was hardly an all-timer but Bing's recording saved the day. The ending phrase, "sumpin' to drink," is sho-'nuff Mercer.

162

When the World Was Young

1951

Music by M. PHILIPPE-GERARD

It isn't by chance I happen to be,
A boulevardier, the toast of Paris,
For over the noise, the talk and the smoke,
I'm good for a laugh, a drink or a joke.
I walk in a room, a party or ball,
"Come sit over here" somebody will call.

"A drink for M'sieur!
A drink for us all!"
But how many times I stop and recall.

Ah, the apple trees,
Blossoms in the breeze,
That we walked among,
Lying in the hay,
Games we used to play,
While the rounds were sung,
Only yesterday
When the world was young.

Wherever I go they mention my name,
And that in itself, is some sort of fame
"Come by for a drink, we've having a
    game,"
Wherever I go I'm glad that I came.
The talk is quite gay, the company fine,
There's laughter and lights, and glamour
    and wine,

And beautiful girls and some of them mine,

But often my eyes see a diff'rent shine.

Ah, the apple trees,
Sunlit memories,
Where the hammock swung,
On our backs we'd lie,
Looking at the sky.
Till the stars were strung,
Only last July
When the world was young.

While sitting around, we often recall.
The laugh of the year, the night of them all.
The blonde who was so attractive that year,
Some opening night that made us all cheer.
Remember that time we all got so tight,
And Jacques and Antoine got into a fight.

The gendarmes who came, passed out like a
    light,
I laugh with the rest, it's all very bright.

Ah, the apple trees,
And the hive of bees
Where we once got stung,
Summers at Bordeaux,
Rowing the bateau,
Where the willow hung,
Just a dream ago,
When the world was young.

A great story-telling lyric that many people still refer to as "Ah, the apple tree." This fine adaptation from a lovely French *chanson* surprised fellow lyricist and Mercer devotee Gene Lees (writing in *High Fidelity* magazine) when he found out that Johnny never learned to speak French. A big record of this song was made by Peggy Lee, another fan and *simpatico* soul. Just consider this picture-book couplet: "Summers at Bordeaux, Rowing the bateau."

Top Banana

1951   Words and music by JOHNNY MERCER

Your big timers and small timers
Don't happen the easy way.
The star comes first,
Then the leading man,
Then the actors in the play.
There are no comics like low comics,
Who finally make the grade.
But recall, sweethearts,
All the phony starts,
And the lousy parts they played!

If you wanna be the top banana,
You gotta start at the bottom of the bunch.
You gotta know the joke about the farmer's
daughter,
Then take it in the kisser with the soda
water,
If you wanna be a burlesque comic,
It's basic trainin' for you to take a punch.
You gotta roll your eyes and make a funny
face,

'N' do a take and holler,
"Dis must be duh place!"
If you wanna be the top banana,
You gotta start from the bottom up.

If you wanna be the top banana,
You gotta start at the bottom of the bunch.
It doesn't matter if the jokes are clean or
shady,
Make fun of anybody, even your old lady.
What's the diff'rence if she's someone's
mother?
She's a straight man who oughta know her
part.
She raised you from an infant
And she's kind and sweet,
But does she know the way to get to Flugel
street?
If you wanna be the top banana,
You gotta start from the bottom up.

There could only be one pal at a time—Hy Kraft wrote the book—so Mercer took on both words and music for this good idea of a Broadway musical. Unfortunately, even the lovable clown Phil Silvers, then at the height of his "Sergeant Bilko" TV fame, couldn't save *Top Banana*, which rattled around in the huge Winter Garden Theatre. In this breezy title song, notice how hip and on-target Mercer is with his reference to "Dis must be duh place!" and "Flugel Street." Deservedly or not, the show is getting a second life in summer stock and places like Las Vegas.

At least the sign was a big splash on Broadway—even Irving Berlin's offices next door are overshadowed.

165

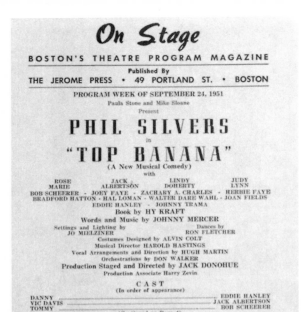
"Whatcha say, Dipper?"
When Jeff was the newest addition.

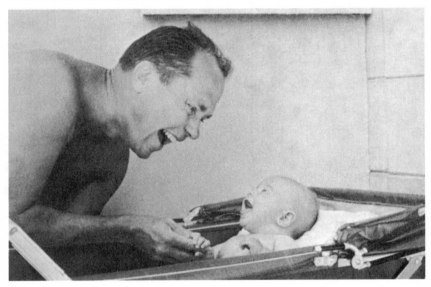

The great Mills Brothers, who helped the "Glow Worm" revival—and vice versa.

Glow-Worm

1952

Music by PAUL LINCKE (1902)

Glow, little glow-worm, fly of fire,
Glow like an incandescent wire,
Glow for the female of the specie,
Turn on the A-C and the D-C;
This night could use a little brightnin',
Light up, you li'l ol' bug of lightnin',
When you gotta glow, you gotta glow,
Glow, little glow-worm, glow

Glow, little glow-worm, glow and glimmer,
Swim through the sea of night, little
    swimmer,
Thou aer-o-nau-tic-al boll weevil,
Il-lu-mi-nate yon woods primeval;
See how the shadows deep and darken,
You and your chick should get to sparkin',
I got a gal that I love so,
Glow, little glow-worm, glow.

Glow, little glow-worm, turn the key on,
You are equipped with tail light neon;
You got a cute vest pocket Mazda
Which you can make both slow or "Fazda";
I don't know who you took a shine to,
Or who you're out to make a sign to,
I got a gal that I love so,
Glow, little glow-worm, glow.

One can only imagine what a ball Mercer had writing this great updating ("tail-light neon," "vest pocket Mazda") and how stunned the original lyricist, Lilla Cayley Robinson, might have been could she have heard it. The Mills Brothers made such a famous record of the modern "Glow-Worm" that they still have to sing it wherever they go (even on American Express commercials) thirty years after its introduction.

Song of India

1953

Text and adaptation by JOHNNY MERCER
From the original by N. RIMSKY-KORSAKOW

And still the snowy Himalayas rise
In ancient majesty before our eyes,
Beyond the plains, Above the pines,
While thru the ever, never changing land,
As silently as any native band
That moves at night, the Ganges shines;

Then I hear the song that only India can
sing,
Softer than the plumage on a black raven's
wing;
High upon a minaret I stand
And gaze across the desert sand
Upon an old enchanted land,
There's the maharajah's caravan,
Unfolding like a painted fan,
How small the little race of Man!

See them all parade across the ages,

Armies, kings and slaves from hist'ry's
pages,
Played on one of Nature's vastest stages.
The turbanned Sikhs and fakirs line the
streets,
While holy men in shadowed calm retreats
Pray thru the night and watch the stars,
A lonely plane flies off to meet the dawn,
While down below the busy life goes on,
And women crowd the old bazaars;

All are in the song that only India can sing,
Softer than the plumage on a black raven's
wing;
Tune the ageless moon and stars were
strung by,
Timeless song that only could be sung by
India,
The jewel of the East!

During the Mercer memorial at the Music Box Theatre (Irving Berlin had donated the use of it) in 1976, Mel Tormé singled this lyric out from among the hundreds of Mercers that had been published. Mel said he had heard a Mario Lanza recording of the song on the radio, had phoned the station to inquire about its modern lyrics, and had been amazed when told they were by Mercer. Even as astute a musician as Tormé is impressed by Mercer's all-round adaptability, represented here by beautifully high-flown, appropriate imagery.

Spring, Spring, Spring

1953   Music by GENE de PAUL

Oh, the barnyard is busy
In a regular tizzy,
And the obvious reason
Is because of the season.
Ma Nature's lyrical
With her yearly miracle,
Spring, Spring, Spring!

All the henfolk are hatchin'
While their menfolk are scratchin'
To insure the survival
Of each brand new arrival.
Each nest is twittering,
They're all baby sittering,
Spring, Spring, Spring!

It's a beehive of budding son and daughter
   life,
Ev'ry family has plans in view.
Even down in the brook the underwater life
Is forever blowing bubbles too.
Ev'ry field wears a bonnet
With some spring daisies on it,
Even birds of a feather
Show their clothes off together.
Sun's gettin' shinery
To spotlight the finery,
Spring, Spring, Spring!

In his hole, though the gopher
Seems a bit of a loafer,
The industrious beaver
Puts it down to spring fever.
While there's no antelope
Who feels that he can't elope,
It's Spring, Spring, Spring!

Slow but surely the turtle
Who's enormously fertile
Lays her eggs by the dozens,
Maybe some are her cousins.
Even the catamount
Is nonplussed at that amount,
It's Spring, Spring, Spring!

Even out in Australia the kangeroos
Lay off butter fat and all French fries.
If their offspring are large it might be
   dangerous,
They've just gotta keep 'em pocket size.
Even though to each rabbit
Spring is more like a habit,
Notwithstanding, the fact is
They indulge in the practice
Each day is mother's day,
The next day some other's day,
It's Spring, Spring, Spring!

To itself each amoeba
Softly croons, "Ach du lieber,"
While the proud little termite
Feels as large as a worm might.
Old poppa dragon fly
Is making the wagon fly,
It's Spring, Spring, Spring!

Ev'ry bug's snuggled snuggy
In its own baby buggy,
And in spite of policing
Seems the tribe is increasing.
'Cause Missus Katydid
Once did what her matey did,
It's Spring, Spring, Spring!

Daddy Long Legs is stretching out his
   creaking joints,
And how busy can a bumble bee?
Flitting hither and thither she keeps seeking
   joints
With a spare room and a nursery.
Each cocoon has a tenant

So they hung out a pennant
"Don't disturb, please keep waiting;
We are evacuating.
This home's my momma's,
I'll soon have my own domicile,"
It's Spring, Spring, Spring!

A natural rhyming trip for Mercer with his long-standing affinity for the animal world (he should have worked for Disney) and things homespun and rural. The movie *Seven Brides for Seven Brothers*, in which this song appeared, has become a classic principally because of Michael Kidd's brilliant choreography. Mercer and his new writing partner Gene de Paul later teamed up again with Kidd for the Broadway show *L'il Abner*; obviously they all worked well together.

The stars of *Seven Brides for Seven Brothers*, Howard Keel and Jane Powell, with Mercer looking rather smallish next to Keel.

170

Capitol Decade

More than a decade ago Johnny Mercer and Glenn Wallichs used to talk about the record business in Wallich's big music store at Sunset and Vine in Hollywood. As one of the nation's leading songwriters ("Lazybones," "Goody Goody," "Jeepers Creepers," etc.), Mercer had many faults to find. Recording artists, he felt, were seldom presented at their best, and arrangements too often did not do justice to his own, or fellow composer's, compositions. And the major companies generally ignored budding talent.

Wallichs, as owner of the Music City, one of the country's largest music emporiums, had his complaints, too. As a record dealer, he disagreed fundamentally with the merchandising and distribution policies of the "big" companies.

The result of their discussions was inevitable. Why not form a record company of their own? At this point, the late B.G. (Buddy) DeSylva, executive producer of Paramount Pictures, endorsed their enterprise and put up $10,000 to get them going. On April 8, 1942, Capitol Records was formed. On April 18 the War Production Board reduced the shellac available to record companies by about 70 per cent. By July 1, Capitol had sold its first records—only to be faced with a curt note from James C. Petrillo, president of the American Federation of Musicians, to the effect that no more records could be made after Aug. 1.

Big Four It was hardly an auspicious birth, and few except Wallichs, Mercer & Co. saw how Capitol could survive, let alone be a threat to the "Big Three"—RCA Victor, Columbia, and Decca. But survive it did, and last week, as Capitol was in full swing celebrating its tenth birthday, the company had not only become a threat to the "Big Three," but forced the industry to recognize there was now a "Big Four" in the business.

In 1942, Capitol grossed $195,000. Last year, total sales exceeded $13,000,000, a gain of more than $1,000,000 over 1950. The company has still to match its all-time high in 1948, when it grossed $16,800,000. But that it bounced back from the horrors of 1949, when the firm netted only $60,000 after taxes, all concerned feel is a miracle made possible only by Capitol's young and aggressive leadership. For 1949 found Capitol caught short in the "Battle of the Speeds," when the record industry was forced to face—and convert to—the new 33⅓ and 45 rpm. The nightmares of this fight for survival were enough to make Wallichs, already a camera enthusiast, take up miniature railroading as an antidote for sleepless nights and worried days.

Camera-bug Wallichs focuses on . . .

When Capitol began, it had nine artists, and its first hits were Ella Mae Morse's "Cow-Cow Boogie" and Johnny Mercer's "Strip Polka." As the years passed there came Mercer's "GI Jive" and "Accentuate the Positive," Betty Hutton's "Doctor, Lawyer, Indian Chief," Peggy Lee's "Golden Earrings" and "Mañana," Nat King Cole's "Mona Lisa" and "Too Young," Tex Williams's "Smoke, Smoke, Smoke, That Cigarette," Les Paul and Mary Ford's "How High the Moon," "Mockin' Bird Hill," "The World Is Waiting for the Sunrise," "Tennessee Waltz," and "Tiger Rag," Kay Starr's "Wheel of Fortune," and, to round out the tenth year, Ella Mae Morse again with "Blacksmith Blues."

Kids and Classics In addition to its extraordinarily strong popular catalogue, Capitol also boasts a kiddie list (the "Bozo the Clown" series as its leader) which accounts for about 20 per cent of the firm's business. And its classical catalogue, initiated with prewar German Telefunken masters, has now increased to include such domestic organizations and artists as the Pittsburgh Symphony, the Hollywood String Quartet, and the young pianist Leonard Pennario.

The aims which Wallichs and Mercer set up in the beginning have been adhered to as far as possible. Wallichs, elected president in 1947, has borne most of the administrative burdens and has seen to it that Capitol's merchandising and distributing policies have followed his progressive ideas.

And Mercer's aims for greater artistic integrity have also been respected. Most major firms supervise—and even dictate—the repertoire and arrangements of their artists. Capitol let Peggy Lee gamble on "Mañana," and it sold 1,500,000 records. Les Paul and his wife Mary Ford last year sold 6,000,000 records.

. . . Capitol recording stars (l. to r.) Les Paul and Mary Ford, and Nat King Cole

Two very successful and musically compatible California gentlemen. Mercer is probably scratching his head over the idea of Arthur Godfrey being on the cover of *Down Beat*.

Something's Gotta Give

1954

Words and music by JOHNNY MERCER

When an irresistible force such as you
Meets an old immovable object like me,
You can bet as sure as you live,
Something's gotta give, something's gotta
   give,
Something's gotta give.

When an irrepressible smile such as yours
Warms an old implacable heart such as
   mine,
Don't say no because I insist
Somewhere, somehow, someone's gonna
   be kissed.

So, en garde, who knows what the fates
   have in store,
From their vast mysterious sky?
I'll try hard ignoring those lips I adore,
But how long can anyone try?

Fight, fight, fight, fight, fight it with all of our
   might,
Chances are some heavenly star spangled
   night,
We'll find out as sure as we live,
Something's gotta give, something's gotta
   give,
Something's gotta give.

Bobby Dolan told us how this hit song came about, which in his professional opinion underlined Mercer's great talent for discovering the clever, original approach to music. There had been a long, stymied script conference in the preparation of *Daddy Long Legs* at 20th Century-Fox. The problem—which might not be a problem today—was what to do about the older man (Astaire) being in love with a much younger woman (Leslie Caron). Mercer solved the impasse, said Dolan, with this sensible but unsensual lyric.

Midnight Sun

1954   Music by SONNY BURKE and LIONEL HAMPTON

Your lips were like a red and ruby chalice,
Warmer than the summer night,
The clouds were like an alabaster palace
Rising to a snowy height.
Each star its own aurora borealis,
Suddenly you held me tight,
I could see the midnight sun.

I can't explain the silver rain that found me,
Or was that a moonlight veil?
The music of the universe around me,
Or was that a nightingale?
And then your arms miraculously found me,
Suddenly the sky turned pale,
I could see the midnight sun.

Was there such a night,
It's a thrill I still don't quite believe,
But after you were gone,
There was still some stardust on my sleeve.

The flame of it may dwindle to an ember,
And the stars forget to shine,
And we may see the meadow in December,
Icy white and crystalline.
But, oh, my darling, always I'll remember,
When your lips were close to mine,
And I saw the midnight sun.

Without question a Mercer tour de force: "Red and ruby chalice" "alabaster palace" "aurora borealis"—who else could put together such rhymes without making it sound contrived? To add to the wonder of this brilliant lyric, Mercer told us that he wrote almost the entire lyric in his head while driving from Palm Springs to Hollywood (two hours) after hearing Lionel Hampton's record on the car radio. That handy modern-day gadget, the car radio, was always one of Mercer's greatest sources of inspiration—and we know how much time Californians spend in their cars, for which hallelujah!

The romantic coupling that caused concern at 20th Century-Fox. Fred Astaire and Leslie Caron in a scene from *Daddy Long Legs*. Mercer's idea for a song pulled them out of the bind.

Lionel Hampton might be telling Johnny a story about their former boss Benny. Mercer's lyrics were a big boost for Hamp's tune "Midnight Sun."

A television interview for Stan Kenton,
Henry Mancini, J.M.

Love in the Afternoon

1957

Music by MATTY MALNECK

Love in the afternoon
Was as sly as a wink and as gay as a pink
    balloon;
We walked along in a kind of trance
And the very streets began to dance.

To think that love nearly passed us by,
Then I happened to be where you
    happened to catch my eye.
And now both our lonely hearts are filled
    with June,
Because of love in the afternoon.

Another title song (movies with full scores of many songs were becoming fewer) with that great chum from the Whiteman days, Matty Malneck. Despite such heavyweights as Gary Cooper, Audrey Hepburn and Maurice Chevalier, with direction by Billy Wilder, this film refused to fly, and the Mercer-Malneck contribution was unusually second rate. (We include it here merely to remind us of the ups and downs in the studios.)

If I Had My Druthers

1956

Lyric by JOHNNY MERCER
Music by GENE de PAUL

If I had my druthers,
I'd druther have my druthers
Than anything else I know
While you'd druther hustle, accumulatin'
    muscle,
I'd druther watch daisies grow.
While they're growing' slow'n
The summer breeze is blowin'
My heart is overflowin' 'n so;
If I had my druthers
I'd druther have my druthers
Than anything else I know.

If I had my druthers,
I'd druther have my druthers
Than work anywheres at all.
It ain't that I hates it, I often contemplates it
While watchin' the raindrops fall.
I sits there for hours,
Developin' my powers
A-figurin' how flowers gets tall.
If I had my druthers
I'd druther have my druthers
Than anything else at all.

Undaunted, Mercer agreed to give Broadway another shot: the company was good (Panama & Frank, Michael Kidd, Gene de Paul) and Hollywood's studios weren't calling as much as they did in the thirties and forties. Then too, the back-country flavor of Al Capp's looney characters was right in Mercer's ballpark. The score, while not up to the high standard of *St. Louis Woman*, has been somewhat unappreciated. The two lyrics we take from it are fun throughout.

Giselle MacKenzie and Stubby Kaye rehearse for the *L'il Abner* recording, but Mercer seems slightly skeptical.

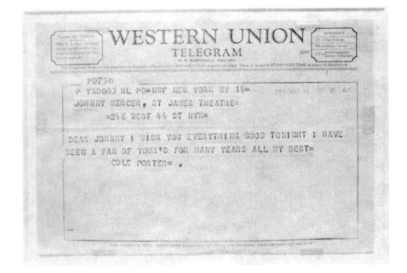

178

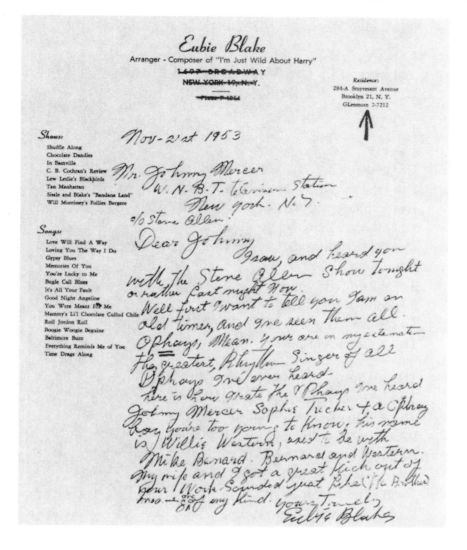

It goes like this (and they ought to know). Noble Sissle, standing, and the remarkable Eubie Blake at the keyboard.

The Country's in the Very Best of Hands

1956

Music by GENE de PAUL

The country's in the very best of hands,
The best of hands, the best of hands.
The treasury says the national debt
Is climbing to the sky.
The government expenditures
Have never been so high.
It makes a fella get
A gleam of pride within his eye.
To see how our economy expands,
The country's in the very best of hands.

The country's in the very best of hands,
The best of hands, the best of hands.
You oughta hear the Senate
When they're drawing up a bill.
Whereas's and to wit's
Are crowded in each codicil.
Such legal terminology
Would give your heart a thrill.
There's phrases there
That no one understands.
The country's in the very best of hands.

Satin Doll

1958

JOHNNY MERCER
DUKE ELLINGTON
BILLY STRAYHORN

Cigarette holder
Which wigs me
Over her shoulder
She digs me
Out cattin'
That satin doll

Baby, shall we go
Out skippin'
Careful, amigo,
You're flippin'
Speaks latin
That satin doll

She's nobody's fool,
So I'm playin' it cool as can be
I'll give it a whirl
But I ain't for no girl catchin' me
Telephone numbers
Well, you know'
Doin' my rhumbas
With uno,
And that's my satin doll.

An alliance of three greats—and their product is becoming more of a pop hit every year (lately, of course, because of the Broadway show *Sophisticated Ladies* and in New York at least because of an incessant TV commercial). Mercer always gets the flavor of both the tune and the subject matter he's writing about (the melody was around awhile without words) and in this case he does it with his usual ease and skill. "Doin' my rhumbas with uno"—Duke must have loved that! Would that they had hooked up more.

Portrait of Mr. Ellington, one third of the "Satin Doll" triumvirate, taken by one of his biggest fans.

1952 TV—"Harry Warren. . . . this is your life!" (Mercer and Warren had just completed *Belle of New York*.)

EVERYTHING IS TICKETTY-BOO

M·G·M Presents
A SOL C. SIEGEL
PRODUCTION

DANNY
KAYE

MERRY ANDREW

Co-Starring
PIER ANGELI · BACCALONI · NOEL PURCELL · ROBERT COOTE
With
PATRICIA CUTTS · ISOBEL LENNART and I. A. L. DIAMOND
Based on a Story by
PAUL GALLICO
Music by
SAUL CHAPLIN · JOHNNY MERCER
Lyrics by
Choreography by
MICHAEL KIDD
In CinemaScope
And METROCOLOR
Associate Producer
SAUL CHAPLIN
Directed by
MICHAEL KIDD

COMMANDER PUBLICATIONS
Hollywood, Calif.

If this shows up on a TV late show, see how Mercer's word juggling can compete with both Danny Kaye and a chimp.

Sketched in a California restaurant by an unknown admirer. "Crazy Oscar" probably refers to a performer known as Crazy Otto, who was then the rage.

A marvelous Gjon Mili study of Mercer waiting out a rehearsal.

JOHNNY MERCER

April 23, 1958

Dear Bob:

Many thanks for the clipping with the complimentary write up of my singing-(?). I guess even an old jazz singer can dig up an old friend or two.

I saw the Benny Goodman show; thought it was very groovy. He is as set in his ways about music as I am. But I thought it really swung when Jo and Ella sang and when Teddy Wilson played. Also thought Norvo was, as usual —— marvelous! All in all a great show. I don't believe you can convince broadcasters that jazz is as big as westerns.

I hope to see you soon, but in any event my love to all. Thanks again for the letter.

Dipper

JM/gw
Mr. Bob Bach
41 East 57th Street
New York 22, New York

A Game of Poker

1959

Music by HAROLD ARLEN

Love is a game of poker
Ev'rything's wild and the chips are down;
One night you may draw the joker,
Next night you may own the town.

One look at the cards they've tossed you,
One look at her you decide to play.
You stay, but they've double-crossed you
And your hunch has cost you more than
    you can pay.
You've won, but oh,
You've lost your heart along the way.

So here goes you and I,
Win or lose, do or die!
But it's sure worth a try
If it's love.

Another opening, another blow: *Saratoga* seemed ready for (finally) an Arlen-Mercer Broadway success, having all the necessary ingredients—Edna Ferber's story, the colorful spa setting, costumes by Cecil Beaton, direction by Morton Da Costa. But, alas, the critics destroyed it, passing quite perfunctorily over the score, which did contain one or two noteworthy items: "Goose Never Be a Peacock" (sung with great depth by concert artist Carol Brice), "One Step Two Step" and the would-be hit "A Game of Poker," the worksheets for which we include to show how diligently Mercer applied himself to the search for the right combination of words.

185

Love

Is a game of poker

Love is a hand of chemin de fer

One night
                    The Joker

Next night
                It's a love affair
                        draw a pair

Etc/more – as I roam & ramble
This life is a lucky gamble
    One
You never knows whose good fortune
            where your luck may starts
                        begin

Each kiss is a sweet preamble

                    to the greatest gamble
                    of the blackest art –
Any man can win   oldest.
        could choose   _ win or lose

Making the most of each shining day
    That ever   magical night
            a gamble when you can lose your heart
Any two cards play
    hearts can ...   is the biggest of
                        them all

Everything wild — and the stakes are high

One night are you holds the joker
    you're a lonely joker

Next night — You can bet the sky

Love is a turn on the wheel of fate

One night — You may hold the joker —

Next night — You're at heaven's gate

You hope — that you'll throw a seven
    for a great big seven

You're home — if you roll a

If anyone thinks that writing lyrics for a musical comedy song is easy, a look at these three handwritten worksheets of Mercer's should dispell that notion. There were a good dozen more pages for "A Game of Poker", which proved only moderately successful in the hapless show *Saratoga*.

CLINT ~~LOVE IS A GAME~~ Love's a game of poker

Love is a game of poker
Everything's wild — and the stakes are high
You lose ....
So you go for broke, or
You win ...
And you own the sky!
You'd swear — that the fates were cheating
Dealing you hands — only fools would play
You raise— and your heart stops beating
But you keep repeating
It's your lucky day .....
You win!
But love is a ~~gamble all the way~~
But love's a game of poker all the way —

CLIO-CLINT
So here goes!
You and I
Win or lose
Do or die
But it's sure — worth a try — if it's love!!!

CLIO

Love is a game of poker
Anything goes — and the chips are down
One night
You may draw the joker
Next night
You may own the town
etc.   ...

187

188

Posed by the fine Savannah photographer Fred Baldwin
in front of the historic Owens-Thomas house.

The Sixties and the Seventies

Does anyone need to be reminded for the hundredth time of what travails the sixties brought us? Probably as great an influence as anything in those turbulent times was the arrival in America of records by four long-haired kids from Liverpool, England—the Beatles. They were British, and that was different. They were kind of clean-cut, even though shaggy-haired, and that was different too. They were not as threatening as some of the scroungy, home-grown rock 'n' rollers, and their songs had some sweetness and charm to them. Thus their success was phenomenal. The Beatles were, thanks to the expanding avenues of communication, many times more powerful in popularity and earnings than had been Rudy Vallee in the twenties, Bing Crosby in the thirties, Frank Sinatra in the forties, and even Elvis Presley in the recent fifties, for they were international in scope and their influence spilled over into areas that changed many life styles of the young. Learned sociologists and musical pundits (Leonard Bernstein among them) gave the Beatles serious consideration, and one can only imagine the feelings of men such as Ira Gershwin, sitting in quiet retirement alongside his Beverly Hills swimming pool, or Jule Styne, pacing around a crowded office in New York's Mark Hellinger Theatre—men who had spent years and years getting to their position of importance in the music world.

But there was some cheer to the situation. Where Elvis and his fellow travellers of the fifties—Chubby Checker, Jerry Lee Lewis, Fats Domino, James Brown—were anathema to ASCAP's songwriting elite because of their remove from the world of Kern and Gershwin, the Beatles got qualified approval from these elders because of their respect for the 32-bar form and for recognizable melody. The Beatles were also miles apart from the yeh-yeh-baby lyrics (lyrics!) of their forerunners in the world of rock. Johnny Mercer, among other survivors, was not ready to throw in the towel.

Throughout America there were the new sounds of stereo in millions of homes and so the record/music business of the sixties held its own against television, movies, paperback books, and the relaxed censorship of both Broadway and Hollywood. In the small nightclubs there were protestors like Lenny Bruce and folksingers in dungarees with guitars. On Broadway there was a musical called *Hair* and another called *Oh Calcutta!* It was a long way indeed from Paul Whiteman at the Biltmore and

189

the *Garrick Gaieties*. And just as Bing had bowed with his usual ease to the changing tastes of audiences, so too did time play a little rough with another pal, Bob Hope, as the sixties saw Mort Sahl, Shelley Berman and the Smothers Brothers moving ahead in popularity.

Song-filled movies such as the ones that kept the writers busy in the thirties were no longer in vogue, but the producers still liked a theme melody to play under the titles, and Johnny Mercer easily tailored his art to those demands. There were two Mercer homeruns right at the beginning of the decade. In 1961 he collaborated with Henry Mancini on a song that Audrey Hepburn was supposed to look as if she were singing while seated on a fire escape and strumming a guitar. The movie was *Breakfast at Tiffany's,* the song was "Moon River," and it was a runaway Oscar winner at the 1962 Academy Awards. The following year it was another Mercer-Mancini success—the title song for a Jack Lemmon movie, *The Days of Wine and Roses*—and Oscar #4 for Johnny Mercer.

By the early sixties the Mercer children, Jeff and Mandy, had grown out of adolescence, California friends were disappearing, and Ginger had found a small apartment, a long-sought pied-à-terre, in New York. The cross-country trains were not as great as they once had been, but for a guy who liked to read so much and jot down ideas so much it was still a kick to travel from coast to coast in a leisurely fashion. In 1963 there was the last attempt at a Broadway show—a Broadway show that opened far, far out of town, in Dawson City, Alaska. The show was titled *Foxy,* based on Ben Jonson's *Volpone,* and it starred the great clown Bert Lahr, with Larry Blyden in a supporting role. The music was again by Mercer's close friend Bobby Dolan (remember *Texas, L'il Darlin'*), and one would be hard pressed today to find any one of the show's songs. Mercer did, however, provide Lahr with a perfect vehicle called "Bon Vivant," in which there is the line, "sailing on the Firth of Forth. . . . or was it Forth of Firth?" Even the clever David Merrick can guess wrong—*Foxy* finally reached New York's Ziegfeld Theatre and closed shortly thereafter.

The New York scene, particularly its swank, never really interested Johnny Mercer much anyway, nor did he care to get involved in the heated political talk of the sixties and early seventies. However, a line here and there in his beautiful Christmas cards of that period show that he cared about the country's plight in Vietnam, about the growth of violence on all sides, and, as a southern country boy, about the ruination of the environment. Margaret Whiting tells of a moment in the early 1970s that seems quite typical of the man: "We were on a train going to Philadelphia for the 'Mike Douglas Show,' and it was a gray, dreary day. As we came out of the tunnel leaving New York—you know those ugly auto graveyards filled with junk that are alongside the tracks just before Newark?—well, Johnny was staring out of the train window and he suddenly said to me, 'Kid, you see that? That's what they're doing to America.' " He rarely let those thoughts out—or at most he kept them wrapped in the gentler philosophy of his song lyrics.

Came the seventies, with so many old friends and collaborators gone, the music business in a completely new bag, and the call for Mercer's services diminished considerably. Therefore the four-time Oscar winner turned to an adjunct of songwriting that had been on his mind for some time—the establishment of a Songwriters' Hall of Fame, an equivalent of the Cooperstown place of honor for the all-time great baseball players. As with the formation of Capitol Records, Mercer's spirit moved things along with class, and before long the organization was housed in a building on New York's Times Square. Old friends Abe Olman and Howie Richmond helped Johnny launch the Hall of Fame. Mercer was immediately elected President, and the first inductees included Irving Berlin, Duke Ellington, Richard Rodgers, Dorothy Fields and Hoagy Carmichael. It was a most impressive beginning, yet Mercer was wise enough and open-minded enough to tell those who would listen how much he liked some of the newer writers—Jimmy Webb was one of the favorites he mentioned.

In 1973 Johnny Mercer embarked on his last full-scale venture. The Mercers moved to London for a year to work on a musical version of J. B. Priestley's *The Good Companions*, with John Mills in the starring role. The music was by André Previn, who was not easy to work with because of his heavy schedule as conductor of the London Symphony Orchestra. But there were frequent visits to the lovely Sussex home of the Previns, where Johnny could also enjoy the company of Previn's pretty wife, Mia Farrow, and their several small children. Despite his bon vivant tastes, Mercer always was a dedicated family man. Things didn't go too well with *The Good Companions* (the London critics singled out Mercer's lyrics as not being English enough), and the ill health that had plagued him for a few years finally took its toll. Johnny Mercer died on June 25, 1976, and people from former maids to the President of the United States sent messages of sadness to Ginger Mercer. Many great tributes were offered at the memorial services in New York and Hollywood—from old friends such as Fred Astaire, Bing Crosby and Dinah Shore—but the collaborators on this book feel that the most moving and accurate estimate of all was written by the columnist Carl Rowan. (See page 231.)

JIMMY McHUGH

February 27, 1968

Dear John Boy,

I would so much appreciate having an autographed photo of yourself, and a copy of BLACK MAGIC. They would both be among my most treasured possessions, I assure you.

As always, it is a real pleasure being with you. Take care and God Bless You.

Love,

JIMMY McHUGH

JFM:m

Mr. Johnny Mercer
10972 Chalon Road
Los Angeles, Calif. 90024

Please autograph the copy of Black Magic too.
J.

Richard Rodgers
598 MADISON AVENUE • NEW YORK 22, N. Y.
Telephone MUrray Hill 8-3640

August 8, 1968

Dear Johnny:

I had seen the New York Times piece on the concert at City Hall but I promise you it gave me no more pleasure than your thoughtfulness in sending it to me and the kind things you said along with it. There seems to be little doubt that you and I belong to a mutual-admiration society. My regard for you and your work is surely no less than your feeling about mine.

Have you plans to come East? Do let me know because I would like very much to see you and talk to you.

Thanks so much for your thoughtfulness and all kindest regards.

Yours sincerely,

Dick.

Richard Rodgers

Mr. Johnny Mercer
10972 Chalon Road
Los Angeles,
California 90024

RR:NS

Bobby Darin, bandleader Billy May and J.M. during the recording session of their "Two of a Kind" duet in 1963.

Christmas Card

THIS blessed time of Jesus' birth
May there be really *Peace on Earth*
Around the tree—amongst our friends
Let's pray this season never ends
And show the way—for all to see
How brave and good mankind can be
The way the world is whirling on
I wonder where the years have gone
But when I think . . . . don't laugh . . . . I do
What pleasant vistas come in view!
Leave it to Beaver—Dan'l Boone . . . . .
How many years of Twilight Zone?
Jack Paar, Jack Benny, Newhart, Hope
Have flashed across our TV-scope
While Ozzie Nelson—how time flies!
Has raised two boys before our eyes
The Smothers Brothers, heads unbowed
Were fired (for speaking up too loud)
Ah, well, we'll have to find the touch
To straighten out this rabbit hutch
The Moon and Mars are now next door
But we're more distant than before
Let's hope, in God's great scheme of things
We find why we've been given wings
So huge and vast the infinite
We must be just a speck in it
So let us all raise humble eyes
To God's immeasurable skies
Then each one pray—"in his own way"
To do the right thing every day
Who wields the knife—who hurls the stone

The risk be his—the neck his own
Let retribution—fast and sure
Revenge the innocent—the pure
(I hope you wiser heads don't find
I tilt at Windmills of the Mind)
Then may we lift the flowing glass
Invite the strangers in who pass
And drink a toast—and have a pause
And spend a while with Santa Claus
We'll take the children on our knee
And tell them how it used to be
And let them know it's really love
That's kept us humans on the move
Then say to God—and mean it too
Thanks for today—and all year through
Thanks for the good things we've all had
Now—help us overcome the bad
Teach us, like children still in school
The facts of life—the Golden Rule
Teach us to know what Jesus meant
Why we are here—why He was sent
With brimming hearts, teach us to say
A Merry, Merry Christmas Day!
And may this Happy New Year too
Be filled with joy the twelve-month through
For goodness, kindness, peace and love
Beats Anybody's treasure trove
So God Bless YOU—and everyone!

THE MERCERS
(GINGER, JEFF AND JOHN).

Moon River

1961

Music by HENRY MANCINI

Moon River,
Wider than a mile:
I'm crossin' you in style
Some day.
Old dream maker,
You heart breaker,
Wherever you're goin',
I'm goin' your way:

Two drifters,
Off to see the world,
There's such a lot of world
To see.
We're after the same
Rainbow's end
Waitin' round the bend,
My huckleberry friend,
Moon River
And me.

Probably his most famous song of all. Even Irving Berlin picked this one out as one of the great American popular songs. He was also curious, in the manner of a complete outsider, as to which came first, the music or the lyrics. Audrey Hepburn, seated on a fire escape, mimed singing this song while strumming a guitar in the movie *Breakfast at Tiffany's* and so it was a shoo-in for Mercer's third Oscar. "Huckleberry friend" is so properly descriptive of our songwriting hero that no one quarreled with the choice of it for the title of this book.

Mancini, Mercer and Miss Reynolds all smile on cue for the battalion of
photographers backstage at the Academy Awards.

The Bilbao Song

1961

English words by JOHNNY MERCER
Music by KURT WEILL

That old Bilbao moon,
I won't forget it soon,
That old Bilbao moon,
Just like a big balloon,
That old Bilbao moon,
Would rise above the dune,
While Tony's beach saloon
Rocked with an old time tune.

We'd sing a song the whole night long
And I can still recall
Those were the greatest,
Those were the greatest,
Those were the greatest nights of them all.

No paint was on the door,
The grass grew through the floor,
Of Tony's two by four
On the Bilbao shore,
But there were friends galore
And there was beer to pour
And moonlight on the shore,
That old Bilbao shore.

We'd sing all night with all our might
And I can still recall
Those were the greatest,
Those were the greatest,
Those were the greatest nights of them all.

Those old Bilbao guys,
They loved to harmonize,
Who stopped to realize
How fast the summer flies!
The moon was on the rise,
We'd catch the ladies' eyes
And whisper Spanish lies,
They never did get wise.

We'd sing a song the whole night long
And I can still recall
Those were the greatest,
Those were the greatest,
Those were the greatest days of them all.

Another Americanized version of an already accepted foreign hit song shows once again Mercer's versatility. The Middle European flavor of Kurt Weill's music and the Brecht background didn't throw the boy from Savannah a bit. "We'd sing a song the whole night long" and "those were the greatest . . . etc . . . etc." are just as beery lines in Chicago or Cincinatti as they might be in Berlin. Bobby Darin was just the right tough-guy singer to make this into a modest native hit.

Days of Wine and Roses

1962

Music by HENRY MANCINI

The days of wine and roses
Laugh and run away
Like a child at play,
Through the meadowland
Toward a closing door,
A door marked "Nevermore,"
That wasn't there before.

The lonely night discloses
Just a passing breeze
Filled with memories
Of the golden smile that introduced me to
The days of wine and roses and you.

This was J.M.'s fourth Oscar winner, and it is unique in that the entire song is encompassed in just two sentences. It was, of course, helped consideraly by the strength of Jack Lemmon's award-winning performance in the movie of the same name. Jack told us that when Mercer first sang this for him and the director it was in a darkened studio under a single spotlight, and the effect was so dramatic that the easygoing Lemmon found tears streaming down his face at the end. Mercer was unquestionably a powerful singer of certain lyrics.

I Wanna Be Around

1962

Words and music by JOHNNY MERCER
SADIE VIMMERSTEDT

I wanna be around
To pick up the pieces,
When somebody breaks your heart;
Some somebody twice as smart as I,
A somebody who will swear to be true,
Like you used to do with me.
Who'll leave you to learn
That mis'ry loves company,
Wait and see!

I wanna be around,
To see how he does it
When he breaks your heart to bits;
Let's see if the puzzle fits so fine.
And that's when I'll discover that revenge is
    sweet;
As I sit there applauding from a front row
    seat,
When somebody breaks your heart
Like you broke mine.

A great human interest story and most revealing (as was the repayment of his father's debts) of Mercer's Southern gentlemanly character. The idea for the song—and certainly a good one—was sent to him in the mail (see illustrations) by the proverbial "little old lady" from Youngstown, Ohio. The very name Sadie Vimmerstedt probably helped a little. Mercer arranged for her to receive a nice 50% of the royalties, made her, by her own account, "a star" around Youngstown, and got his publishing company to line up Tony Bennett for a terrific record.

Johnny Mercer Splits Royalties On New Song With 'Cinderella'

By WILLIAM D. LAFFLER

NEW YORK (UPI)—Life has a new meaning for Sadie Vimmerstedt because she wrote a letter to singer-composer Johnny Mercer.

She is coauthor of one of the nation's top songs even though she did not write either its music or lyrics. Her almost unbelievable success has earned her the title of "the Cinderella girl of Tin Pan Alley."

Cinderella was a young girl; Sadie is 58 and a grandmother.

The story of Sadie, who lives in Youngstown, Ohio, began five years ago when she wrote a letter to Mercer suggesting that he write a song called "I wanna be around to pick up the pieces when somebody breaks your heart."

"Two years later he answered my letter and apologized for his tardiness," Sadie said in a telephone conversation from her home.

When months and then years went by without another word from Savannah - born Mercer, Sadie apparently forgot about her idea. Then one day she heard again from Mercer.

"He said he didn't want to record the song until he got the best singer," Sadie said. "When he told me that Tony Bennett was going to record it, I really got excited."

Bennett at that time had just become the hottest seller at Columbia Records with the single, "I Left My Heart in San Francisco."

Today Bennett's recording of Sadie's "I Wanna be Around" is moving toward the top of the best-seller charts.

Sadie is grateful to Mercer, because Johnny wrote the music and lyrics but gave her credit as cocomposer and split the royalties with her on 50-50 basis.

"He is a most unselfish man," Sadie said of Mercer. "To me he was a person you could talk to."

Sadie's song sold 15,000 copies the first day it was released. It appears that she will net about $50,000 in royalties by June.

While Sadie is not a professional musician and does not pretend to be anything more than an average Youngstown citizen, she sings in the choir at St. Ann's Roman Catholic Church.

"My husband passed away four years ago, but I don't like being called a widow," Sadie said. "I now sell cosmetics and I love my job."

Her ambition now is to see two men who mean so much to her.

"We are a little trio," she said, "but I've never met Tony Bennett or Johnny Mercer."

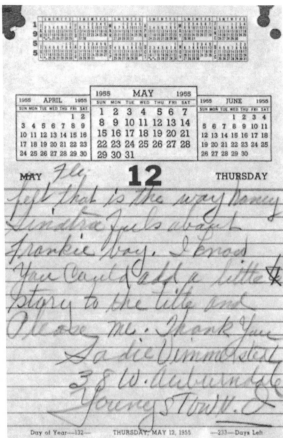

MAY *Fri* **12** THURSDAY

felt that is the way Nancy Sinatra feels about frankie boy. I know you could add a little story to the title and Please me. Thank You

Sadie Vimmerstedt
38 W. Auburndale
Youngstown O.

Day of Year—132—   THURSDAY, MAY 12, 1955   —233—Days Left

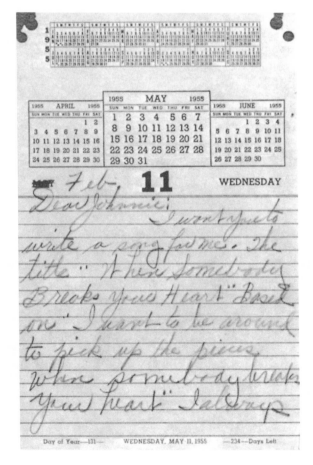

Feb. **11** WEDNESDAY

Dear Johnnie:

I want you to write a song for me. The title "When Somebody Breaks your Heart" Based on "I want to be around to pick up the pieces when somebody breaks your heart" I always

Day of Year—131—   WEDNESDAY, MAY 11, 1955   —234—Days Left

199

Fun on the boulevard: Mercer enjoyed the company of his new friend, Michel Legrand, particularly the visits to the country home of the Legrands where he would play with the kids.

Jack Klugman (pre-"Odd Couple" and "Quincy") helped Jack Lemmon in his Academy Award performance, and the theme song helped a bit too.

Mercer in his favorite
Greek fisherman's cap near Savannah in 1970.

Once Upon a Summertime

1962

Original lyric by EDDIE MARNAY   English lyric by JOHNNY MERCER
Music by EDDIE BARCLAY and MICHEL LEGRAND

Once upon a summertime, if you recall,
We stopped beside a little flower stall.
A bunch of bright forget-me-nots was all
I'd let you buy me.

Once upon a summertime, just like today,
We laughed the happy afternoon away
And stole a kiss in ev'ry street café.

You were sweeter than the blossoms on the
   tree.
I was as proud as any girl could be,
As if the Mayor had offered me the key
To Paris!

Now, another wintertime has come and
   gone.
The pigeons feeding in the square have
   flown,
But I remember when the vespers chime
You loved me once upon a summertime.

The first collaboration with French composer Michel Legrand, who was later to become a good friend with whom Mercer worked on several projects. The song was originally titled ''Valse de Lilacs'' and was brought to Mercer's attention by Blossom Dearie, an enthusiasm of his from the sixties on. This very pretty song is still generally unappreciated despite records by Sinatra, Barbra Streisand, George Shearing and Anita O'Day.

Charade

Music by HENRY MANCINI

When we played our Charade
We were like children posing,
Playing at games,
Acting out names,
Guessing the parts we played.

Oh, what a hit we made.
We came on next to closing
Best on the bill,
Lovers until
Love left the masquerade.

Fate seemed to pull the strings,
I turned and you were gone.
While from the darkened wings
The music box played on.

Sad little serenade,
Song of my heart's composing,
I hear it still,
I always will
Best on the bill Charade

The Mercer-Mancini magic diminished a little this time out, although the song got an Academy Award nomination. Movie title songs were the name of the game for bigtime songwriters in Hollywood of the sixties. With the Beatles mania still raging, Mercer, like so many others of his craft, was forced to spend most of his time on the sidelines. Even in this less-than-golden period musically "Charade" is a good solid song, nothing to be shrugged off.

Emily

1964

Music by JOHNNY MANDEL

Emily, Emily, Emily
Has the murmuring sound of May.
All silver bells, coral shells, carousels
And the laughter of children at play say.

Emily, Emily, Emily
And we fade to a marvelous view.
Two lovers alone and out of sight
Seeing images in the firelight.

As my eyes visualize a family,
They see dreamily,
Emily too.

The last movie theme song of any importance for Mercer, this one has some tender and poetic pictures in its opening lines. He had a special fondness for children, although this feeling rarely showed up in his lyrics. The movie was *The Americanization of Emily*, starring Julie Andrews and James Garner, and the strong melodic line is by former jazz trumpeter Johnny Mandel, who also wrote "The Shadow of Your Smile," which award-winning song Mercer winningly admits he failed to write acceptable lyrics for. Musicians seem to be drawn to this song a lot (no lyrics necessary generally).

Bon Vivant

1964   Music by ROBERT EMMET DOLAN

Now for the life men dream about,
Days that a king might scheme about.
Once I have got
My palatial yacht,
I shall slowly steam about the brine.
Fie on the word economy,
I'll live a life of bonhomie,
Sail into port
For a night pour le sport
Full of rare gastronomy and wine.

Manchester and Dorchester
And Chichester and Perth
Sailing on the Firth of Forth
Or is it Forth of Firth?

Woppington on Battersea,
The shire of me birth,
In a thatched home of modest worth
  (unpaid for).

Birmingham and Nottingham
And Sandringham and Crewe
Shrewesbury and Tewkesbury
And Shaftsbury and Lewe
Where I starred as Portia
In "The Taming of the Shrew."
As we would say in school,
I've been around the pool
So I'm the bon vivant you want.

A perfect wow of a Mercer fun lyric, during which you can practically hear Bert Lahr foghorning his way through it. It was written for the wonderful Lahr when the show *Foxy* (with Bobby Dolan again) began its pre-Broadway run in—of all places—Dawson City, Alaska. In talking about Lahr much later, Mercer told the audience at New York's 92nd Street "Y": "He endeared me to him." (Haven't you always heard it the other way—"he endeared himself to me"?) The use of British town names was duck soup for Mercer, so much so that he repeated the trick later when writing the London musical *Good Companions*. But even producer David Merrick can guess wrong, and so *Foxy* failed, though one reason, we're told, was Merrick's lack of advertising support.

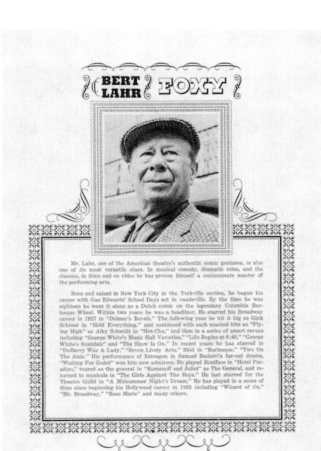

Summer Wind

1965

English words by JOHNNY MERCER
Music by HENRY MAYER

The summer wind came blowing in across
    the sea,
It lingered there to touch your hair and walk
    with me.
All summer long we sang a song and strolled
    the golden sand.

Two sweethearts and the summer wind.
Like painted kites the days and nights went
    flying by.
The world was new beneath a blue umbrella
    sky.
Then, softer than a piper man
One day it called to you.

I lost you to the summer wind.
The autumn wind, the winter winds
Have come and gone
And still the days, the lonely days
Go on and on
And guess who sighs his lullabyes
Through nights that never end.

My fickle friend, the summer wind,
The summer wind, the summer wind.

The last truly "Hit Parade" sort of success for Mercer, this one was helped through the miasma of rock 'n' roll thanks to records by Wayne Newton and Frank Sinatra. Walter Rivers, Johnny's cousin and boyhood pal, wonders from whence came the expression "a piper man"—is there or was there such a thing? This is a perfectly wonderful song to use as a marker of sorts for the passage of Mercer from one period of creativity to another.

Trees
(With sympathy for Joyce Kilmer)

1969

I think that never shall I see
A poem loveless as a tree

A tree whose hungry mouth is pressed
Against some scientific breast

A tree which from no acorn springs
But comes from Mother's barkless rings

A tree that looks to Vitamin A
And lifts her leafless arms to pray

A tree whose beauty life and soul
Starts in some laboratory bowl

A tree who may at birth be found
With nests of nutrients all around

Who must, as one non-sexual cell,
In niacin and thiamine dwell

A tree who may in winter wear
No rain nor snowflakes in her hair

Whose thirst is slaked—if slaked at all
When auxins and cytokinins fall

Who'll feel no sunshine kiss of love
Just an electric light above

A tree, whose very birth may have
Joyce Kilmer whirling in his grave

While GOD, (if he's alive, of course)
Accepts retirement pay by force

A tree improved in every way
For each undappled summer's day

A tree that's neither he nor she
Who'll know no dog, who'll know no bee

Poems are made by fools in love
But only Dr. Linus Winton, biologist of the
    Institute of Paper Chemistry
    —out there in Appleton, Wisconsin—
    can make an entire non-sexual aspen
    grove!

"Four unusual little trees. . . . produced from a tiny plug of unspecialized non-sexual tree cells, began their existence in a laboratory dish at the Institute of Paper Chemistry in Appleton, Wisconsin, today."

The New York Times, April 18, 1969

207

At Christmas time, it's hard to say
The old-time wish a brand-new way
For fashions rise, and fashions fall
But Christmas is the best of all
So prayerfully I lift my pen
To welcome Santa once again
Old Santa of the cherry nose
The apple cheeks, the swirling snows
Who, yearly, with his reindeer comes
To shacks and condiminiums
The only payment for his ride
The knowledge there is love inside
For though love makes the world go round
It's getting harder to be found
And in our riot, war torn land
The Scrooges have the upper hand
We oldsters who were youngsters then
Must set examples once again
And make our fun so unalloyed
That underneath — they're overjoyed!
It's like a man who walks a wire
Above a sea of molten fire
While balancing on cattail stalks
Your Aunt's best china as he walks
For how can anything be solved
If no one smiles — or gets involved?
But I — in my dimwitted way —
Sing out, "A Merry Christmas Day"
The blessing old still ringing true
For you — and you — and you — and you!

While seated 'round your Christmas tree
Think of the trees that used to be
The happy faces of old friends
Whose roles are through — whose playlet ends
Remember how they used to smile
Their glow lit up the world a while
And welcome little ones at birth
Who've just now joined us all on Earth
The old and new — a lovely sight
They made almost as bright a light
As that far tree in Viet Nam
Whose one bright bauble is a bomb
Then go to church and sing — off key!
(. . . as every hymn in church must be!)
Against our good friends wise advice
We'll sing the loudest at the part;
"Still stands thine ancient sacrifice,
"An humble and a contrite heart"
So, friends and neighbors . . . Nashville style
I send you all a great big smile
A great big hug that's full of love
A great big blessing from above
I wish you — in imperfect rhyme
The perfect wish at Christmastime:
Just for a moment — now and then
Be ...little children once again
Get on the floor with all your toys
And be one of the girls and boys!
Remember — when the tinsel's gone
The Mercers — Ginger, Jeff and John

208

December 17, 1965

Mr. Johnny Mercer
10972 Chalon Road
Los Angeles, California 90024

Dear Johnny:

What a good warm Christmas card!
But then I would not expect anything less
from a good warm man like yourself. Many
many thanks and the happiest of holidays
to you and Ginger.

Sincerely,

Frank

FL:kp

IRVING BERLIN

December 22nd, 1965

Dear Johnny:

    Only God can make the tree
    Where presents lie for you and me
    But only Mercer makes the rhyme
    That cheers us all at Christmas time

Thanks for the couplet you inscribed and best
Holiday wishes to you and Ginger from us,

        As always,

Mr. Johnny Mercer
10972 Chalon Road
Los Angeles, California

JACK LEMMON

December 28, 1971

Dear John:

    A quick note in the midst of the
Holiday madness just to voice my personal
opinion and that of the rest of my family,
that you should be the first man to receive
an Academy Award for a Christmas card.

    It is absolutely marvelous and far and
away the greatest card that any of us has
ever received. As a matter of fact, I may
frame the damn thing and put it on the piano!
(Surrounded by Mercer songs.)

    Hope to see you soon, and in the mean-
time, pull yourself together--- and may the
coming year bring you all possible happiness,
which, of course, includes another Oscar.

        Best always,

        The Human Hinge.

JL:bg

Mr. Johnny Mercer
1092 Chalon Road
Los Angeles, Calif.

The message is more than the medium.

209

Interview with Johnny Mercer, March 14, 1971:

Part of the New York 92nd Street "Y" Series of
Lyrics and Lyricists. The interviewer is Maurice
Levine, host of the series.

Q: I'd just like to ask you a couple of questions, relative to today's songwriters versus those of the past. Were you and your colleagues reworking the single emotion of romantic love? Were you being superficial and impersonal, were you not concerned with the quality of life?

JM: I think we were in more of a rut than the kids are, though I think ours was a more attractive rut.

JM: I think it all springs from the war. They're all scared and they want to tell everybody what they know. They're really children philosophers. They're talking about . . . philosophically, they're trying to say to you, what they want everybody to hear, and so they don't write any tunes. They write to the same tune, they have new words, and I just think it's appalling, but I think that out of it all, there will come a lot of great writers, because there are so many people writing. Almost everybody is a songwriter. There used to be maybe a hundred songwriters or five hundred, now there are maybe fifty thousand or five million. Maybe eight, I don't know. But some of them are good. A few of them have a lot of integrity, like Jimmy Taylor. He's brand new—he sings like he means it. The kid with Blood, Sweat and Tears—he's a marvelous singer. The writers I'm not so nutty about. I'm not so nutty about the Beatles. I think Stephen Sondheim is a wonderful writer. And I think some of these folk writers, the kids, are good, but there's nothing very new. Woody Guthrie wrote before that—before him, Vernon Dalhart used to sing "The Death of Floyd Collins" and those narrative songs, "The Wreck of the Old 97." This whole folk bag is overdone.

This is a kind of a dull answer. When I get serious about things, it's dreary.

Q: Johnny, the unique thing about the *Greatest Songs of the Sixties* is it contains one helluva great tune called "Moon River." Johnny, you may have touched on this and I guess you have, but I'd still like to ask it as a general question, what were your great influences?

JM: Well, I guess, as I say, I started to sing when I was six months old. When I was in dresses, I remember cylindrical records—before the big flat Edison records. And I think in those days, Victor Herbert—the first ones I remember were Victor Herbert and Harry Lauder. Big impression on me. And then as I got a little older, Berlin, although I didn't know who he was, Donaldson, I did know who *he* was—Walter Donaldson—and then later on, Harry Warren.

Then I got up to New York and I became a little more—well, a little more educated, I guess. I found out about Porter and the Gershwins and particularly Rodgers and

Hart. So, when you live in a rural community, you like pop songs and that's what you learn how to write. When you come to New York, it's like starting all over again. So that's my Southern background.

Q: Johnny, surely you must know that now you're the model and the inspiration for a generation of younger lyricists, and here are just a couple of questions I'm going to ask on their behalf and actually at their request, and they're a little more specific, having to do with lyric writing. And here's one I was asked to ask you. What qualities do you look for in a collaborator?

JM: In a collaborator? First of all, great talent and integrity, that's what I like. I like a guy who writes his way and his way is so high that it starts where other guys leave off. I've written with a few like that. I think Kern is everybody's favorite. I think Harold Arlen is an enormous talent. I think Hoagy Carmichael, in his way, starts where most guys stop. And that's the best thing in a music writer, I think.

Other guys may have a little gift this way or that way and they're all different. I prefer to write not with them but away from them. I don't like to get too mixed up with them—very delicate, collaboration.

Q: That leads to that classic question which everyone asks, what comes first, the melody or the lyric, and I gather from what you've said, that you like to have a good melody——

JM: With me, I prefer that.

Q: Yip Harburg said the same thing.

JM: Well, you know why? He feels music like a composer and so do I, so we understand the music. We know where the accents should come, and I don't mean to sound conceited when I say this, but I've often had a lot of good lyrics loused up by writing them first because the guy doesn't understand the meter that I wrote. I'd rather try and catch the mood of his tune than—now, there are some exceptions. Mr. Rodgers is magnificent at writing to words. But I think most guys would rather do it the other way.

Q: You may have answered this next question, which one of the other writers——

JM: I feel like John Jay Anthony. Remember him? Or The Answer Man. What did Durante say? These are the answers, you figure out the questions.

Q: This question is, how did your various composers differ in approach?

JM: They're all different. Every one is different, but you know, there's something funny about songs—it's elusive, it's like you're going out looking for the snark or something that you never heard of, the golden fleece. You don't know where it is, it's just up there somewhere and you can tune in on it, and you get a little glimmer, and you say, ah—you don't even know if it's a word and then it begins to—it's like you're tuning in to a musical instrument that's miles away, and you say, oh, there's something there, if I just dig hard enough, I know it'll come. I think that's the way I write. I think that's the way Yip writes too.

Q: Here's a good question. How do you write for a character and yet emerge with a hit?

JM: Well, it's not easy, but sometimes it helps. For instance, if you're going to write a song for Helen Morgan, you've got to write with a limited range and the qualifications sometimes are an asset, really. Or if you're going to write for Crosby, you know that he's very casual, he sort of talks his songs. If you're going to write for a big singer, then you write a little more operetta. You adapt, you adapt to the artist.

Q: One of the songwriters and lyricists out in the audience wants to know what was the most difficult lyric problem you ever encountered?

JM: Well, I think the thing that scared me the most was when I was about twenty-one, I couldn't even write yet, I was trying to write a show with Vincent Youmans. I would come in petrified every day, and of course I didn't write it. And the next one, I think, was working with Harold on *Saratoga*—outside of meeting that darling Teague DaCosta, that show was a dreary show. Hey, Harold?

Q: Which leads me to another question, which is my own question. Your greatest hits—I'm talking numerically, the greatest number of hits—came from straight pop songs or from the movies, and can you give us some indication of why this did not happen in your Broadway shows? Numerically, I'm talking about.

JM: I don't know. Frank Loesser said "Boy, I wish you could write (he wanted to be my publisher, I think, before he died) I can show you how to get those big songs in shows."—Well, I never had the shows at the time I had my big songs. And you can't let a song hang around too long, somebody else is going to write it. I could never wait. Unless you're a recluse. I just don't think I'm that gifted a show writer, I just don't think I am. I think Lerner is a marvelously gifted show writer. He's literate, he writes scenes well, he writes business songs well. I don't think he knows too much about popular songs, but he gets hits anyway.

Q: Do you think that popular songs and the musical theater are the antithesis of each other?

JM: Sort of. For instance, you talk about the kids writing folk songs. That's the bedrock, that's the grass roots, and if you write something and you say the same thing, you have bad rhymes, but you have a kind of a folk quality. That's the man in the street. But the theatre is as cultivated as you can get. You're going in and you're paying sometimes $50 a ticket nowadays, and you expect to hear music that's comparable to Kern or Arlen and you expect to hear witty, inventive, great lyrics, and I think you're entitled to that for that money.

Q: Well, Johnny, your catalogue in ASCAP is just one of the largest there is, and I took off a day last week just to read your song titles. There seems to be nothing but winners in that catalogue. Tell us about your losers.

JM: Oh, I've had a lot of those. I've got a trunk full of those. Would you like to hear about a real new loser?

It's like how it was with Buddy DeSylva. I used to play him songs and he'd laugh and say "Oh, that's wonderful—can't use it." That's what happened to the lyric I wrote for the song that became "The Shadow of Your Smile." They sent it back and said they couldn't use it. I said, "Well, get Paul Francis Webster" and they did and had a great big hit.

Q: Johnny, what are the three greatest moments in a songwriter's life?

JM: Well, I think the three greatest moments in a songwriter's life are when he first knows he can write a song, when he writes his first song, even when he's fifteen, in my case. The second time is when he gets his first song published, and he's in print, like an author. And then the third time is when he gets his first hit, a real hit song that you hear—you go down the street and people are singing it that don't know who you are, they just love the song—and that's really a thrill. It's still a thrill, right now. Which somehow reminds me of something sort of funny: A few years ago my wife went to Japan with her sister while I was gallivanting around out in California, and she was dancing with a gentleman on the boat and he said, "By the way, what does your husband do?" And she said, "Oh, he's a songwriter?" And he said, "Yeah, but what does he do for a *living*?"

Speaking of which—a few years ago a lady sent me a song title. She worked in a cosmetic counter in Youngstown, Ohio, and I finally wrote the song and I told her we had a record by Tony Bennett. Well, she was thrilled. She's the cutest thing,—she writes me letters all the time:—She says, "You've changed my life, Mr. Mercer, you just don't know." People are coming in the store asking for my autograph, next week I have to go on the radio in Cleveland, and two weeks later, I'm going to Cincinnati. I'm getting to be so famous. Finally, she came to New York and she was on "To Tell the Truth" or something and then she goes to Europe and she says, "Mr. Mercer, I gotta work every day next week—I'm tired, I'm going to get out of show business." [Two stories about a couple of hit songs will wrap it up]

About "Blues In the Night." You know, when I wrote the lyric "My Mama done tol' me" that was way down at the end and Harold said, "Why don't you take that and put it up in the front?"

Another song had a funny beginning: They had a preview of this picture, *Breakfast at Tiffany's,* in San Francisco, and we had one of those conferences afterwards. Didn't go too well. Of course, it was a big hit, but it didn't go too well at this preview, so the producer, Marty Ragin, said, "Well, I don't know what you guys are going to do, but I'll tell you one thing—that damn song can go." That song was, of course, "Moon River."

Happy Ever After

1971

Music by DICK HYMAN

Second mortgage man
Showed me a plan
Easy to swing—with a single little down
    payment,
So I'm savin' up,
Found an old cup,
Makin' it clang—with a gang o' nickels 'n'
    dimes. . . .

Happy ever after,
Are ya gettin' the picture—same as me?
Kids on every rafter,
Runnin' over the nice clean floors,
All mine and yours.
A tiny station wagon,
Automatic disposal in the sink.
When I bring you home a dragon,
You'll fix us both a drink!

Mondays, I'll be off and slavin',
Stashin' stuff in the bank.

You'll be shoppin', blue-chip savin',
Puttin' gas in the tank.
Ajax, Brillo, Instant Bourbon,
TV dinners at night.
Kids all bussin', interurban,
Too darn busy to fight.

Sunshine, flowers, laughter,
What a beautiful lifetime—wait and see.
Happy ever after,
After you say you'll marry me!

Second mortgage man,
Coppin' your plan,
Buyin' a ring with a single little down
    payment.
For it to succeed
Whadda I need?—Little more greed and a
    "Yes indeedy" from you!

What amounts to a posthumous song that composer Dick Hyman only recently began performing. Interestingly, both Hoagy Carmichael and Mercer picked up on this melody when it was released on Enoch Light's record label and easygoing Johnny at first said he would step aside to let his former writing partner do it.

"SATCHMO"

Dear Ginger & Johnny:

I sincerely appreciate your beautiful letter and
your kind expressions of love and sympathy.

Louis and I often talked about you both and the
wonderful memories we shared of your friendship.

Love,

LUCILLE

August 1971

Lucille

Shortly after Louis Armstrong's death, his widow, remembering their mutual admiration, sent this letter to the
Mercers. One of Johnny's favorite stories concerned the
time that Satchmo was emceeing a stage show in a
predominately Black theatre. Satch started to introduce
the next act—a white tap-dancing team—but then, looking into the wings, realized he had forgotten their names.
He grinned, hemmed and hawed for a moment or two,
and then announced, "And now, folks . . . here they are
. . . The Two Ofays!"

215

Untitled Poem

JOHNNY MERCER

Ain't you proud of me?—I'm a man
I spoil everything that I can
And I'll never be satisfied
Till I've ruined the countryside
I catch all the fish in the seas
Burn up forests and chop down trees
Fill the rivers with sludge and oil
Wash the minerals from the soil
I kill tigers and leopards, too
I put everything in the zoo
(Those I haven't destroyed, I save
To remind me that I'm so brave!)
Soon not one of them will be here
I make everything disappear
Giant turtles and blue sperm whales
Now are rarer than nightingales
I shoot eagles and bears from planes
They're all gone with the whooping cranes
I have mountaintops leveled down
For one ticky-tack hi-rise town
Soon the air will be black as ink
All the water unfit to drink
I raise cattle and pigs for meat
Ducks and chickens are good to eat
As for hummingbirds—they're no loss
They're delicious with bearnaise sauce!
I kill sables and minks for furs
—Some are his'n—and some are hers—
I stuff everything else I can
Ain't you proud of me? . . . . . . I'm a man!
When I've got 'em all on a shelf
I may even destroy myself!

I have children my wife adores
So I send 'em all off to wars

Where they shoot someone else's sons
Ain't that wonderful?—That sells guns
That ain't all—I been on the moon
Like a fly on a macaroon
But them planets are no damn good
Ain't no animals there for food.

Some damn dreamers—and I mean damn
Think they're better than what I am
Say by usin' the sense God gave
There's no species they couldn't save
If we only killed one apiece
We might even make things increase!
Did you ever hear such damn rot?
They don't know of the plans I got
Like the buffalo and the gnu
Like the passenger pigeons too
I plan startin' in on the shrew
Soon, ol' buddy, I'll start on you!
Then, imperious, I will stand
In a waterless, treeless land
On a planet of sand and stone
Picked as clean as a chicken bone!

Well, I'd like to just stay and "jaw"
But in Africa I just saw . . . . . .
Say! . . . . . they tell me in Timbucktoo
There's a panda or two in view
And I know—'cause I seen the map—
Oil lies under the polar cap
So I'm takin' my blastin' rig
That uranium's tough to dig!
Well, ol' buddy, I'll see you roun'
Don't take nothin' that ain't nailed down

216

No music here. . . . Ginger Mercer found this poem among
Johnny's papers. It goes to show the mostly hidden serious side
of his nature.

Some day when you instruct your son
Tell the little chap what I've done
He'll be sort of impressed, I bet
Hell, I haven't got started yet!

There ain't nothin' that man can't do
Ain't you proud of me?
You're one too!

SHINING HOURS

Mercer and Bach in the garden of
La Residence du Bois, Paris, 1973

GINGE & JOHN Glass Pants

Johnny loved this joke: two guys forming a business partnership on New York's lower East Side during the early
1900s decide to have their picture taken together to celebrate the event. The photographer, though very good at his
craft, speaks very little English. He poses the two guys this
way and that, keeps saying "Glass pants." They don't know
what he's driving at. Finally the photographer comes out
from behind the camera, takes one guy's hand and places it
in his partner's hand in a pose of fraternal togetherness.
"Dot's nice," says the photog. "Glass pants."

Frazier

1972

Music by JIMMY ROWLES

Frazier was an aging lion
Living in a cage of iron
In a circus out of Tia Juana.
Frazier was their main attraction
And he gave them satisfaction,
Doing it with talent and with honor.
Growling for his daily dinner,
Frazier kept on getting thinner
On a measly can of Spam and tuna.
Days were lean but he got leaner
So one night in Pasadena
Through the bars he split for South Laguna.
Oh, cruel is fate but it's never too late, said
    Frazier.
I'm ninety-one and I haven't a son, thought
    Frazier,
The blue-eyed truth is I'm ready for
    eusthanasia.
Though matted and tarry, a local safari
    rescued poor old Frazier.

First they combed his tangled tresses,
Housed him with the lionesses,
Thinking him a harmless old grandpapa.
Fed him niocyn and fluoride, B-1, 2, 612
    and chloride,
Clams, cod liver oil and copper.
Younger studs brought in for breeding
Wound up beaten, bruised and bleeding.
Every day the same thing kept occurring.
Stretched out on an old serape
There lay Frazier tired and happy,

All his ladies on the list and purring
Oh, cruel is fate but it's never too late, said
    Frazier,
Announce the feast, I'm king of the beasts,
    grinned Frazier,
But king or not I am certainly hot, yawned
    Frazier
Well, when you're hot and you're hitting the
    spot their action might amaze-ya.

Children by his wives eleven added up to
    sixty-seven.
What nocturnal bliss he must have tasted
For no matter what the night time
Any night time seemed the right time.
Daytime found him fast asleep, just wasted.
When the circus owner found him,
Brought a lawsuit to impound him
Claiming you cats have to go where we go.
Frazier roared hasta la vista
You think all these chicks my sister?
I'm in business for myself, amigo,
Oh, cruel is fate but it's never too late, said
    Frazier,
I thank my stars I'm not behind bars, said
    Frazier.
They pay to see what comes naturally in
    Asia,
No African cat ever had it like that
And that goes for Malaysia.
He's up above, dear Frazier . . . Raising
    cubs, oh Frazier . . . Bless his heart, happy
    Frazier.

A lion isn't a bird but it's still part of the animal kingdom and therefore this story, which got quite a bit of play in the California press and on TV, appealed to Mercer. He had great fun with it and was able to stretch the storyout through several choruses. Jimmy Rowles, the great pianist who sometimes accompanied Mercer, brought it to his attention, wrote the music, and still performs it almost as well as his co-author did.

I'm Shadowing You

1973

Music by BLOSSOM DEARIE

Everywhere you go
I think you ought to know
I'm shadowing you.
Turn around 'n' find
I'm half a step behind,
I'm shadowing you.
You lug, you,
I wouldn't bug you
Except whenever I can.
You see, love,
You are to me, love,
The indispensable man.
After you decide
You want me for a bride
The deed'll be done.
Both of us'll be
So independent we
Will live on the run,
Picketing for every cause,
Fighting all the unjust laws,
Happy as can be,
Just you, J. Edgar Hoover and me.
I'm shadowing you.

Like I said before,
I'm campin' at your door,
I'm shadowing you.
How can you escape,
I'm getting out a tape
And video too.
In Venice
I'll be a menace
In your Italian motel.
In Paris,
I shall embarrass
You on the rue de Chappelle.
After you decide
You wanna be my bride
The deed'll be done.
Both of us'll be
So independent we
Will live on the run,
Picketing for every cause,
Fighting all the unjust laws,
Happy as can be,
Just you, the Secret Service and me.
I'm shadowing you.

Mercer always had an open door for those with special talents, and that certainly worked in favor of someone as unique as Blossom Dearie. She is not only a fine musician but funny and cute to boot. The song may be obscure (only Blossom is known to perform it), but it does represent one of the master's last few examples of the old fashioned boy-girl pop song lifted out of the ordinary with some tricky rhymes and references.

March, 1967: Meeting of the "in crowd", here composed of Blossom Dearie, JM, Jean Bach, and great comedy writer Goodman Ace.

M & M in high good humor. The beard and the glasses remind us of the passing years.

Good Companions

1974

Music by ANDRÉ PREVIN

Good companions stick together,
Sunny skies or stormy weather,
Birdies of uncommon feather,
Come what may.
Even when the rain drops tumble
Good companions never grumble.
Them's the breaks,
As William Shakespeare used to say.
Through the highways
And the byways
Of our native land,
Playing both the big time
And the one-night stand,
Hand in hand,
Good companions that's the ticket,
This old life's a game of cricket,
Sitting duck or sticky wicket,
Work or play,
We're good companions all
And we're on our way.

Frustration clouded a great deal of the period during which Mercer worked with André Previn for the
British production *Good Companions*. Previn was often away with the London Symphony Orchestra,
making their collaboration difficult, but Mercer was a big admirer of J. B. Priestley, on whose novel the
musical was based, and so he hung in there. The result was pleasant and charming if not blockbuster,
with Mercer capturing a few nice Britishisms such as "sitting duck and sticky wicket" here. Mercer's old
pal Bing recorded the song—which makes for a fitting salute.

221

Proprietors:
A.T.P. (London) Ltd.

Chairman:
SIR LEW GRADE

Managing Director:
TOBY ROWLAND

Deputy Chairman:
LOUIS BENJAMIN

General Manager: RAYMOND LANE
Box Office: 01-930 6606

Bernard Delfont Richard M Mills and Richard Pilbrow on behalf of the Bernard Delfont Organisation Ltd
present

John MILLS *The* **Judi DENCH**

GOOD COMPANIONS

The Musical of the Novel by J.B. Priestley

Christopher GABLE · Marti WEBB

Hope JACKMAN · Malcolm RENNIE
Roy SAMPSON · Jeannie HARRIS · Bernard MARTIN
Ray C. DAVIS

Music by
André PREVIN · Lyrics by **Johnny MERCER** · Book by **Ronald HARWOOD**

Choreography by
Jonathan TAYLOR · Orchestrations by **Herbert W. SPENCER & Angela MORLEY**

Designed by
Malcolm PRIDE · Lighting by **John B. READ** · Sound by **David COLLISON** · Musical Supervision by **Marcus DODS**

Production Associate Peter Rowley
Directed by **Braham MURRAY**

First performance at Her Majesty's Theatre, Thursday 11th July 1974

222

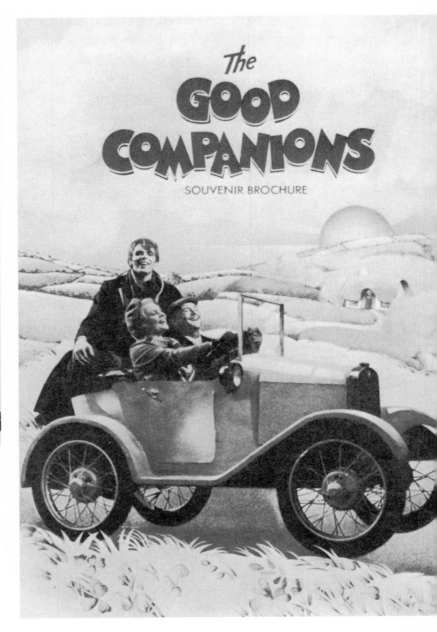

The GOOD COMPANIONS

SOUVENIR BROCHURE

How 'bout your old Da
Dancing for you?   Dancing for two?
O-ho and a-ha   Terping

You sing oom-pah-pah
I'll dance for two   Top   a few
                          Terp.

Dig my entrechat   Middle ... pipe my entrechat luv
                                    Also my pas-des-deux

And etcetera, luv   Oo-la-la   While
                           Sing tra-la, luv   When I entrechat luv
                                                You passe-partout!

                           Til you go on   turky-trot
                           Put a proper show on
                           Or

I'll entertain the queue
And then ..... ta-ta! luv   Tra-la-la, luv .... Here's
A great big hurrah, luv!   Ooo-la-la, luv
Ta, luv .... for you!   Watch my entrechat, luv

Go and put the face on   While you   My ......
                              I'll

Like Paris, lass .   Heel & toe &
See, lass oui, lass   Rockettes in a row
(Just-) If you follow me, lass   And on the stage we go
    I'll bring you in on cue -   In the spot " "
1, 2, 3. lass, Keep following me, lass.

Ta, luv
Ta, luv
How 'bout your old Da, luv
Dancing for you?

Oom-pah-pah, luv
When I entrechat, luv
You pas des deux!

One, two, three, lass
Just you follow me, lass
I'll bring you in on cue!

And then ...... tada! luv
A great big hurrah, luv
Ta, luv
For you!

When I pas des deux, luv
You pas des too!

First we entrechat, luv
Then pas des deux!

Heel and toe, lass
Down the stairs we go, lass
Wait for the proper cue
(Climb through the window too!)
(Circle the table too!)

Another example of the word puzzling that goes on when putting together a good song. This one became "Ta Luv" in *Good Companions*, but we might wonder whose phone number is at top right.

223

My New Celebrity Is You

1976   Music by BLOSSOM DEARIE

I dig Modigliani,
Jolson doing "Swanee,"
Several Maharanee are my intimates too.
I played with Mantovani,
And that's a lot of strings to get through.
But anyone can *see*
My new celebrity is you.

I've sung with Ethel Merman,
Swung with Woody Herman,
Played a gig in Germany with Ogerman too.
I nodded at a sermon
Billy Graham barely got through.
But anyone can see
My new celebrity is you.

I'm not a bit
Ashamed of it,
My rapier wit
Kept Serge Koussevitzky in line.
I'd reprimand
The Dorsey band
And right on the stand,
'Cause Annie's cousin Fanny was a sweetie
    of mine.

I've golfed with Lee Trevino,
Won at the casino,
Danced the Piccolino,
When the movie was new.
Spent the night with Dino,
Had to sleep with Jerry Lewis too.
But anyone can *see*
My new celebrity is you.

I've swooned at Mia Farrow,
Angular and narrow,
Drove her Pierce Arrow
To a Gatsby review.
Though frozen to the marrow,
Who would dream of leaving that queue?
But anyone can see
My new celebrity is you.

Her husband André Previn
Absolutely heaven,
Even Herman Levin
Wants to hire him too.
And as for Lady Bevan
We were both in labor that's true.
But anyone can see
My new celebrity is you.

I played the uke
With Vernon Duke
So well in Dubuque
That Vladimir Dukelsky
Said "Gee!"
My fingering
A certain string
Was such a big thing
That Fanny's cousin Annie's taking lessons
    from me.

I'm quite a fan of Lena,
Close to Katerina,
Very fond of Gina
Lollobrigida too.
And as for Pasadena

Everybody there's an old shoe,
But anyone can see
My new celebrity is you.

I've drunk with Willie Harbach,
Also Roger Staubach,
Wiggled pretty far back,
When you start to pursue.
And talk about your star back,
Tarkenton can scramble some too.
But anyone can see
My new celebrity is you.

I see Muhammad Ali,
Clanking goes my trolley.
Starred in "Hello Dolly"
When it ran out of glue.
And Salvador Dali
Did a little sketch of me too.
But anyone can see
My new celebrity is you.

You need a pair
To give an air
Of fashion and flair,
Have Bob and Danny Zarem fly down.
The older set
Will need a pet
So who do you get?
Well Danny
Has a granny
Who's the talk of the town.

The incidents are many,
Jack and Mary Benny,
Nick and Sister Kenny
Made the scene for me too.
And little Lotte Lenya
Helped to entertain at chez nous
Where everyone could see
My new celebrity is you.

By rights "Good Companions" should be the last song in the book but chronologically this one follows and how can you leave out a tour de force such as this one? Can you believe that the same man who wrote such commercial hits as "Moon River" and "Laura" could take the time to construct a laundry-list song of hip and inside references? But that's our Huckleberry Friend for you—they don't make 'em much anymore.

Having a good time despite the chilly weather in his native Savannah. The window display tells the period.

The Last Christmas Card

THIS Christmas card, I think, may be
The last you people hear from me
The reason being, not because
I don't believe in Santa Claus,
But I most strongly disapprove
Of how you gallivanters . . . MOVE!
A half a year is what it took
To change around my address book!
In January cards come back
All saying, "Moved"—"Not here"—"Lost
    track"
In February, one or two
Return across the ocean blue
In March and April, people call
To say "Your card came, after all"
In May and June, I start to think
And get out paper, pen and ink
And stew and wonder how on earth
I'll celebrate our Saviour's birth
And then, as summer wanly smiles,
I busily correct my files!
Old friends deceased, this couple wed
That pair no longer shares a bed
Those children now have different names
Their parents too—have different dames!
With all these different "libs" in sight
The sex is incidental, right?
So I perspire, type, erase
Recalling some forgotten face
And pretty soon the summer's gone
And Autumn puts her colors on
The Bears, the Lions and the Rams

Are at each other's diaphragms
And soon it's time to "have a Merry"
To spike yourselves a Tom and Jerry
So, here is looking at you, pal
Out seated on the old corral
Or in the traffic's roaring boom
The silence of your lonely room
Safe in your boudoir, or your den
There in your tent of oxygen
Before the IRS men catch you
Ol' pal o' mine, here's looking at you!
Like in your bathroom—all enamely
Amid the bosom of your family
Be thankful that's your home address
The world out there is in a mess
So, bank the fire, jump in bed
Await the reindeer overhead
And picture Santa, cheeks aglow
Tiptoeing through the fallen snow
Then, down the chimney noiselessly
To leave his toys beneath the tree
Can you recall when all were young
And Christmas carols first were sung?
How deep the snow! . . . and everywhere!
But now the snow is in our hair
So . . . to the tasks we have to do
While getting kissed—and loaded too
Remembering, thanks to the Lord
There's one gift we can all afford
And here it is . . . from these old versers
The gift of love—from all the Mercers—
                    Merry Christmas!

February 16, 1976

Mrs. Johnny Mercer
10972 Chalon Road
Los Angeles, Ca. 90024

Dear Mrs. Mercer:

I just thought you might be interested in the reaction to our recent show, "The Songs of Johnny Mercer".

I, personally, have had more wonderful comments on this show than almost any show we've ever done. Our mail also reflects the same sentiment. Many people have remarked that such a tribute was long over-due. Others were amazed to learn that Johnny had written so many great songs. I tell them what George Thow has often said, "We could do a whole season of Johnny Mercer songs, without repeating ourselves, and every show would be good."

I felt that both you and Johnny would be happy to know how well this show turned out. I hope Johnny was able to see it, and if not, I trust that by now you will have received the Video-tape Cassette Marshall Robbins had asked for.

All of us are hoping that Johnny is making progress, and that his recovery will be quick and complete.

With warmest personal regards to you both.

Sincerely,

Lawrence Welk
LW:ll

July 15, 1976

Dear Mr. Adams:

Johnny Mercer once said he had a "feeling for tunes". No one who ever heard his songs doubts those words. His mellow voice revealed that he was a child of the South; but his phrases were full of affection for people everywhere.

Johnny Mercer's talent was just too big to be applied to any one area of show business. As a performer, he had a special warmth that reached out and made a friend of every audience. We sang his wonderful songs and we listened as his music caught the precise mood of the moment in many motion pictures. Johnny Mercer had a gift all could enjoy.

Today, let me join with countless others in expressing my appreciation for Johnny Mercer's unique and loving contribution to the performing arts. He will long be remembered.

Sincerely,

Gerald R. Ford

Mr. Stanley Adams
ASCAP
One Lincoln Plaza
New York, New York 10023

S I D N E Y   Z I O N

Blues in the Night

June opened by giving us Jimmy Carter and ended by taking Johnny Mercer. If there's a better reason for getting out of town I don't want to hear it, and to make sure I don't hear it I'm going so far into the hills that even the meadowlarks won't bother. I never thought I'd pick an apple tree over Sardi's bar, but then who thought we'd have a coronation in New York on the bicentennial? And who could dream that Jimmy Carter's "ideas" on foreign policy would be a headline while Johnny Mercer died on the obit page?

I suppose it's strictly romance, but there must have been a time in this country when people preferred writing popular songs to making unpopular laws. If so, it was in the Twenties, when John Mercer of Savannah, Ga. — see why I put him in the same sentence with a guy like Carter? — came to Tin Pan Alley to go up against the poets in the Brill Building. He was one of the few Southerners ever to make it in that wondrous world, where everything that counted lived in 32 bars; surely he was the only lyricist then or now to write with a true touch of the South. "Lazy Bones," "Pardon My Southern Accent," and "Moon River" were to the South what "Manhattan" was to New York.

Mercer never lost that flavor, the scent of roots that made him the most American of all our song writers, Irving Berlin included. For all his imitators, anyone who knew his stuff could always tell a Mercer lyric; however sophisticated the story line, there was the lovely patented fragment and everybody has his favorite. Mine: "Like the lights home before me ..." Has any kid ever come back from college or the army who didn't feel something the first time he caught the home fire on the way down the block?

It was his knack—his genius—to conjure up novels in a word, a phrase, which however otherwise curious was always perfect in context. Was there ever a better one than "my huckleberry friend" from "Moon River"?

A few years ago, Johnny went back home to be honored at a municipal celebration. "Savannah's still like it used to be," he said later. "Everybody goes around and sings songs, drinks, and loves one another."

Just like Plains, right baby? But Johnny Mercer had no cross to bear; all he could do was sing and write songs. For my money he was one of the best jazz singers ever; if you can find his sides with Jack Teagarden or Bing Crosby, you'll know. But they are almost impossible to get; more likely, though difficult to pick up, is his LP, "The Best of Johnny Mercer" on Capitol, which label, incidentally, he founded. There is also a great LP he made with Bobby Darin called "Two of a Kind" on Atco, and a recent English disc, "Johnny Mercer Sings Johnny Mercer" by Pye Records.

Still, his lyrics are his immortality, and he wrote for the best composers in the country, including Harold Arlen, Duke Ellington, Richard Whiting, Jerome Kern, Harry Warren, Jimmy Van Heusen, Hoagy Carmichael, Walter Donaldson, Henry Mancini, Gene DePaul, Arthur Schwartz, Bobby Dolan and Michel LeGrand. He also composed a few tunes, like "Something's Gotta Give," "Dream," and "Strip Polka."

Few people under forty know much about Mercer's lyrics, and few over forty know he wrote them, however much they may have fallen in love to them. So herein a brief, hardly all-inclusive list:

Too Marvelous For Words
Satin Doll
That Old Black Magic
Days of Wine and Roses
You Must Have Been a Beautiful Baby
Come Rain or Come Shine
Skylark
I Want To Be Around To Pick Up the Pieces
Jeepers, Creepers
Goody, Goody
Ac-Cent-Tchu-Ate the Positive
Laura
Autumn Leaves
Summer Wind
You Were Never Lovelier
Dearly Beloved
I'm Old Fashioned
The Atchison, Topeka and the Santa Fe'
Hooray for Hollywood
When The World Was Young ("Ah, the Apple Tree")
One For My Baby (And One More For the Road)

Hardly comparable to the Grateful Dead, even if I did leave out "Blues In The Night," which if you want to know why I have 'em, well baby look at you now. ●

230   The Mercer tribute, July 22, 1976, on the stage of the Music Box Theatre, New York. Carl Rowan reads his column about Mercer while (left to right) Jimmy Rowles, Margaret Whiting, Harold Arlen, William B. Williams, Alec Wilder, Mel Tormé and Albert Hibler listen.

Carl Rowan's Tribute

WASHINGTON—Ask me how I'd prefer to judge a society. By its preachers and politicians, its authors or architects? No, I'd first like a look at the output of those who write its popular songs.

In war or peace, hard times or good, it is the popular lyricists who tell us so much about the heart and soul of a nation.

That's why a little bit of me died the other day with the passing of Johnny Mercer. And I'm disappointed that a greater fuss wasn't made over this man who for more than four decades put magical words to tunes and touched, even helped shape, the lives of millions of us.

As a boy of 8 in Tennessee, wading barefoot in a creek looking under rocks for crawfish, I learned about "the work ethic" from Johnny Mercer.

I truly believed that he was telling me something when I sang lines from his "Lazybones":

"You'll never get your day's work done resting in the morning sun. You'll never get your cornmeal made sleeping in the noonday shade."

Now, it seems, Americans learn about the work ethic only from politicians who seek power by berating welfare recipients.

I was 15 and had suffered through at least one high school crush before Mercer wrote a beautiful lyric which taught me that romance is a risky situation where only "Fools Rush In."

"Fools rush in where wise men never go, but wise men never fall in love—so how are they to know?"

But when I was 17, Johnny Mercer let me know that he wasn't really putting down romance. So my heart pounded as I sat in the movie *The Fleet's In*. I've almost forgotten Dorothy Lamour, Bob Eberle, Helen O'Connell, Betty Hutton, Eddie Bracken and William Holden, the stars of that Paramount hit. But I've never forgotten a single word of Mercer's simple but haunting lyric, "I Remember You":

"When my life is through . . . and the angels ask me to recall . . . the thrill of them all. Then I shall tell them I remember you."

231

That was the same year, 1942, when a college freshman would take two looks at a pretty coed and wonder if he had been struck by what Mercer described so eloquently as "That Old Black Magic" called love.

Someone is forever writing to ask me to list "the six books that most influenced your life." Why don't they ever ask me to list the songs that most influenced me?

That summer of '42, while doing household work for a vacationing family up near Monteagle, Tenn., I read a book I recall as *The Quest Eternal* by E. Phillips Oppenheim. It moved me greatly, but today I don't recall how or why.

But I'm sure no book writer influenced me more than did Mercer, whose gloomy hero would in 1943 tell the bartender that he was drinking "to the end of a brief episode . . . Make it one for my baby and one more for the road."

People often wonder whether novelists write biography. I was asking that about Mercer when he wrote: "From Natchez to Mobile, from Memphis to St. Joe, wherever the four winds blow. I been in some big towns. I heard me some big talk. But there is one thing I know: a woman's a two-face. A worrisome thing who'll leave you to sing the blues in the night."

I lot of us learned from Mercer, without paying Dale Carnegie a dime, that you make things happen when you "Ac-Cent-Tchu-Ate the Positive."

And how many millions of Americans must have kissed, loved, broken up, cried to those unpretentiously beautiful lyrics Mercer wrote about "Autumn Leaves":

"Since you went away the days grow long, and soon I'll hear old winter's song. But I miss you most of all, my darling, when autumn leaves start to fall."

It is almost incredible that from boyhood depression days in the early '30s, when I sang "Lazybones," right up till these days when I delight in crooning "Moon River," it has been Johnny Mercer psyching me up, making me a romantic, sending up warning signals about that other sex—yet always telling me that "we're after the same rainbow's end, waiting round the bend."

Johnny Mercer, thank you. I hope you make it to rainbow's end.

232

(Overleaf) The real Moon River: This is Mercer's home on the outskirts of Savannah; in the rear it faced onto a winding stream that the city renamed in honor of the award-winning song.

233

This compendium of known lyrics and songs by or attributed to Johnny Mercer is based upon the original listing which appeared in *Johnny Mercer: The Life, Times and Song Lyrics of Our Huckleberry Friend*, written by Bob Bach and Ginger Mercer and published by Lyle Stuart in 1982. This listing is as complete as possible as of November 1, 2008.

It has been compiled from and cross-checked by comparing information available on the websites of the American Society of Composers and Publishers (ASCAP), Broadcast Music, Inc. (BMI), the Johnny Mercer Collection at Georgia State University, the Songwriters Hall of Fame, the Johnny Mercer Educational Archives and the Johnny Mercer Foundation, as well as a host of additional websites posted by performers' representatives, lyric collectors and others with an abiding interest in *The Great American Song Book* and Johnny specifically. Compiled by Dianne S. Thurman with assistance from Lee Maltenfort.

Please address any additions, comments or discrepancies to:
Friends of Johnny Mercer via www.friendsofjohnnymercer.com.

Johnny Mercer's Songs: Composers and Collaborators

Song Title	Composers/Collaborators

A

About Face *(Unpub)* .... Edward Albertson

Absentminded Executive, The .... Johnny Mercer

Ac-cent-tchu-ate The Positive *(see Mister In-Between)* .... Harold Arlen

Affable, Balding Me .... Robert Emmett Dolan

After All These Years *(Unpub)* .... Johnny Mercer

After Twelve O'Clock *(see Rockin' After Midnight)* .... Hoagy Carmichael

Afterbeat, The .... Fred Astaire

Ah Juliette *(see Jeepers Creepers)* .... Harry Warren

Ah Love Ya .... Harold Arlen

Ah The Apple Trees *(see Chevalier De Paris* and *When The World Was Young) (JM & Anfele Vannier)* .... M. Philippe-Gerard

Ain't Nature Grand .... Arthur Schwartz

Air-Minded Executive, The .... Bernie Hanighen

Al Fresco .... Harold Arlen

All Mucked Up .... Andre Previn

All Over The World *(Unpub)* .... Johnny Mercer

All Through The Night .... Arthur Schwartz

All Tied Up .... Hoagy Carmichael

Alphabet Of Love Begins And Ends With You, The .... *(Johnny Mercer & Hilda Gottlieb)* .... Lewis E. Gensler

Amazing What Love Can Do .... Hoagy Carmichael

Ambiguous Means I Love You *(see Word A Day, A)* .... Johnny Mercer

Amour Et La Rose *(see Days Of Wine And Roses)* .... Henry Mancini

And Points Beyond .... Andre Previn

And So To Bed .... Robert Emmett Dolan

And The Angels Sing *(see And The Angels Sing)* .... Ziggy Elman

Angel Face *(Draft Lyrics)* .... Unknown

Angeli Cantano *(see And The Angels Sing)* ... Ziggy Elman

Angels Cried, The .... Johnny Mercer

Anne *(Unpub)* .... Edward Albertson

Anota Esta Noche *(see Moon River)* .... Henry Mancini

Another Case of Blues .... Richard Myers

Anthony And Cleopatra Theme *(see Nile, The)* .... Alex North

Antonia .... Howard Jackson

Any Old Day *(Unpub)* .... Johnny Mercer

Any Place I Hang My Hat Is Home .... Harold Arlen

Any Similarity Is Just Coincidental .... Hoagy Carmichael

Any Way The Wind Blows *(Unpub/Draft Lyrics)* .... Johnny Mercer

Apache Love Song *(see Love Song)* .... David Raskin

Are You Gonna Throw Me Down? *(Unpub/Draft Lyrics)* .... Johnny Mercer

Aren't You The Charming One? .... Milton Samuels

Ariane .... Matt Malneck

Around The Bend .... Johnny Mercer

Art Of Conservation Has Declined, The ..... Alan Bergman

Arthur Murray Taught Me Dancing In A Hurry .... Victor Schertzinger

As Fair As Her Name .... Robert Emmett Dolan

As Long As You Live *(You'll Be Dead When You Die)* .... Bernie Hanighan

At Last .... Barry Manilow

At The Jazz Band Ball .... D.J. LaRocca, Larry Shields

Au Giulietta *(see Jeepers Creepers)* .... Harry Warren

Audition Dance .... Jerome Kern

Augie Is A Nachural (Natural) Man *(see Li'l Augie Is A Natural Man* and *Natchul Man)* .... Harold Arlen

Augie Is A Travelin' Man .... Johnny Mercer

Aus Lauter Liebe *(see P.S. I Love You)* ..... Gordon Jenkins

Autumn Leaves *(see Feuilles Mortes Les* and *Feuilles Mortes* and *Hojas Muertas Las)* ....Joseph Kosma

Autumn Twilight .... Joseph S. Dubin

Aw Come On Now .... Johnny Mercer

Aye Lad .... Andre Previn

B

Baby .... Steve Allen

Baby Doll .... Harry Warren

Baby Don't You Quit Now .... Jimmie Rowles

Baby O'Mine *(Draft Lyrics)* .... Unknown

Baby-O .... Johnny Rotella

Baby's Born, A .... Harold Arlen

Bachelor Dinner Song .... Harry Warren

Back Stretch Rambler .... Harold Arlen

Song Title	Composers/Collaborators
Bad Humor Man, The (see Ting-a-ling Man) .... Jimmy McHugh	
Ballad Of A Private Eye (Unpub/Draft Lyrics) .... Johnny Mercer	
Ballad Of Alvarez Kelly, The .... Johnny Green	
Barefoot In The Park (see Pieds Nus Dans Le Parc) .... Neal Hefti	
Barrelhouse Beguine .... Jerome Kern	
Bathtub Ran Over Again, The .... Michael H. Cleary	
Be Happy (Unpub/Draft Lyrics) .... Johnny Mercer	
Be My Guest .... Johnny Mercer	
Beautiful Forever (Draft Lyrics) .... Frederic Spielman	
Beauty From Ashes .... Unknown	
Bees 'N Flowers (Bees n' Flowers) .... Harold Arlen	
Before We Start (Draft Lyrics) .... Unknown	
Bells Of Honolulu........................... Franz Steininger	
Beneath The Curtain Of The Night (see Ninfa de Ojos Brujos) (Johnny Mercer & Alfredo Brito) ......Alfredo Brito	
Bernardine .... Johnny Mercer	
Best Love Of All, The (Unpub) .... Robert Emmett Dolan	
Betsy And Me (Unpub/Draft Lyrics).......... Johnny Mercer	
Better Days (Johnny Mercer & Gilbert Martinez).................Gilbert Martinez	
Betting Calls........................... Harold Arlen	
Beyond The Moon (Johnny Mercer & Johnny Gruelle)........ Guy Stevens	
Biarn's Song (see The Piney Woods and Theme From The Missouri Traveler) ....Jack Marshall	
Bi-Focal Fred .... Johnny Mercer	
Big Beautiful Ball, A................................John Williams	
Big Movie Show In The Sky, The ... Robert Emmett Dolan	
Big Time In A Small Town Lyrics (In Script)...... Unknown	
Bilbao Song, The ....Kurt Weill	
Biography – BG Cues.......Gene De Paul, Joseph J. Lilley, Nelson Riddle	
Birmingham Bertha................................ Johnny Mercer	
Bittersweet .... Mike Corda	
Black Magic (see That Old Black Magic and Ce Diable Noir) .... Harold Arlen	
Blasted King Of England, The (see Phony King Of England, The)...Traditional	
Bless Your Beautiful Hide .... Gene De Paul	
Bless Your Heart................................... Johnny Mercer	
Blind Man................................... Harold Arlen	
Blossom ....Duke Ellington and Billy Strayhorn	
Blow De Whistle .... Harold Arlen	
Blue And Lazy Days, The (Draft Lyrics)............Unknown	
Blue Rain ....Jimmy Van Heusen	
Bluebird (Draft Lyrics) ....n/a	
Blues Della Notte (see Blues In The Night)... Harold Arlen	
Blues Improvisation (Unpub) .... Johnny Mercer	

Song Title	Composers/Collaborators
Blues In The Night (see My Mama Done Tol' Me) .... Harold Arlen	
Blues Theme (Instrumental) .... Johnny Mercer	
Bob White (see Whatcha Gonna Swing Tonight?)..................... Bernie Hanighen	
Boit A, Bois La (Unpub) .... Johnny Mercer	
Bon Apetit I (see Menu Song) .... Harold Arlen	
Bon Apetit II (see Menu Song) .... Harold Arlen	
Bon Apetit III (see Menu Song)................... Harold Arlen	
Bon Apetit IV (see Menu Song) .... Harold Arlen	
Bon Vivant .... Robert Emmett Dolan	
Bouquet ....Percy Faith	
Boy Meets Girl................................Harry Warren	
Boyhood Daze (see Captains Of The Clouds).................Harold Arlen	
Boys Will Be Boys–Girls Will Be Girls ....Lewis E. Gensler	
Brasilia (Serenata Negra) ....Panano & Madinez & Loti	
Break It Up, Cinderella .... Hoagy Carmichael	
Bride's Wedding Day Song, A (see Thank You, Mr. Currier, Thank You, Mr. Ives) ....Harry Warren	
Broadway (Composer) .... Johnny Mercer	
Bully Boys, The (Unpub/Draft Lyrics) .... Johnny Mercer	
Buona Fortuna (see Here's Cheers and see Salud)...........Saul Chaplin	
Busy Little Bumble Bees ....Harry Warren	
But I Never Know When To Stop (see I Can Spell Banana) .... Geoff Clarkson	
But They Better Not Wait Too Long .... Hoagy Carmichael	
By Jove (Unpub/Draft Lyrics)......... Robert Emmett Dolan	
By The Way...Vernon Duke	
Bye Bye Baby (see Hit The Road To Dreamland) .... Harold Arlen	

C

Song Title	Composers/Collaborators
Ca Va Ca Va (see Goody Goody) (Johnny Mercer & Matt Malneck) ....Johnny Mercer & Matt Malneck	
Ca Va Exlater (see Immer noch einmal and Something's Gotta Give)................................ Johnny Mercer	
Cake Call .... Harold Arlen	
Cake Song.. Harold Arlen	
Cake Walk (see Cakewalk Your Lady).......... Harold Arlen	
Cakewalk Your Lady (see Cake Walk).......... Harold Arlen	
California's Melodyland........................... Johnny Mercer	
Call Him Dad (Draft Lyrics) ....Unknown	
Call Him Daddy (see Old Man, The) (Draft Lyrics)........... Johnny Mercer	
Calling All Squares............................. Bernie Hanighen	
Calypso Song .... Harold Arlen	
Camaraderie .... Andre Previn	
Camptown Races................................. Stephen Foster	

Song Title	Composers/Collaborators

Can't Teach My Old Heart New Tricks (1937)................... Richard A. Whiting

Can't Teach My Old Heart New Tricks (1988)................... Barry Manilow

Can't Ya Take A Joke? (see Holy Smoke)...... Royal Marsh

Captains Of The Clouds (see Boyhood Daze)........................... Harold Arlen

Caribees, The .... Robert Emmett Dolan

Carnival In Rio (Instrumental)................. Johnny Mercer

Carnival Stall Song.................................... Andre Previn

Case Of Rape, A...................... Robbert Emmett Dolan

Cast Your Bread Upon The Water .... Johnny Mercer

"C-A-T" Spells Cat.............................. Johnny Mercer

Cat With Nine Lives, A (Unpub/Draft Lyrics).................. Johnny Mercer

Ce Diable Noir (see That Old Black Magic)... Harold Arlen

Cedar Point Parade .... Robert G. Friedman

Celestial Caliope (Instrumental)................. Johnny Mercer

Celia's First Essay......................... Robert Emmett Dolan

Celia's First Lament (see Celia's Lament) .... Robert Emmett Dolan

Celia's Lament (see Celia's First Lament) .... Robert Emmett Dolan

Central Park .... Matt Malneck

C'est La Guerre .... Arthur Schwartz

Champagne Fo' De Lady .... Harold Arlen

Charade (see Et Le Bateau En Va)...........Henry Mancini

Charleston (Unpub) .... Johnny Mercer

Charmed Existence, A ....Saul Chaplin

Cheat On Me... Gene di Novi

Chevalier De Paris (see Ah, The Apple Trees and see When The World Was Young) (JM & Anfele Vannier)...... M. Philippe-Gerard

Chez L Pere Nazaire (Unpub) .... Johnny Mercer

Child Of The Wild, A..................... Robert Emmett Dolan

Chimney Corner Dream .... Robert Emmett Dolan

Chin Up, Stout Fellow ....Saul Chaplin

Chinquapin Bush .... Harold Arlen

Christmas Spirit, The (Unpub/Draft Lyrics)................... Johnny Mercer

Cinderella Waltz .... Al Mack

Cindy (adapted by Johnny Mercer) Lyricist: Jo Stafford, Paul Weston.......................... Jo Stafford, Paul Weston

Circus Is Coming To Town .... Bernie Hanighen

Clink Your Glasses .... Sammy Cahn

Close Your Eyes (Draft Lyrics)..........................Unknown

Clouds In The Sky (see Like Clouds In The Sky) .... Harold Arlen

College November....................................Lew Quadling

Come On, Li'l Augie .... Harold Arlen

Come Rain Or Come Shine .... Harold Arlen

Come Rain Or Come Shine (Reprise) .... Harold Arlen

Come Up And See Me Sometime (Unpub)...................... Robert Emmett Dolan

Comes The Revolution Baby ....Lewis E. Gensler

Comet In The Sky, A........................... Ronnell L. Bright

Confidentially (Johnny Mercer & Al Dubin).................... Harry Warren

Conjur Man .... Harold Arlen

Conservation While Dancing....................... Paul Weston

Corn Pickin' ....Harry Warren

Could Be .... Walter Donaldson

Countin' Our Chickens .... Harold Arlen

Country's In The Very Best of Hands, The ... Gene De Paul

Cowboy From Brookyln...........................Harry Warren

Crawled Up A Rainbow (see Rainbow) .... Harold Arlen

Cream Puff...Henry Mancini

Cross The River, Round The Bend .... Johnny Mercer

Crying Eyes And An Empty Heart (Unpub) .... Rich Barcellona

Cuando Estas As Enamorad (see When You're In Love) ... Gene De Paul

Cuckoo In The Clock.......................... Walter Donaldson

Cure, The.. Harold Arlen

Curse .... Harold Arlen

D

Daddy Long Legs................................... Johnny Mercer

Daddy Long Legs Cues........................... Johnny Mercer

Dame Sans Coeur (see Satin Doll)................................. Duke Ellington and Billy Strayhorn

Dance Of Life, The ....Andre Previn

Dancing Through Life .... Johnny Mercer

Dangerous When Wet (see Fifi) (Songwriter's Hall of Fame).. Arthur Schwartz

Dangerous When Wet Cues .... Arthur Schwartz

Dark Is The Night......................................Joseph Meyer

Darkest Before The Dawn...........................Andre Previn

Darling Lili ....Henry Mancini

Darling Lili Cues ....Henry Mancini

Darn Clever These Chinee.................. Hoagy Carmichael

Day After Day After Day......................Barry Manilow

Day In – Day Out .... Rube Bloom

Daybreak Blues, The ....Walter Weschler

Daydreaming (All Night Long) ....Harry Warren

Days Of Wine And Roses (see Vino E Rose).................. Henry Mancini

De Right Answer.................................... Harold Arlen

Dear Mirium .... Johnny Mercer

Dearest Darling (Draft Lyrics) ....Unknown

Dearly Beloved (see Decoly Beloved) .... Jerome Kern

Deaux Amoureux (Unpub) .... Johnny Mercer

Song Title	Composers/Collaborators

Decoly Belsved *(see Dearly Beloved)*............ Jerome Kern

Deep South In My Heart.......................... Archie Bleyer

Deirde....................................... Michael Masser

Della's Entrance .... Harold Arlen

Derry Down Dilly ....Johnny Green

Dig It *(see I Ain't Hep To That Step But I'll Dig It!)*.............
.... Hal Borne

Dig You Most.. Hal Borne

Dis Is De Day *(see This Is Our Day and This Is The Day)* .....
.... Harold Arlen

Dis Little While *(see This Little While)* .... Harold Arlen

Dixie's Dream *(see I Remember You) (Songwriter's Hall Of
Fame)*.. Victor Schertzinger

Dixie Isn't Dixie Anymore........................... Rube Bloom

Dixieland Band, The .... Bernie Hanighen

Do My Eyes Deceive Me? *(Johnny Mercer & Dave
Dreyer)*...................Johnny Mercer & Dave Dreyer

Doctor Watson And Mister Holmes *(see Dr. Watson & Mr.
Holmes)* .... Bernie Hanighen

Dog Eat Dog .... Harold Arlen

Dog Is Man's Best Friend, A.................... Johnny Mercer

Dog Patch Dance .... Gene De Paul

Don't Ask Too Much Of Love............. Emmerich Kalman

Don't Play Me Cut Rates *(Unpub/Draft Lyrics)*....................
.... Johnny Mercer

Don't Run Away From The Rain .... Johnny Mercer

Don't Stop Me If You've Heard It *(Unpub)* ...Henry Souvaine

Don't That Take The Rag Off'n The Bush *(see Rag Offen
The Bush)*..Gene De Paul

Don't Think It Ain't Been Charming........ Jimmy McHugh

Don't Use A Bridle.................................... Harold Arlen

Don't You Come Crying To Me *(Unpub)* .... n/a

Down A Long, Long Road *(Johnny Mercer & Margot
Millham)*...................Johnny Mercer & Margot Millham

Down In The Dumps *(Unpub/Draft Lyrics)*................. n/a

Down In The Valley...................... Robert Emmett Dolan

Down T' Uncle Bill's *(Johnny Mercer & Hoagy
Carmichael)*..........Johnny Mercer & Hoagy Carmichael

Down Through The Ages......Phil Charig and Richard Myers

Dr. Watson And Mr. Holmes *(see Doctor Watson And
Mister Holmes)* .... Bernie Hanighen

Drat 'Em ....Gene De Paul

Dream *(see Ensueno and Solo Un Sogno)*.....Johnny Mercer

Dream Awhile...Phil Ohman

Dream Peddler's Serenade, The............John Rufus Sharp

Drinking Again ....Doris Tauber

Druthers *(see If I Had My Druthers and Si Tu M Aimais)*
.... Gene De Paul

Duration Blues...................................... Johnny Mercer

E

E Flat Ballad .... Johnny Mercer

Early Autumn *(see Finalement L'Automne Est)*...............
......................................Ralph Burns, Woody Herman

Easy Street .... Harold Arlen

Ebenezer McAfee III .... Robert Emmett Dolan

Echo Of A Dream, The.............................Serge Walter

Echoes .... Johnny Mercer

Eeny Meeny Meiny Mo *(Johnny Mercer & Matt
Malneck)* .... Johnny Mercer and Matt Malneck

El Camino .... Michael Shanklin

El Rio De La Luna *(see Moon River)*..........Henry Mancini

Elevator Song .... Johnny Mercer

Emily ....Johnny Mandel

Empty Tables .... James Van Heusen

Ensueno *(see Dream and Solo Un Sogno)*. Johnny Mercer

Equivalent Of A Haa-vud Education, The *(Unpub/Draft
Lyrics)* .... Johnny Mercer

Et Le Bateau En Va *(see Charade)* ....Henry Mancini

Even If I Say It Myself .... Hoagy Carmichael

Every So Often ....Harry Warren

Every Step Of The Way *(see I Fought Every Step Of
The Way)* .... Johnny Mercer

Everybody Is Your Partner In New York .... Johnny Mercer

Everybody Knows Those Old Jokes – Parody ....
.... Johnny Mercer

Everything Happens To Me................. Hoagy Carmichael

Everything Is Tickety-Boo ....Saul Chaplin

Exercise Your Prerogative .... Gene De Paul

Extravaganzia .... Andre Previn

Eyes Of The Beloved *(Unpub/Draft Lyrics)*.....................
.... Johnny Mercer

F

Facts Of Life, The .... Johnny Mercer

Falling Off The Wagon *(Johnny Mercer &
E. Y. Harburg)* ....Lewis E. Gensler

Fancy Free... Harold Arlen

Fare-The-Well To Harlem .... Bernie Hanighen

Fate Moves In Mysterious Ways .... Andre Previn

Feuilles Mortes Les *(see Autumn Leaves)* ...Joseph Kosma

Fever Heat *(Unpub/Draft Lyrics)* .... Archie Bleyer

Fifi *(see Dangerous When Wet) (Songwriter's Hall Of
Fame)*.. Arthur Schwartz

Finale *(Blues Opera)*................................. Harold Arlen

Finale *(Foxy)* .... Robert Emmett Dolan

Finale *(Li'l Abner)* .... Gene De Paul

Finale *(Saratoga)* .... Harold Arlen

Finale *(Top Banana)* .... Johnny Mercer

Song Title	Composers/Collaborators	Song Title	Composers/Collaborators

Finalement L'Automne Est *(see Early Autumn)*................
......................Ralph Burns, Woody Herman

Finders Are Keepers *(Unpub)* ....Barry Manilow

Finders Are Keepers (Draft Lyrics, 1935) ...... Carl Sigman

Fine Thing!............................. Robert Emmett Dolan

First Auto Theme *(Instrumental)* .... Johnny Mercer

First Chinese Theme *(Instrumental)*......... Johnny Mercer

First Last and Always ....Barry Manilow

Fix Yo'Self Up *(Fix Yourself Up)* .... Harold Arlen

Fleet's In, The.................... Victor Schertzinger

Fleet's In, The Cues...................... Victor Schertzinger

Fleur De Lys .... Hoagy Carmichael

Floating Lei .... Johnny Mercer

Flower Call .... Harold Arlen

Fool That I Am .... Matt Malneck & Frank Signorelli

Fools Rush In *(see Pazzo di Te* and *Where Angels Fear To Tread)* .... Rube Bloom

Footloose .... Andre Previn

For Lovers Only *(Johnny Mercer & Al Dubin)* .... Harry Warren

Foremost Dairy Commercial .... Victor Schertzinger

Forever Amber............................David Raskin

Forget Me Not *(Unpub/Draft Lyrics)* .... n/a

Fountain In The Rain........Milton Samuels & Charles Hale

Foxy............................ Robert Emmett Dolan

Frasier *(see The Sensuous Lion)*.............. Jimmie Rowles

Fred Astaire Salutes Fox Musicals *(Unpub)* .... Johnny Mercer

Free And Easy .... Harold Arlen

French Waltz *(Unpub)*............................ Johnny Mercer

Freshman Song, The *(see Welcome Egg-head)* .... Johnny Mercer

Friend Of The Family .... Hoagy Carmichael

F'Rinstance *(Unpub/Draft Lyrics)* .... Johnny Mercer

Funeral Scene – A Prelude......................... Harold Arlen

G

G. I. Jive................................. Johnny Mercer

Gamblers, The .... Harold Arlen

Game Of Poker, A .... Harold Arlen

Game Of Poker *(Reprise)* .... Harold Arlen

Garden Of The Moon *(Johnny Mercer & Al Dubin)*......... ....Harry Warren

Gasoline Gypsies .... Richard A. Whiting

Gee I Wish I'd Listened To My Mother ..... Jimmy McHugh

Gee, But It's Good To Be Home Again *(Unpub)*.............. .... Robert Emmett Dolan

General Bullmoose *(see What's Good For General Bullmoose)* .... Gene De Paul

Gentle Art Of Murder, The *(Unpub)*.............................. .... Robert Emmett Dolan

Georgia Georgia .... Johnny Mercer

Gerfunkt .... Johnny Mercer

Get A Horse ....Henry Mancini

Gettin' A Man............................ Harold Arlen

Ghost Of Love ....Harold Spina

Girl Friend Of The Whirling Dervish, The *(Johnny Mercer & Al Dubin)*...........................Harry Warren

Girl In No Man's Land, The.......................Henry Mancini

Girl Of All Nations .... Johnny Mercer

Give Me Back My Heart *(Unpub)*................Joseph Wiess

Glow Worm *(The Glow Worm) (original lyrics: Lilla C.Robinson)*............................. Paul Lincke

God Is Love (And Love Is God) *(Unpub)* .... Ida Thomas

Goin' Co'tin' ....Gene De Paul

Golden Bells *(Unpub)*.................... Robert Emmett Dolan

Good Companions........................Andre Previn

Good Companions/And Points Beyond ....Andre Previn

Good-bye ....Andre Previn

Goody Goody *(see Ca Va, Ca Va) (Johnny Mercer & Matt Malneck)* .... Johnny Mercer & Matt Malneck

Goose Never Be A Peacock .... Harold Arlen

Gossip Song, The *(see Have You Heard?)*.... Harold Arlen

Got To Wear You Off My Weary Mind .... Harold Arlen

Gotta Get Some Shuteye *(see Shut Eye)* .... Walter Donaldson

Great Guns...............................Harry Warren

Great North Road ....Andre Previn

Greetings Gate .... Hoagy Carmichael

Guardian Angel........................... Johnny Mercer

Guitar Country *(Johnny Mercer & Willard Robison)* ....Johnny Mercer & Willard Robison

H

Hail To MacCrackens *(see McCracken's)* ... Johnny Mercer

Half-zies .... Rube Bloom

Hands Of Fate *(Unpub)* .... n/a

Handy With Your Feet .... Richard A. Whiting

Hang On To Your Lids, Kids *(see Here We Go Again)* .... Harold Arlen

Hangin' Loose .... Sammy Nestico

Hangin On To You................................ Harold Arlen

Hank............................... Frank S. Perkins

Happy Bachelor .... Gene De Paul

Happy Endings *(Unpub/Draft Lyrics)* .... n/a

Happy Ever After *(Unpub)* .... Dick Hyman

Happy New Year To You .... Hoagy Carmichael

Happy Times .... Sylvia Fine

Hare Piece *(Instrumental)* .... Johnny Mercer

Song Title	Composers/Collaborators
Harlem Butterfly	Johnny Mercer
Harlem To Hollywood	n/a
Harvey Girls	Harry Warren
Harvey The Victory Garden Man	Harold Arlen
Have A Heart	Gene Di Novi
Have A Nice Day	Sammy Nestico
Have You Got Any Castles, Baby?	Richard A. Whiting
Have You Heard? (see The Gossip Song)	Harold Arlen
Have You Written Any Good Books Lately?	Johnny Mercer
Havin' A Ball	Johnny Mercer
Hayride	Harry Warren
Haystacks On A Hill (Draft Lyrics)	Unknown
He Didn't Have The Know — How No How	Robert Emmett Dolan
He Loved Me Till The All Clear Came	Harold Arlen
He Never Even Knew What Hit Him (Draft Lyrics)	Unknown
He Never Knew What Hit Him (Draft Lyrics)	Johnny Mercer
He Shouldn't-a, Hadn't-a, Oughtn't-a Swang On Me!	Henry Mancini
Headed For Big Things	Harold Arlen
Headless Horseman	David Raksin
Hear Them Bells (Arrangement Johnny Mercer)	Johnny Mercer
Heart Of Mine Cry On	Barry Manilow
Hello, Out There Hello (Hello Out There, Hello)	Wingy Manone
Her First Evening Dress	Michael Cleary
Here Come The British	Bernie Hanighen
Here Come The Waves	Harold Arlen
Here Comes The Groom	Hoagy Carmichael
Here Goes Nothing	Harold Arlen
Here We Are (Unpub)	Robert Emmett Dolan
Here We Go Again (see Hang On To Your Lids, Kids)	Harold Arlen
Here You Are (Draft Lyrics)	Unknown
Here's Cheers (see Buona Fortuna and Salud)	Saul Chaplin
Here's To My Lady	Rube Bloom
He's Dead But He Won't Lie Down	Hoagy Carmichael
Higgledy Piggledy	Marshall L. Robbins
High Society	Gene De Paul
High, Low, Jack And The Game	Harold Arlen
Higher Den De Moon (see Higher Than The Moon and see On Top Of The World)	Harold Arlen
Higher Than The Moon (see Higher Den De Moon and On Top Of The World)	Harold Arlen
Hip Little World (Unpub)	Johnny Mercer
History Of The Beat (see That'll Get It)	Johnny Mercer
Hit The Road To Dreamland (see Bye, Bye Baby)	Harold Arlen

Song Title	Composers/Collaborators
Hoe Down The Bayou (see Poor Mr. Chisholm)	Bernie Hanighen
Hojas Muertas Las (see Autumn Leaves)	Joseph Kosma
Holy Smoke (see Can't Ya Take A Joke?)	Royal Marsh
Holy Smoke! Can't You Take A Joke	Royal Marsh
Homecoming	Walter Donaldson
Honey (Unpub/Draft Lyrics)	n/a
Honeymoon Is Over, The	Robert Emmett Dolan
Hong Kong Café (Instrumental)	Johnny Mercer
Honolulu	Johnny Mercer
Honor Bright	Jimmy McHugh
Hoody Do To You	Harold Arlen
Hooray For Hollywood	Richard A. Whiting
Hooray For Spinach	Harry Warren
Hootin' Owl Trail	Robert Emmett Dolan
Hoping	Al Hansen
Horseshoes Are Lucky	Robert Emmett Dolan
House-Raising Dance	Gene De Paul
How Do You Say Auf Wiedersehn?	Tony Scibetta
How I Wish That You Were In My Place (Unpub)	Johnny Mercer
How Little We Know	Hoagy Carmichael
How Long Has This Been Going On?	Archie Bleyer
How Nice For Me	Hoagy Carmichael
How Nice For Me (Reprise)	Hoagy Carmichael
How To Commit Marriage (Instrumental)	Johnny Mercer, J. Lilley, G. Levene and V. Cleave
Howdy Do To You	Harold Arlen
Howdy Stranger	Richard A. Whiting
Howdy, Friends And Neighbors	Gene De Paul
Human Race Is Human After All, The (Unpub)	Robert Emmett Dolan
Hymn (see Man In My Life, The)	Harold Arlen

I

Song Title	Composers/Collaborators
I Ain't Down Yet (Unpub/Sound Recording)	Johnny Mercer
I Ain't Heard	Harold Arlen
I Ain't Hep To That Step But I'll Dig It! (see Dig It)	Hal Borne
I Boogied When I Should Have Woogied	Bernie Hanighen
I Can Spell Banana (see But I Never Know When To Stop)	Geoff Clarkson
I Can't Believe My Eyes (Draft Lyrics)	n/a
Ichabod (Johnny Mercer & Don Raye)	Gene De Paul
I Could Kiss You For That	Jimmy McHugh
I Did It For The Red, White and Blue	Rube Bloom
I Don't Believe In Signs	Harry Warren
I Don't Wanna Be Alone Again	Howard Smith

I Feel My Luck Comin' Down (see *Luck Just Go Down*) ... . Harold Arlen

I Fought Every Step Of The Way (see *Every Step Of The Day*).. Johnny Mercer

I Got Out Of The Bed On The Right Side....Arthur Schwartz

I Guess It Was You All the Time .... Hoagy Carmichael

I Guess There Ain't No Santa Claus............................... .... Barry Manilow and Edward Arkin

I Had Myself A True Love/I Wonder What Became Of (see *True Love*).. Harold Arlen

I Hear A Song In My Heart .... Paul Weston

I Knew .... Rube Bloom

I Know Your Kiss By Heart .... Johnny Mercer

I Like Men .... Arthur Schwartz

I Love To Beat The Big Bass Drum............. Harry Warren

I Love You (I Think)............................ Johnny Mercer

I Never Knew .... Johnny Mercer

I Never Saw A Better Night....................Lewis E. Gensler

I Never Wanna Look Into Those Eyes Again ....Milton Raskin

I Owe It All To You.............................. Johnny Mercer

I Pray .... Johnny Mercer

I Promise You .... Harold Arlen

I Really Get A Message From You (*Unpub/Draft Lyrics*)..n/a

I Remember You (see *Dixie's Dream*) (*Songwriter's Hall Of Fame*).. Victor Schertzinger

I Sang A Love Song (*Draft Lyrics*) .... Unknown

I Saw Her At Eight o'clock (*Johnny Mercer & Matt Malneck*)...................... Johnny Mercer and Matt Malneck

I Saw You Dancing In My Dreams .... Matt Malneck & .... Frank Signorelli

I Shall Remember (*Draft Lyrics*) .... Unknown

I Still Remember The Masquerade (*Unpub/Draft Lyrics*)..n/a

I Struck It Lucky (*Draft Lyrics*) .... Unknown

I Think We Need A Drink (*Unpub/Draft Lyrics*) .... n/a

I Thought About You ....Jimmy Van Heusen

I Walk With Music .... Hoagy Carmichael

I Walk With Music (*Reprise*).................. Hoagy Carmichael

I Wanna Be A Dancin' Man..................... Harry Warren

I Wanna Be Around (see *J Aimerais Etre La*) (*JM & Sadie Vimmerstedt*)....... Johnny Mercer & Sadie Vimmerstedt

I Wanna Be In Love Again .... Johnny Mercer

I Want You (*Draft Lyrics*) ....Unknown

I Wind Up Taking a Fall (*Johnny Mercer & Robert Emmett Dolan*).............Johnny Mercer & Robert Emmett Dolan

I Wish I Had Someone Like You....................Al Hansen

I Wish It Could Be Otherwise (see *Otherwise*).................. .... Gene De Paul

I Wonder What Became Of Me? .... Harold Arlen

I'd Know You Anywhere .... Jimmy McHugh

If Dis De Race.. Harold Arlen

If I Could Have My Way ....Serge Walter

If I Could Only Read Your Mind................. Peter Tinturin

If I Didn't Love You ....Lorelei Tripper

If I Had A Million Dollars .... Matt Malneck

If I Had My Druthers (see *Druthers* and *Si Tu M Aimais*)...... ....Gene De Paul

If It Can't Be You (*Unpub*)......................Barry Manilow

If It Can't Be You (*Unpub*)................... Bernie Hanighen

If Mother Could Just See Me Now...... Robert Emmett Dolan

If Someday Comes Ever Again .... Alec Wilder

If The Moon Could Talk (*Unpub*) ....n/a

If You Build A Better Mousetrap......... Victor Schertzinger

If You Can Imagine Such A Thing (*Unpub*)................. n/a

If You Come Through............................... Rube Bloom

If You Were Mine (*Johnny Mercer & Matt Malneck*) ..... Matt ....Malneck and Johnny Mercer

I'll Be Free (*Unpub*) (*Johnny Mercer & Howard Dietz*)..... ....Henry Souvaine

I'll Be Respectable .... Harold Arlen

I'll Cry Tomorrow.. Alex North

I'll Dream Tonight .... Richard A. Whiting

I'll Get Even .... Robert Emmett Dolan

I'll Give You Three Guesses.....................Henry Mancini

I'll Hate Myself Tomorrow (*Draft Lyrics*)............Unknown

I'll Never Forgive Myself.............................Al Kaufman

I'll Tell The World................................Andre Previn

Illusion .... Johnny Mercer

I'm A Stranger In These Parts (*Unpub*).....Henry Souvaine

I'm An Old Cowhand (From The Rio Grande)................. .... Johnny Mercer

I'm Building Up For An Awful Letdown ....Fred Astaire

I'm Doin' It For Defense........................... Harold Arlen

I'm Going Back To The Farm .... Johnny Mercer

I'm Gonna Shoot Yuh............................... Harold Arlen

I'm Happy About The Whole Thing ....Harry Warren

I'm Headed For Big Things (*Saratoga*)......... Harold Arlen

I'm Like A Fish Out Of Water .... Richard A. Whiting

I'm Off The Wagon ....Hoagy Carmichael

I'm Old Fashioned (I'm Old-Fashioned) .... Jerome Kern

I'm Past My Prime (see *Past My Prime*).......Gene De Paul

I'm Shadowing You .... Blossom Dearie

I'm The Worrying Kind (*Johnny Mercer & Pinky Tomlin*)...... .... Johnny Mercer & Pinky Tomlin

I'm Too Durn Bashful ....Gene De Paul

I'm Way Ahead Of The Game .... Robert Emmett Dolan

I'm With You.. Bobby Troup

Immer Noch Einmal (see *Ca Va Exlater* and *Something's Gotta Give*).. Johnny Mercer

In A Café In Montmartre ....Joseph Meyer

In A Moment Of Weakness ....Harry Warren

In Loving Memory.................... Robert Emmett Dolan

In My Wildest Dreams.......................... Arthur Schwartz

Song Title	Composers/Collaborators
In Society	Gene De Paul
In The Back Of My Liddle Ol' Cadill-Lo-Lac *(see My Cadill-Liddle-Ol-Lac)*	Hoagy Carmichael
In The Cool, Cool, Cool Of The Evening	Hoagy Carmichael
In The Late Afternoon	Rich Barcellona
In The Mornin' Blues *(Unpub)*	Johnny Mercer
In The Valley *(see Where The Evening Sun Goes Down)*	Harry Warren
In Waikiki	Arthur Schwartz
Indian Summer	Peter Tinturin
Indiscretion	Matt Malneck
Injun Giver	Robert Emmett Dolan
International Playboy *(Instrumental)*	Johnny Mercer
Isadore Shapiro & Sons *(Unpub)*	Robert Emmett Dolan
It Had Better Be Tonight *(see Meglio Stasera)*	Henry Mancini
It Happened One Night	Gene De Paul
It Takes One To Know One *(Draft Lyrics)*	Unknown
It's A Great Big World	Harry Warren
It's A Nuisance Having You Around	Gene De Paul
It's A Typical Day *(see Typical Day)*	Gene De Paul
It's A Woman's Prerogative *(see Woman's Prerogative, A)*	Harold Arlen
It's About Time	Peter Tinturin
It's Easy When You Know How	Robert Emmett Dolan
It's Great To Be Alive	Robert Emmett Dolan
It's Out Of My Hands *(Unpub)*	Johnny Mercer
It's Somebody Else's Moon Above, Not Mine *(see Not Mine)*	Victor Schertzinger
I've Got A Heartful Of Music	Richard A. Whiting
I've Got A Lot In Common With You *(see Lot In Common With You, A)*	Harold Arlen
I've Got A Lot To Live For *(Unpub)*	Ted Helms
I've Got a One-Track Mind	Jimmy McHugh
I've Gotta Be On My Way	Eddie Miller, Hilton Lamare & M. Matlock
I've Hitched My Wagon To A Star	Richard A. Whiting
I've Nothing To Hide *(Unpub)*	Alfred Opler
I've Waited For A Waltz	Johnny Rotella

JJ

Song Title	Composers/Collaborators
J Aimerais Etre La *(see I Wanna Be Around)* *(JM & Sadie Vimmerstedt)*	Johnny Mercer & Sadie Vimmerstedt
Jack-O-Lantern	Hoagy Carmichael
Jamboree Jones	Johnny Mercer
Je T'Aime *(Commercial)*	Johnny Mercer
Jeepers Creepers	Harry Warren
Jezebel	Harry Warren
Joanna	Henry Mancini

Song Title	Composers/Collaborators
Jockey Lineup	Harold Arlen
John Henry *(Draft Lyrics)*	Unknown
Johnny Mercer's Melody *(see Stop The Presses)*	Johnny Mercer
Johnny Tiger Cues *(ASCAP Here Come The Waves)*	Johnny Green
Join The Navy *(classicalmoviemusicals.com)*	Harold Arlen
Jo-Jo The Cannibal Kid	Rube Bloom
Jubilation T. Cornpone	Gene De Paul
Julie's Dream *(Instrumental)*	Johnny Mercer
June Bride	Gene De Paul
June Comes Around Every Year	Harold Arlen
Just A Fair Weather Friend	Matt Malneck
Just A Quiet Evening	Richard A. Whiting
Just Across The Mountain	Arthur Kent
Just For Tonight	Hoagy Carmichael
Just Like A Falling Star	Ralph Bolton
Just Like Taking Candy From A Baby	Barry Manilow
Just Remember (1937)	Carl Sigman
Just Remember (1988)	Barry Manilow
Just The Letter 'Q'	Johnny Mercer
Just To Keep The Record Straight *(Draft Lyrics)*	Robert Emmett Dolan
Just To Remind You *(Unpub/Draft Lyrics)*	Howard Jackson

KK

Song Title	Composers/Collaborators
Keep A Twinkle In Your Eye	Rube Bloom
Keep Your Pigs Out Of My Potatoes *(Unpub/Draft Lyrics)*	Johnny Mercer
Keeper Of My Heart, The	Matt Malneck
Killing Sequence	Harold Arlen
Kiss And Tell *(Unpub)*	Johnny Mercer
Kiss From You, A *(see Lydia and The Virginian)*	Benny Carter
Know Where De Wind Blows *(Unpub/Lyrics in Script Only)*	Harold Arlen
Kubla's Soliloquy *(Unpub)*	Robert Emmett Dolan

LL

Song Title	Composers/Collaborators
La Valse Des Lilas *(see Once Upon A Summertime)*	Eddie Barclay & Michel Legrand
Ladies and Gentlemen	Harold Arlen
Lady On The Two-Cent Stamp, The *(Johnny Mercer & Al Dubin)*	Harry Warren
Lake Saint Mary	Louis Alter
Lalita	Harry Warren
Lament *(see Lonesome Polecat)*	Gene De Paul

Land Where The Old Dreams Go, The .... Matt Malneck

Larceny and Love .... Robert Emmett Dolan

Last Dream Home, The ....Barry Manilow

Last Laugh .... Henry Mancini, Danny Swain

Laura .... David Raskin

Lawd, I Give You My Children (see Lord, I Give You My Children) .... Bernie Hanighen

Lazy Bones.............................Hoagy Carmichael

Lazy Mood (see Love's Got Me In A Lazy Mood) ....
.... Eddie Miller

Le Meddiants De Sourires (Unpub) .... Johnny Mercer

Least That's My Opinion .... Harold Arlen

Leave The Key In The Mailbox (Draft Lyrics) .... Unknown

Leavin' Time................................... Harold Arlen

Legalize My Name................................ Harold Arlen

Legend Of Old California, The .... Harry Warren

Les Feuilles Mortes (see Autumn Leaves) ...Joseph Kosma

Les P'tits Oiseaux (see Little Birds, The)....Henry Mancini

Lesson In Jazz (Unpub)........................... Wingy Manone

Lesson In Love .... Harold Arlen

Lest You Forget (Draft Lyrics) ....Unknown

Let That Be A Lesson To You .... Richard A. Whiting

Let's Go Sailor (see Shore Leave) .... Harold Arlen

Let's Have Another On Me (see Skol) ....Henry Mancini

Let's Knock On Wood (Draft Lyrics)................. Unknown

Let's Take The Long Way Home .... Harold Arlen

Letter Of The Law, The................. Robert Emmett Dolan

Life Is What You Make It...................... Marvin Hamlisch

Life's Darkest Moment .... Robert Emmett Dolan

Life's So Complete (Johnny Mercer & Richard Himber) ...
.............................Johnny Mercer & Richard Himber

Lights of Home, The ....Lew Quadling

Like Clouds Up In The Sky (see Clouds In The Sky) ....
.... Harold Arlen

Like the Fella Once Said .... Jimmy McHugh

Li'l Abner .... Johnny Mercer

Li'l Abner Cues..................................... Johnny Mercer

Li'l Abner Selection................................. Johnny Mercer

Li'l Abner Underscore ......Gene De Paul, Joseph J. Lilley,
.... Nelson Riddle

Li'l Augie Is A Natural Man (see Augie Is A Natural (Natchural) Man and Natchural Man) .... Harold Arlen

Li'l Ol' Tune .... Johnny Mercer

Li'l Tune (Unpub) (Lyrics n/a) .... Johnny Mercer

Lim' ricks .... Harold Arlen

Liquapep... Arthur Schwartz

Little Acorns..Arthur Kent

Little Birds, The (see Les P'tits Oiseaux and Petits Oiseaux)..Henry Mancini

Little Bit O' Country (Unpub/Draft Lyrics) ....
.... Robert Emmett Dolan

Little Boats Of Barcelona, The .... Peter Tinturin

Little Cowboy Blues .... Walter Donaldson

Little Ingenue................................... Jimmie Rowles

Little Lost Dream ....Andre Previn

Little Man With The Hammer, The........ Bernie Hanighen

Little Ol' Tune...................................... Johnny Mercer

Little Old Cross-Road (Crossroad) Store ...... Peter Tinturin

Little Traveling Music, A ....Andre Previn

Living In The Used To Be (Unpub/Draft Lyrics) .Alfred Opler

Loca Illusion .... Xavier Cugat

Lock The Barn Door .... Johnny Mercer

Lonelyheart (Unpub)...................... Robert Emmett Dolan

Lonesome Polecat (see Lament) ....Gene De Paul

Long Goodbye, The .... Johnny Williams

Long Of It, The–Short Of It, The (Unpub) ....n/a

Longing..Don Borzage

Longtime, No See .... Walter Donaldson

Look At You (see Something Tells Me I'm Falling In Love)...
.... Barry Manilow

Look In The Mirror .... Allie Wrubel

Lord, I Give You My Children (see Lawd, I Give You My Children).. Bernie Hanighen

Lorna.. Mort Lindsey

Lost (see Rings Of Melody) (Johnny Mercer, Phil Ohman, and Macy O. Teetor) .... Johnny Mercer, Phil Ohman &
....Macy O. Teetor

Lost In The Sun (Unpub/Draft Lyrics) (Johnny Mercer & E.Y. Harburg) ....Henry Souvaine

Lot In Common With You, A (see I've Got A Lot In Common With You)............................... Harold Arlen

Love Held Lightly................................... Harold Arlen

Love In A Home (see You Can Tell When There's Love In A Home) .... Gene De Paul

Love In The Afternoon ....Matty Malneck

Love Is A Merry Go Round .... Rube Bloom

Love Is For The Birds (Unpub/Draft Lyrics) ...Johnny Mercer

Love Is On The Air Tonight .... Richard A. Whiting

Love Is Where You Find It (1988) ....Barry Manilow

Love Is Where You Find It (1938) (Johnny Mercer & Al Dubin)..Harry Warren

Love Like Yours (Johnny Mercer & Luiz Bonfa) ....
.... Johnny Mercer & Luiz Bonfa

Love Me With Your Heart (Unpub) ....Gilbert Martinez

Love Me, Love My Dog (Reprise)...... Robert Emmett Dolan

Love Of My Life, The .... Artie Shaw

Love Song (see Apache Love Song) .... David Raskin

Love With The Proper Stranger ....Elmer Bernstein

Love Woke Me Up This Morning................Harry Warren

Lovers In The Dark .... Gordon Jenkins

Love's Got Me In A Lazy Mood (see Lazy Mood) ....
.... Eddie Miller

Song Title	Composers/Collaborators

Luck Just Go Down (see I Feel My Luck Comin' Down)... .... Harold Arlen

Lullaby .... Harold Arlen

Lydia (see Kiss From You, A and Virginian) (Song Writer's Hall of Fame) ....Benny Carter

Lyrics On The Spot Melody (Unpub) (Johnny Mercer, Mel Blanc & Bobby Troup) ....
...................Johnny Mercer, Mel Blanc & Bobby Troup

M

Ma Belle Cherie .... Robert Emmett Dolan

Made For Each Other (Draft Lyrics).................Unknown

Magic In The Moon Light ....Lewis E. Gensler

Magic Island (Far From The Sea) ....Bernie Wayne

Make Believe Ballroom....................Al Jarvis, Leon Rene

Make Believe Ballroom Cues...........Al Jarvis, Leon Rene

Make With The Kisses ....Jimmy Van Heusen

Mama Torpedo (Draft Lyrics) .... Johnny Mercer

Mambo (Instrumental)............................ Johnny Mercer

Man In My Life, The (see Hymn) .... Harold Arlen

Man Of The Year This Week, The .... Johnny Mercer

Mandarina (see Si Tu Veux and Tangerine) ....
.... Victor Schertzinger

Mandy Is Two .... Fulton McGrath

Man's Best Friend (see Nobody Understands Me) ....
.... Johnny Mercer

Man's Favorite Sport................................Henry Mancini

Man's Gotta Fight, A .... Harold Arlen

Many, Many Ways To Skin A Cat .... Robert Emmett Dolan

March Of The Dogies, The ....Harry Warren

Mardi Gras (see While We Danced) .... Alfred Opler

Mary Ellen...Billy Vaughn

Matador...Howard Jackson

Matrimonial Stomp, The (see Stomp)..........Gene De Paul

May I Have The Pleasure Of Your Company? (see Pleasure Of Your Company, The)........................Andre Previn

Maybe You Know What I Mean .... Hoagy Carmichael

McCracken's (see Hail To MacCrackens) ... Johnny Mercer

Me and Mom Cues (ASCAP)...........................
..............................Richard De Benedictis, Hal Borne

Me And The Ghost Upstairs................. Bernie Hanighen

Meant To Tell Yuh...................Charles Dant & Al Rinker

Meddiants De Sourires Le........................ Johnny Mercer

Medium (Couldn't Get Through), The (Unpub/ Draft Lyrics) .... Bernie Hanighen

Medium, The (Draft Lyrics).............................Unknown

Meet Miss America (Johnny Mercer & Matt Malneck)......
...............................Johnny Mercer & Matt Malneck

Meet Miss Blendo.................................. Johnny Mercer

Song Title	Composers/Collaborators

Meglio Stasera (see It Had Better Be Tonight)................
....Henry Mancini

Melopee Dans La Nuit (see Blues In The Night)...............
.... Harold Arlen

Memories Will Linger (Unpub)...... Erwin Lee, Ted R. Creech

Memory Song .... Paul Weston

Men Who Run The Country, The .... Harold Arlen

Menu Song (see Bon Apetit I) .... Harold Arlen

Menu Song (see Bon Apetit II) .... Harold Arlen

Menu Song (see Bon Apetit III) .... Harold Arlen

Menu Song (see Bon Apetit IV).................... Harold Arlen

Mercer's Melody (Lyrics n/a) .... Johnny Mercer

Merci Beaucoup (Unpub/Draft Lyrics)........... Ray Navarre

Merry Andrew ....Saul Chaplin

Merry-Go-Round In The Rain ....John Green

Mexican Moon (Johnny Mercer & Charles Rinker) ....
....Walter Gross

Midnight Sun ....Sonny Burke & Lionel Hampton

Minor Nursery (Instrumental)................... Johnny Mercer

Mio Autunno (see Whistling Away The Dark)..................
....Henry Mancini

Miracle Of Christmas.............................Gilbert Martinez

Miriam (Pepsodent Commercial).............. Johnny Mercer

Mirror, Mirror, Mirror .... David Raskin

Misguided Faith (see Sanctifying Grace)....... Brian Minard

Mister In-Between (see Ac-cent-tchu-ate The Positive) ......
.... Harold Arlen

Mister Meadowlark .... Walter Donaldson

Mister Pollyanna (see Mr. Pollyanna)....Hoagy Carmichael

Mistletoe Mansion (Johnny Mercer & Vern Hansen) ....
....Vern Hansen

Moment Of Truth, The .... Robert Emmett Dolan

Moment To Moment................................Henry Mancini

Money Isn't Everything .... Robert Emmett Dolan

Montage Theme (Instrumental) .... Johnny Mercer

Month Of Sundays, A.................. Robert Emmett Dolan

Month Of Sundays, A (Repsise) ..... Robert Emmett Dolan

Moon And The Night, The (Unpub/Draft Lyrics) ....
.... Johnny Mercer

Moon Country (see Moon Country Is Home To Me) (Johnny Mercer & Hoagy Carmichael) ....
............................Johnny Mercer & Hoagy Carmichael

Moon Country Is Home To Me (see Moon Country) (Johnny Mercer & Hoagy Carmichael) ....
............................Johnny Mercer & Hoagy Carmichael

Moon Dreams.............................Chummy MacGregor

Moon In The Mulberry Tree ....George Motola

Moon River (see El Rio De La Luna) ....Henry Mancini

Moon Shines Down, The .... Emmerich Kalman

Moonlight On The Campus................ Richard A. Whiting

Moonlight Waltz...Al Rinker

Morning Star .... Jimmie Rowles

Song Title	Composers/Collaborators
Mouthful O'Jam	Archie Bleyer
Mr. Crosby Mr. Mercer *(Unpub/Draft Lyrics)*	n/a
Mr. T From Tennessee	Matt Malneck
Murder Of J. B. Markham *(Sound Recording)*	Johnny Mercer
Music From Across The Sea	Peter Tinturin
Music In The Barn	Hoagy Carmichael
Musica Di Roma	Gilbert Martinez
Musical Chairs	Johnny Mercer
Mutiny In The Nursery	Harry Warren
My Adventure	Harry Warren
My Cadill-Liddle-Ol-Lac *(see In The Back Of My Liddle Ol' Caddill-Lo-Lac)*	Hoagy Carmichael
My Crazy Old Subconscious Won't Leave You Alone *(Unpub/Draft Lyrics)*	Johnny Mercer
My Future Just Passed	Richard A. Whiting
My Home Is In My Shoes	Johnny Mercer
My Inamorata	John Williams
My Intuition	Harry Warren
My Jekyll Island *(Johnny Mercer & Ida Thomas)*	Ida Thomas
My Love For You	Stan Hoffman
My Mama Done Tol' Me *(see Blues In The Night)*	Harold Arlen
My Mamma Thinks I'm a Star	Harold Arlen
My Mother's Love	Jimmy Rowles
My Name Is Love – Fly Me	David Raskin
My New Celebrity Is You	Johnny Mercer
My Night To Howl *(see This Is My Night To Howl)*	Robert Emmett Dolan
My Old Man	Bernie Hanighen
My Piano Won't Play	Lewis E. Gensler
My Resistance Is Low	Jimmy McHugh
My Shining Hour	Harold Arlen
My Valentine Letter	Johnny Mercer
My Weight In Gold	Robert Emmett Dolan

N

Song Title	Composers/Collaborators
Namely You	Gene De Paul
Natchul Man, A *(see Augie Is A Natural (Nachural) Man and Natchural Man, A)*	Harold Arlen
Natural Man	Harold Arlen
Naughty But Nice	Harry Warren
Naughty But Nice Cues	Harry Warren
Navy Blues	Arthur Schwartz
Navy Song, The	Harold Arlen
News Chant	Harold Arlen
Night Over Shanghai	Harry Warren
Night Song	Hal Borne
Nightcap Song	Walter Donaldson

Song Title	Composers/Collaborators
Nile, The *(see Anthony And Cleopatra Theme)*	Alex North
Nine Thorny Thickets *(Rolfe Humphries – Lyricist)*	Johnny Mercer
Ninfa de Ojos Brujos *(see Beneath The Curtain Of Night) (Johnny Mercer & Alfredo Brito)*	Alfredo Brito
No Late Racehorse	Harold Arlen
No Wonder It's Banned In Boston *(Unpub/Draft Lyrics)*	Johnny Mercer
Nobody Asks Me *(Draft Lyrics)*	Unknown
Nobody Understands Me *(see Man's Best Friend, A)*	Johnny Mercer
Nodaway Road *(see On The Nodaway Road)*	Charles Bates
Not For Sale	Johnny Mercer
Not Mine *(see It's Somebody Else's Moon Above, Not Mine)*	Victor Schertzinger
Not With My Wife You Don't	John Williams
Nothing Up My Sleeve *(Unpub/Draft Lyrics)*	Archie Bleyer
Now It's A Thing Of The Past *(Unpub/Draft Lyrics)*	Alexander Fogarty

O

Song Title	Composers/Collaborators
O.K. (Okay) For T.V. *(see You're OK For TV)*	Johnny Mercer
Oasis *(Johnny Mercer & Samuel Schwartz)*	Donald Borzage
October Twilight	Josef Myrow
Oh Happy Day *(see Piu Bel Giorno)*	Gene De Paul
Oh What A Horse Was Charlie	Harry Warren
Oh What A Memory We Made	Eddy Samuels
Oh, Boy! *(Draft Lyrics)*	Unknown
Oh, I Wanna Be Back *(Draft Lyrics)*	Unknown
Oh, Johnny	Jimmy McHugh
Oh, You Kid	Harry Warren
Ohio	Johnny Mercer
Old Aunt Kate	Archie Bleyer
Old Black Magic *(see That Old Black Magic)*	Harold Arlen
Old Brown Thrush, The	Alfred J. Thieme
Old Glory	Harold Arlen
Old Guitaron	Laurindo Almeida
Old King Cole	Richard A. Whiting
Old Man Rhythm	Lewis E. Gensler
Old Man Rhythm Cues	Lewis E. Gensler
Old Man, The *(Call Him Daddy) (Unpub/Draft Lyrics)*	Johnny Mercer
Old Music Master, The	Hoagy Carmichael
Old Reporters Never Die	Gene De Paul
Old Rob Roy	Robert Emmett Dolan
Old Skipper	Hoagy Carmichael

Song Title	Composers/Collaborators
On Behalf Of The Traveling Salesmen (Dream/Play) .... Walter Donaldson	
On Behalf Of The Visiting Firemen.......	Walter Donaldson
On My Way	Andre Previn
On Our Golden Wedding Day (Unpub).........	Carl Sigman
On The Atchison, Topeka And The Santa Fe (see Petit Train Du Far West) ....Harry Warren	
On the Beam......................................	Jerome Kern
On The Bridge Of Avignon....................Lewis E. Gensler	
On The Merry Go Round (see When We Ride On The Merry Go Round) (Johnny Mercer & Earl McCarron)... .... Ralph W. Bolton	
On The Nodaway Road (see Nodaway Road) .... Charles Bates	
On The Swing Shift	Harold Arlen
On Top Of The World (see Higher Than The Moon and Higher Den De Moon)...........................	Harold Arlen
On With The Dance	Richard A. Whiting
Once Upon A Summertime (see La Valse Des Lilas)........ .... Eddie Barclay & Michel Legrand	
One For My Baby (And One More For The Road and Saloon Song)	Harold Arlen
One Step-Two Step	Harold Arlen
One Step-Two Step (Introduction)	Harold Arlen
One, Two, Three..............Phil Charig and Richard Myers	
Only If You're In Love............................	Johnny Mercer
Ooh! What You Said	Hoagy Carmichael
Oops!.....................................Harry Warren	
Opening A – Saratoga...............................	Harold Arlen
Opening B – Saratoga...............................	Harold Arlen
Opening C – Saratoga...............................	Harold Arlen
Opening D – Saratoga...............................	Harold Arlen
Opus 1..	Rich Barcellona
Otherwise (see I Wish It Could Be Otherwise)................ .... Gene De Paul	
Our Family Tree...........................	Robert Emmett Dolan
Our Man In Paradise (Unpub/Draft Lyrics) .... Johnny Mercer	
Out Of Breath (And Scared To Death Of You) .... Everett Miller	
Out Of This World....................................	Harold Arlen
Overture (Unpub).....................................	Gene De Paul
Overture (Foxy)	Robert Emmett Dolan
Overture From Top Banana	Johnny Mercer

P

Song Title	Composers/Collaborators
P. S. I Got The Job (Unpub/Draft Lyrics)	n/a
P. S. I Love You (see Aus Lauter Liebe) ...	Gordon Jenkins
Paesan	Ray Sinatra
Palsy Walsy...................................	Harold Arlen

Song Title	Composers/Collaborators
Papa Good Times (Could Be)	Leslie C. McCann
Pardon My Southern Accent	Matt Malneck
Paresseaux (see Lazy Bones)...............	Hoagy Carmichael
Parks Of Paris, The..................................	Harold Arlen
Parting Is Such Sweet Sorrow	Joseph Meyer
Parting Song	Nat Shilkret
Passe (Unpub/Draft Lyrics)	n/a
Past My Prime (see I'm Past My Prime).......	Gene De Paul
Pazzo di Te (see Fools Rush In and Where Angels Fear To Tread)	Rube Bloom
Peekaboo To You.. .... Johnny Mercer, Carl Sigman, Joseph Meyer	
Perfect Paris Night, A	Hoagy Carmichael
Person To Person (Songwriter's Hall Of Fame)............... .... Johnny Mercer	
Peter Piper	Richard A. Whiting
Petit Train Du Far West (see On The Atchison, Topeka and Santa Fe).....................................	Harry Warren
Petits Oiseaux (see Little Birds)	Henry Mancini
Petticoat High..	Harold Arlen
Petty Girl Cues..	Harold Arlen
Petty Girl Number	Harold Arlen
Petty Girl, The	Harold Arlen
Phone Call To The Past	Henry Mancini
Phony King Of England, The (see Blasted King Of England, The)....................................	Traditional
Picadilly Circus.......................................	Andre Previn
Pieds Nus Dans Le Parc (see Barefoot In The Park)........ .... Neal Hefti	
Pine Top Boogie	Johnny Mercer
Pineapple Pete.......................................	Johnny Mercer
Piney Woods, The (see Biarn's Song and Piney Woods, The)...................................	Jack Marshall
Pink Panther Theme	Henry Mancini
Pipes Of Pan, The..................................	Saul Chaplin
Piu Bel Giorno (see Oh, Happy Day)	Gene De Paul
Play With My Deck....................................	Harold Arlen
Playgirl (Draft Lyrics).....................................	Unknown
Pleasure Of Your Company (see May I Have The Pleasure Of Your Company?)	Andre Previn
Poker, The...	Harold Arlen
Politics	Robert Emmett Dolan
Pools, The...	Andre Previn
Poor Miriam	Johnny Mercer
Poor Mister (Mr.) Chisholm (Hoe Down The Bayou) .... Bernie Hanighen	
Pot and Pan Parade, The	Howard Jackson
Poupee De Satin (see Satin Doll)............................ ....Duke Ellington and Billy Strayhorn	
Power Of Love, The	Robert Emmett Dolan
Pretty Please.......................................	Walter Donaldson

Song Title	Composers/Collaborators

Progress Is The Root Of All Evil .... Gene De Paul
Prologue (Foxy) ....Robert E. Dolan
Promenade (Sweet Cries) .... Harold Arlen
Propaganda .... Johnny Mercer
P'tit Bec Un (Unpub) .... Johnny Mercer
P'tit Gars D Chez Nous .... Johnny Mercer
Put 'Em Back The Way They Wuz .... Gene De Paul
Put Every Dollar....................................... Harold Arlen

Q

Qu Ahong Ren San (see Sweetheart Tree, The)...............
....Henry Mancini
Que Le Vaya Bien (Unpub) ....Fabian Andre
Queen Of The May .... Gene De Paul
Queenie The Quick-Change Artist....... Hoagy Carmichael
Quierme Y Veras ....Jose Antonio Mendez

R

Rabbit's Foot............................... Robert Emmett Dolan
Race .... Harold Arlen
Racin' Form.. Harold Arlen
Rag Offen The Bush (see Don't That Take The Rag Off'n
The Bush?) .... Gene De Paul
Railroad Fight, The .... Harold Arlen
Rainbow (see Crawled Up A Rainbow) .... Harold Arlen
Rainbows In The Night .... David Raskin
Rainy Night .... Matt Malneck
Raise A Ruckus Tonight .... Robert Emmett Dolan
Reading The News .... Harold Arlen
Ready, Willing And Able .... Richard A. Whiting
Ready, Willing And Able Cues............ Richard A. Whiting
Reap The Harvest (see Sow The Seed And Reap The Har-
vast and Sow The Seed) .... Harold Arlen
Red Apple (Unpub)................................ Johnny Mercer
Red Sky At Morning.......................... Billy Goldenberg
Remember Dad On Mother's Day (Remember Dad).........
....Harry Warren
Respectability.............................. Robert Emmett Dolan
Revenge Is Sweet .... Robert Emmett Dolan
Ride 'em Cowboy......................... Robert Emmett Dolan
Ride Tenderfoot, Ride...................... Richard A. Whiting
Ridin' On The Moon .... Harold Arlen
Ridin' Our Luck .... Harold Arlen
Riffin' The Scotch ....Benny Goodman, Dick McDonough,
.... Fred Buck
Rings Of Melody (see Lost) (Johnny Mercer, Phil Ohman,
Macy O. Teetor) .... Johnny Mercer, Phil
................................Ohman, Macy O. Teetor

Song Title	Composers/Collaborators

Rock In A Weary Land, A .... Johnny Mercer
Rockin' After Midnight (see After Twelve O'Clock)..........
....Hoagy Carmichael
Rocky Mountain Moon .... Johnny Mercer
Rollin' In Gold........................... Robert Emmett Dolan
Rosie... Harry Warren
Roxanne (Draft Lyrics) ....Unknown
Royce Hall Blues (Sound Recording)......... Johnny Mercer
Rumba Jumps!, The .... Hoagy Carmichael
Run, Run, Run Cinderella .... Robert Emmett Dolan

S

S. S. Commodore Ebenezer McAfee the Third, The.........
.... Robert Emmett Dolan
Sad Little Rain Of China................ Robert Emmett Dolan
Sadie Hawkins Day (Ballet) .... Gene De Paul
Saloon Song (see One For My Baby And One More For
The Road) .... Harold Arlen
Salud (see Buona Fortuna and Here's Cheers).. Saul Chaplin
Sanctifying Grace (see Misguided Faith)....... Brian Minard
Sans Sousi.. Johnny Mercer
Santa Claus Came In The Spring............. Johnny Mercer
Saratoga.. Harold Arlen
Satan's Li'l Lamb (Johnny Mercer & E.Y. Harburg)..........
.... Harold Arlen
Satin Doll (see Dame Sans Coeur and Poupee De Satin).....
....Duke Ellington, Billy Strayhorn
Say It With A Kiss ....Harry Warren
Says Who? Says You, Says I....................... Harold Arlen
Scarecrow Ballet .... Gene De Paul
SCUSA (see Sorry)................................ Gene De Paul
Second Auto Theme (Instrumental) .... Johnny Mercer
Second Wind .... Harold Arlen
Seeing's Believing ....Harry Warren
Selections From Seven Brides For Seven Brothers
(Unpub).. Gene De Paul
Senorita Diaz....................................... Johnny Mercer
Sensuous Lion, The (see Frasier) .... Jimmie Rowles
Sentimental and Melancholy .... Richard A. Whiting
Seven Little Steps To Heaven (Johnny Mercer & Hilda
Gottilieb)..Lewis E. Gensler
Shake It, But Don't Break It .... Erroll Garner
Shameless .... Robert Emmett Dolan
Share and Share Alike.................. Robert Emmett Dolan
Sharp As A Tack.................................... Harold Arlen
Shooby Dooin'..Jerry Gray
Shore Leave (see Let's Go Sailor)............... Harold Arlen
Shorty George, The .... Jerome Kern
Shotgun Wedding.................................. Gene De Paul
Show Me How To Cry (Unpub) .... Johnny Mercer

Song Title	Composers/Collaborators
Show Your Linens, Miss Richardson	Bernie Hanighen
Shut Eye (see Gotta Get Some Shut Eye)	Walter Donaldson
Si Tu M Aimais (see Druthers and If I Had My Druthers)	Gene De Paul
Si Tu Veux (see Tangerine)	Victor Schertzinger
Sighs	Nestor Amaral & Laurindo Almeida
Silhouetted In The Moonlight	Richard A. Whiting
Silver Luck, Golden Luck	Harold Arlen
Simpatico (Unpub)	Joseph Meyer
Sing Me To Sleep (Unpub/Draft Lyrics)	Del Cleveland
Sing, You Son Of A Gun	Richard A. Whiting
Singin' In The Moonlight	Johnny Mercer
Singing Marine (Johnny Mercer & Al Dubin)	Harry Warren
Single-O	Donald Kahn
Sinner or Saint (Draft Lyrics)	Unknown
Skol (see Let's Have Another One On Me)	Henry Mancini
Skylark	Hoagy Carmichael
Sleep Peaceful, Mr. Used-To-Be	Harold Arlen
Sleepyhead	Lewis E. Gensler
Slippin' Around The Corner	Andre Previn
Slogan Song	Johnny Mercer
Sluefoot (see Zahnweh)	Johnny Mercer
Small Petrushka	Louis Alter
Smarty Pants	Walter Donaldson
Smile Away Each Rainy Day	Henry Mancini
Smile For The Press	Hoagy Carmichael
Snake Eyes (Unpub/Draft Lyrics)	Harold Arlen
So Many Kinds Of Love	Harold Arlen
Soap Commerical	Johnny Mercer
Sobbin' Women	Gene De Paul
Solo Un Sogno (see Dream and Ensueno)	Johnny Mercer
Some Place Of My Own	Gene De Paul
Something Tells Me	Harry Warren
Something Tells Me I'm Falling In Love (see Look At You)	Barry Manilow
Something's Gotta Give (see Ca Va Exlater and Immer Noch Einmal)	Johnny Mercer
Somethint You Gotta Find Out For Yourself	Harold Arlen
Song Of India	N. Rimsky-Korsakov
Song Of Long Ago, The	Hoagy Carmichael
Songs Of Delta Delta Delta	Johnny Mercer
Sorry (see SCUSA)	Gene De Paul
Sounds Around The House, The	Alec Wilder
Sounds Of The Night, The	Gerald Fried
South Wind (1936)	Rube Bloom
Southern Cross, The (Unpub)	Robert Emmett Dolan
Southwind (1976)	Barry Manilow
Sow The Seeds (see Reap The Harvest)	Harold Arlen
Sow The Seeds And Reap The Harvast (see Reap The Harvest)	Harold Arlen

Song Title	Composers/Collaborators
Speak To The Heart (Unpub)	Collen Tex Satterwhite
Spelled Backwards I Love You (Unpub)	Robert Emmett Dolan
Splendor Of You, The (Unpub/Draft Lyrics)	Johnny Mercer
Spring Is In My Heart Again	William Woodin
Spring Reunion	Harry Warren
Spring, Spring, Spring	Gene De Paul
Square Dance, The (Theme Of)	Robert Emmett Dolan
Square Of The Hypotenuse, The	Saul Chaplin
St. Louis Woman	Harold Arlen
Stage Door John	Andre Previn
Stage Struck	Andre Previn
Star Sounds	Johnny Mercer
Step To The Rear Of The Car, Please	Johnny Mercer
Stomp (see Matrimonial Stomp)	Gene De Paul
Stop The Presses (see Johnny Mercer's Melody) (Lyricist: Archie Lebrecht)	Johnny Mercer
Storm, The	Milt Raskin
Strawberry Lane	Jimmy McHugh
Streak Of Lightnin' (see Lightning)	Harold Arlen
Strip Polka (see Take It Off! Take It Off!)	Johnny Mercer
Sudsy Suds	Hoagy Carmichael
Summer On The Cape	Al Dero
Summer Rain	Johnny Mercer
Summer Wind	Henry Mayer
Susie For Everybody	Andre Previn
Sweater Number (see Sweater, A Sarong And A Peek-a-boo Bang, A)	Harold Arlen
Sweater, A Sarong And A Peek-a-boo Bang, A (see Sweater Number)	Harold Arlen
Sweet Little Lady Next Door	Alfred Opler
Sweet Tidings (Draft Lyrics)	Unknown
Sweetenin'(Sweetening) Water	Harold Arlen
Sweetheart Tree, The (see Qu Ahong Ren San)	Henry Mancini
Swing Into Spring	Bob Swanson
Swing Is The Thing, The	Rube Bloom
Swing Your Partner Round And Round	Harry Warren

T

Song Title	Composers/Collaborators
Ta Luv	Andre Previn
Tailgate Ramble, The	Wingy Manone
Take A Crank Letter	Robert Emmett Dolan
Take It From A Lady	Robert Emmett Dolan
Take It Off! Take It Off! (see Strip Polka)	Johnny Mercer
Talk To Me, Baby	Robert Emmett Dolan
Talkin' Glory	Harold Arlen
Talking In My Sleep	Harry Archer & Margot Millham
Tangerine (see Mandarina and Si Tu Veux)	Victor Schertzinger

Tango *(Instrumental)* .... Johnny Mercer

T'Avoir Connu *(Unpub)* .... Johnny Mercer

Technique .... Johnny Mercer

Temporarily .... Gene De Paul

Tender And True Love *(Unpub)* .... Joe Dubin

Tender Loving Care .... Ronnell Bright

Texas March *(Instrumental)* .... Johnny Mercer

Texas Millionaire *(Instrumental)* .... Johnny Mercer

Texas Romp And Square Dance .... Johnny Mercer

Texas Waltz *(Instrumental)* .... Johnny Mercer

Texas, Li'l Darlin' .... Robert Emmett Dolan

Thank You Mr. Currier, Thank You Mr. Ives *(see Bride's Wedding Day Song, A)* .... Harry Warren

Thank Your Lucky Stars *(Unpub)* .... Robert Emmett Dolan

Thanks But No Thanks *(Unpub/Draft Lyrics)* .... Johnny Mercer

Thanksgivin' .... Hoagy Carmichael

That Old Black Magic *(see Black Magic and Ce Diable Noir)* .... Harold Arlen

That'll Get It *(see History Of The Beat)* .... Johnny Mercer

That's For Sure .... Johnny Mercer

Theme From The Missouri Traveler *(see Biarn's Song and Piney Woods, The)* .... Jack Marshall

Then Suddenly .... Harold Arlen

There She Was .... Hoagy Carmichael

There's A Fella Waiting In Poughkeepsie ..... Harold Arlen

There's A Little Old House .... Richard A. Whiting

There's A Love Song *(Draft Lyrics)* .... Unknown

There's A Ring Around The Moon .... Johnny Green

There's A Sunny Side To Every Situation ..... Harry Warren

There's No Forgetting You *(Unpub/Draft Lyrics)* .... Johnny Mercer

There's Nothing Like A College Education .... Lewis E. Gensler

There's Room Enough For Us .... Gene De Paul

There's Something Mighty Peculiar Goin' On .... Gene De Paul

These Orchids .... Jerome Kern

They Talk A Different Language *(see Yodel Blues, The)* ... . Robert Emmett Dolan

They Used To Call Him Preacher *(Draft Lyrics)* .... Unknown

They're Pavin' California .... Jimmie Rowles

Third Day Rag (3rd Day Rag) *(Instrumental)* .... Johnny Mercer

Thirteenth Street Rag (13th Street Rag) .... Wingy Manone

This Is My Night To Howl *(see My Night To Howl)* .... Robert Emmett Dolan

This Is Our Day *(see This Is The Day and Dis Is De Day)* .... Harold Arlen

This Is The Day *(see This Is Our Day and Dis Is De Day)* .... Harold Arlen

This Is The Night *(Unpub/Draft Lyrics)* ..... Johnny Mercer

This Little While *(see Dis Little While)* .... Harold Arlen

This Time The Dreams On Me .... Harold Arlen

Three Guesses ....Phil Charig and Richard Myers

Three Of A Kind *(Unpub)* .... Bobby Darin

Thumbin' a Ride .... Gene De Paul

Thunderbird .... Johnny Mercer

Till It Goes Out Of Style .... Robert Emmett Dolan

Time Marches On *(Unpub)* .... Matt Malneck

Time To Smile .... Geoff Clarkson, Les Brown, J.Hill

Ting-A-Ling *(see Bad Humor Man, The)* .. Jimmy McHugh

Toastin' Sequence .... Harold Arlen

Today I Am A Glamour Girl .... Hoagy Carmichael

Tomorrow Never Comes *(Cimarron Strip TV show)* .... Morton Stevens

Tomorrow You Belong To Uncle Sam *(see Uncle Sammy)* .... Victor Schertzinger

Tonight Is Mine .... Sammy Fain

Tonight May Have To Last Me All My Life.... Don Borzage

Too Good To Be True (1967) .... George Shearing

Too Good To Be True *(Unpub/Draft Lyrics)* .... Florence Ledtwich

Too Marvellous For Words *(see Too Marvelous For Words and You're Just Too Marvelous For Words)* .... Richard A. Whiting

Too Marvelous For Words *(see Too Marvellous For Words and You're Just Too Marvelous For Words)* .... Richard A. Whiting

Top Banana .... Johnny Mercer

Top Banana Ballet .... Johnny Mercer

Toss A Song In The Deep Blue Night *(Unpub/Draft Lyrics)* .... n/a

Train Must Be Fed, The .... Harry Warren

Trav'lin Light ....Jimmy Mundy & Trummy Young

True Love *(see I Had Myself A True Love/I Wonder What Became Of)* .... Harold Arlen

Truly .... Antone Iavello

Twilight Reflections (My Reflections) *(Unpub)* .... Joseph Meyer

Twilight World .... Marian McPartland

Two Hearts Are Better Than One .... Jerome Kern

Two Of A Kind *(Johnny Mercer & Bobby Darin)* ....Johnny Mercer and Bobby Darin

Typical Day *(see It's A Typical Day)* .... Gene De Paul

U

Uncle Sammy *(see Tomorrow You Belong To Uncle Sam)* .... Victor Schertzinger

Unnecessary Town .... Gene De Paul

Until We Kiss .... Emmerich Kalman

Song Title	Composers/Collaborators

V

Valse Des Lilas (see Once Upon A Summertime) .... Eddie Barclay & Michel Legrand

Vecchio Cow Boy (see I'm An Old Cow Hand (From The Rio Grande)) .... Johnny Mercer

Velvet Night .... Michel Legrand (adapted from Mozart)

Venice In Spring (Unpub) .... Robert Emmett Dolan

Very Important Man, A (Unpub) ..... Robert Emmett Dolan

Village (Johnny Mercer & Roy Kaplan) (Unpub) .... Harold Arlen, Roy Kaplan

Vino E Rose (see Days Of Wine And Roses) .... Henry Manicini

Virginian, The (see Kiss From You, A and Lydia) (Songwriters Hall of Fame) .... Benny Carter

Vocal Selections From The Good Companions .... Andre Previn

Vocal Selections From Saratoga .... Harold Arlen

W

Wait and See .... Harry Warren

Wait For The Wagon (Wait For The Hoedown) .... Robert E. Dolan

Wait No More .... Elizabeth Firestone

Wait Till It Happens To You .... Harold Arlen

Wait Till You See Me In The Morning ..... Hoagy Carmichael

Waiter, And The Porter And The Upstairs Maid, The .... Johnny Mercer

Wait'll It Happens To You .... Harold Arlen

Wake Me When You Leave (Draft Lyrics) .... Unknown

Walkin' With My Shadow .... Bernie Hanighen

Waltz With Me (Draft Lyrics) .... Unknown

Wanted Man, A (Draft Lyrics) .... n/a

Watch A Darky Dance (Unpub/Draft Lyrics, Sound Recording) .... Peter Tinturin

Way Back In 1939 A.D. .... Hoagy Carmichael

Way It Is, The (Unpub) .... Johnny Mercer

Way Of A Maid With A Man, The (Unpub/Draft Lyrics) ... . Robert Emmett Dolan

Way To A Man's Heart, The .... Gene De Paul

We Can All Make Mistakes (Unpub/Draft Lyrics) .... Carl Sigman

We Do It On A Horse (Unpub) .... Robert Emmett Dolan

We Shall Meet To Part, No Never .... Harold Arlen

We Stayed In Love Too Long (Unpub/Draft Lyrics) .... Archie Bleyer

We Won't Worry Till Fall (Unpub/Draft Lyrics) .... Henry Souvaine

Weary Shoulders (Unpub/Draft Lyrics) ..... Henry Souvaine

Wedding Dance .... Gene De Paul

Wedding In The Spring .... Jerome Kern

Wedding Song .... Gene De Paul

Weekend (Week End) Of The Private Secretary, The .... Bernie Hanighen

Welcome Egghead (Egg-head) (see Freshman Song, The) .... Johnny Mercer

Welcome Stranger .... Johnny Mercer

We're In Wonderland (Unpub/Draft Lyrics) .... Carl Sigman

Were Those The Days? .... Johnny Mercer

We're Working Our Way Through College .... Richard A. Whiting

Whacha Sayin' Biglow (Whatcha Saying, Bigelow) .... Harold Arlen

What A Revoltin' Development This Is ...... Johnny Mercer

What Have I Done? (Johnny Mercer, Fritz Rotter & Desmond Carter) .... Walter Jurmann

What The Well Dressed World Will Wear (Draft Lyrics) .... Unknown

What Was Your Name In The States .... Robert E. Dolan

What Will I Do Without You (Johnny Mercer & Hilda Gottlieb) .... Lewis E. Gensler

Whatcha Gonna Swing Tonight? (see Bob White) .... Bernie Hanighen

What-cha Ma Call It (Whatcha-Ma-Call-It) ... Gene De Paul

Whatcha Sayin' Della? .... Harold Arlen

What'll They Think Of Next? .... Hoagy Carmichael

What's Good For General Bullmoose (see General Bullmoose) .... Gene De Paul

Wheel'Em Deal'Em (Wheel'Em ' N Deal'Em) .... Harold Arlen

When Your College Days Are Gone .... Richard A. Whiting

When A Man Loves A Woman .... Bernard D. Hanighen, ... Gordon Jenkins

When A Woman Loves A Man (Blues In The Night-Play) .... Bernie Hanighen & Gordon Jenkins

When Are We Going To Land A Broad? ..... Arthur Schwartz

When I'm A Bust In The Hall Of Fame (Draft Lyrics) .... Unknown

When I'm Out With The Belle of New York (see When You're Out With The Belle Of NY) .... Harry Warren

When Love Walks By .... Hoagy Carmichael

When October Goes .... Barry Manilow

When Sally Walks Along Peacock Alley ...... Harry Warren

When The Meadow Was Bloomin' .... Barry Manilow

When The World Was Young (Ah, The Apple Trees and Chevalier De Paris) (Johnny Mercer & Anfele Vannier) .... M. Philippe-Gerard

When We Ride On The Merry Go Round (see On The Merry Go Round) (Johnny Mercer & Earl McCarron) ... . Ralph W. Bolton

When You Are In My Arms .... Lewis E. Gensler

When You Hear The Time Signal .... Victor Schertzinger

Song Title	Composers/Collaborators
When Your College Days Are Gone....	Richard A. Whiting
When You're In Love (see Cuando Estas As Enamorad)...	Gene De Paul
When You're Out With The Belle Of New York (see When I'm Out With The Belle Of New York).....	Harry Warren
Where Angels Fear To Tread (see Fools Rush In)..	Rube Bloom
Where The Evening Sun Goes Down (see In The Valley)..	Harry Warren
Where You Looking, Della?....................	Harold Arlen
Where's The Happy Ending (Unpub/Draft Lyrics)..	Ted Helms
Which-a-way'd They Go................	Robert Emmett Dolan
While We Danced At The Mardi Gras (see Mardi Gras)....................................	Alfred Opler
Whistling Away The Dark (see Mio Autunno).................	Henry Mancini
Whistling For A Kiss (Johnny Mercer & E. Y. Harburg)..................................	Richard Myers
Who Knows (Unpub/Draft Lyrics)............	Johnny Mercer
Who, But You (Unpub)...........................	Johnny Mercer
Whoopin' And A-Hollerin'............	Robert Emmett Dolan
Who's Excited......................................	Johnny Hodges
Why Can't It Be Me?......................	Rube Bloom
Why Didn't I Tell Him? (Unpub/Draft Lyrics)..	Johnny Mercer
Why Didn't She Tell Me? (Unpub/Draft Lyrics)..	Johnny Mercer
Why Fight This?..........................	Harold Arlen
Wide Place In The Road, A................	Johnny Mercer
Wild Wild West, The........................	Harry Warren
Will O' The Wisp (Unpub).............	Robert Emmett Dolan
Willie The Wolf Of The West................	Harold Arlen and Joseph Lilley
Windmill Under The Stars....................	Jerome Kern
Windows Of Paris, The........................	Tony Osborne
Wings Over The Navy............................	Harry Warren
Winter In My Heart........................	Nat Shilkret
With My Lover Beside Me....................	Barry Manilow
With You With Me................................	Johnny Green
Without Benefit Of Clergy (Unpub/Draft Lyrics).........	n/a
Woman's Prerogative (see It's A Woman's Prerogative)..	Harold Arlen
Woman's Work Is Never Done, A................	Harold Arlen
Wonderful, Wonderful Day....................	Gene De Paul
Won't Dat Be De Blessed Day....................	Harold Arlen
Word A Day, A (see Ambiguous Means I Love You)..	Johnny Mercer
Word To The Wise Will Do, A................	Archie Bleyer
Work Hard, Love Hard............................	Harold Arlen
Working Now For Me............................	Harold Arlen
Workman's Song....................................	Harold Arlen
World Is My Apple, The....................	Richard A. Whiting

Song Title	Composers/Collaborators
World Of Maurice Chevalier, The...	Robert Emmett Dolan
World Of My Heart, The........................	Johnny Green
Would'ja For A Big Red Apple (Johnny Mercer & Everest Miller)....................................	Henry Sovaine
Wrap Yourself In Cellophane..............	Hoagy Carmichael

Y

Song Title	Composers/Collaborators
Ya'Pushin' Yo Luck, Gal...........................	Harold Arlen
Yearly Consular Ball, The........................	Johnny Mercer
Yodel Blues, The (see They Talk A Different Language)......	Robert Emmett Dolan
Yogi (Who Lost His Will Power), The.......	Jimmy McHugh
You..	Joseph Meyer
You And Your Love................................	John Green
You Best Take Lila Back............................	Harold Arlen
You Came Along (Unpub/Draft Lyrics)..	Robert Emmett Dolan
You Can Have Your Wine and Women (Draft Lyrics)..	Unknown
You Can Say That Again (You're The Difference) (Johnny Mercer & Carl Sigman)...........................	Freddie Slack
You Can Tell When There's Love In A Home (see Love In A Home)................................	Gene De Paul
You Can't Always Have What You Want......	Saul Chaplin
You Can't Lose (Unpub/Draft Lyrics)........	Johnny Mercer
You Can't Run Away From It....................	Gene De Paul
You For Me....................................	Harold Arlen
You Go Your Way................................	Johnny Mercer
You Gotta Be A Grandparent (Unpub/Draft Lyrics)..	Johnny Mercer
You Gotta Have A Slogan........................	Johnny Mercer
You Grow Sweeter As The Years Go By.......	Johnny Mercer
You Have Taken My Heart......................	Gordon Jenkins
You Know You Don't Want Me......	Robert Emmett Dolan
You Know You Don't Want Me (So Why Don't You Leave Me Alone?)................	Robert Emmett Dolan
You Must Have Been A Beautiful Baby.......	Harry Warren
You Never Miss The Water Till The Well Runs Dry (Unpub/Draft Lyrics)...........................	Peter Tinturin
You Or No One..........................	Harold Arlen
You Take After Your Mother (composed for Seven Brides For Seven Brothers but not used).......	Gene De Paul (?)
You Took The Words Right Out Of My Heart..	Johnny Mercer
You Were Never Lovelier...........................	Jerome Kern
You'll Find Out......................................	Jimmy McHugh
Young and Free..	Johnny Rotella
Your Good Will Ambassador....................	Henry Mancini
Your Heart and Mine................................	Rube Bloom
Your Heart Will Tell You So..........	Robert Emmett Dolan

Song Title	Composers/Collaborators

Your Make-Believe Ballroom *(Johnny Mercer, Leon Rene, Al Jarvis)* .... Johnny Mercer, Al Jarvis, Leon Rene

You're A Natural .... Arthur Schwartz

You're Just Too Marvelous For Words *(see Too Marvelous For Words* and *Too Marvellous For Words)* ....Richard Whiting

You're My Love *(Unpub)* .... Robert Emmett Dolan

You're OK For TV *(see O.K. For T.V.)*........ Johnny Mercer

You're So Beautiful – That .... Johnny Mercer

You're The One (For Me) .... Jimmy McHugh

You're The One (For Me) Cues .... Jimmy McHugh

Yours For Keeps ....Vernon Duke

You've Got Me This Way .... Jimmy McHugh

You've Got Me This Way (Whatta-Ya-Gonna Do About It)..... ....Jimmy McHugh

You've Got Me Where You Want Me.......... Harry Warren

You've Got Something There .... Richard A. Whiting

Z

Zahnweh *(see Sluefoot)* .... Johnny Mercer

Filmography
Johnny Mercer's Contribution to the Movies

1933

Movie	Song	Composer
Bombshell	*Lazybones*	Hoagy Carmichael
College Coach	*What Will I Do Without You (Johnny Mercer & Hilda Gottlieb)*	Lewis E. Gensler

1934

Movie	Song	Composer
The Dude Rancher	*Howdy Stranger*	Richard A. Whiting
Transatlantic Merry-Go-Round	*If I Had A Million Dollars*	Matty Malneck

1935

Movie	Song	Composer
Broadway Gondolier	*For Lovers Only (Johnny Mercer & Al Dubin)*	Harry Warren
Lazybones	*Lazybones*	Hoagy Carmichael
Old Man Rhythm	*Boys Will Be Boys – Girls Will Be Girls*	Lewis E. Gensler
	Comes The Revolution Baby	Lewis E. Gensler
	I Never Saw A Better Night	Lewis E. Gensler
	Old Man Rhythm	Lewis E. Gensler
	There's Nothing Like A College Education	Lewis E. Gensler
	When You Are In My Arms	Lewis E. Gensler
Too Beat The Band	*Eeny Meeny Meiny Mo (JM & Matt Malneck)*	Johnny Mercer & Matt Malneck
	I Saw Her At Eight o'clock (JM & Matt Malneck)	Johnny Mercer & Matt Malneck
	If You Were Mine (JM & Matt Malneck)	Johnny Mercer & Matt Malneck
	Meet Miss America (JM & Matt Malneck)	Johnny Mercer & Matt Malneck
	Santa Claus Came In The Spring	Johnny Mercer

1936

Movie	Song	Composer
Rhythm on the Range	*I'm An Old Cowhand (From the Rio Grande)*	Johnny Mercer
The CooCoo Nut Grove, *Cartoon*	*My Old Man*	Bernie Hanighen

1937

Movie	Song	Composer
For Auld Lang Syne	*Ride Tenderfoot, Ride*	Richard A. Whiting
Hollywood Hotel	*Bob White (Whatcha Gonna Swing Tonight?)*	Bernie Hanighen
	Can't Teach My Old Heart New Tricks	Richard A. Whiting
	Have You Got Any Castles, Baby?	Richard A. Whiting
	Hooray For Hollywood	Richard A. Whiting
	I'm Like A Fish Out Of Water	Richard A. Whiting
	I've Got A Heartful Of Music	Richard A. Whiting
	I've Hitched My Wagon To A Star	Richard A. Whiting
	Let That Be A Lesson To You	Richard A. Whiting
	Silhouetted In The Moonlight	Richard A. Whiting
	Sing You Son Of A Gun	Richard A. Whiting
Little Red Walking Hood, *Cartoon*	*Have You Got Any Castles, Baby? (uncredited)*	Richard A. Whiting
	Old King Cole (uncredited)	Richard A. Whiting

1937 (continued)

Movie	Song	Composer
Love Is On The Air	*Love Is On The Air Tonight*	Richard A. Whiting
Ready, Willing And Able	*Gasoline Gypsies*	Richard A. Whiting
	Handy With Your Feet	Richard A. Whiting
	Just A Quiet Evening	Richard A. Whiting
	Ready, Willing And Able	Richard A. Whiting
	Sentimental and Melancholy	Richard A. Whiting
	There's A Little Old House	Richard A. Whiting
	Too Marvelous For Words	Richard A. Whiting
	World Is My Apple, The	Richard A. Whiting
The Singing Marine	*Night Over Shanghai*	Harry Warren
	Singing Marine, The (Johnny Mercer & Al Dubin)	Harry Warren
Varsity Show	*Gasoline Gypies*	Richard A. Whiting
	Have You Got Any Castles, Baby?	Richard A. Whiting
	Let That Be A Lesson To You	Richard A. Whiting
	Love Is On The Air Tonight	Richard A. Whiting
	Moonlight On The Campus	Richard A. Whiting
	Old King Cole	Richard A. Whiting
	On With The Dance	Richard A. Whiting
	We're Working Our Way Through College	Richard A. Whiting
	When Your College Days Are Gone	Richard A. Whiting
	You've Got Something There	Richard A. Whiting

1938

Movie	Song	Composer
A Star Is Hatched, *Cartoon*	*Hooray For Hollywood*	Richard A. Whiting
Boy Meets Girl	*Boy Meets Girl*	Harry Warren
Cinderella Meets Fella, *Cartoon*	*Boy Meets Girl (uncredited)*	Harry Warren
Cowboy From Brooklyn	*Cowboy From Brooklyn*	Harry Warren
	I'll Dream Tonight	Richard A. Whiting
	I've Got A Heartful Of Music	Richard A. Whiting
	Ride Tenderfoot, Ride	Richard A. Whiting
Four's A Crowd	*Daydreaming (All Night Long)*	Harry Warren
Garden Of The Moon	*Confidentally (Johnny Mercer & Al Dublin)*	Harry Warren
	Garden Of The Moon (Johnny Mercer & Al Dublin)	Harry Warren
	Girl Friend Of The Whirling Dervish, The (JM & Al Dubin)	Harry Warren
	Lady On The Two-Cent Stamp, The (JM & Al Dubin)	Harry Warren
	Love Is Where You Find It	Harry Warren
Going Places	*Jeepers Creepers*	Harry Warren
	Mutiny In The Nursery	Harry Warren
	Oh, What A Horse Was Charlie	Harry Warren
	Say It With A Kiss	Harry Warren
Gold Diggers In Paris	*Daydreaming (All Night Long)*	Harry Warren
	My Adventure	Harry Warren
Hard To Get	*Love Is Where You Find It*	Harry Warren
	There's A Sunny Side To Every Situation	Harry Warren
	You Must Have Been A Beautiful Baby	Harry Warren
Have You Got Any Castles?, *Cartoon*	*Have You Got Any Castles, Baby?*	Richard A. Whiting
	Old King Cole	Richard A. Whiting
Jezebel	*Jezebel*	Harry Warren
Katnip Kollege *cartoon*	*Let That Be A Lesson To You*	Richard A. Whiting
Larry Clinton & His Orchestra, *Musical Short*	*Corn Pickin'*	Harry Warren
Mr. Chump	*As Long As You Live (You'll Be Dead When You Die)*	Bernie Hanighan
	Daydreaming (All Night Long)	Harry Warren
Porky's Five & Ten, *Cartoon*	*Hooray For Hollywood*	Richard A. Whiting
Woody Herman And His Orchestra, *Musical Short*	*You Must Have Been A Beautiful Baby*	Harry Warren

1939

Movie	Song	Composer
A Day At The Zoo, *Cartoon*	*Munity In The Nursery*..Harry Warren	
Babes In Arms	*Bob White (Whatcha Gonna Swing Tonight)* ....Bernie Hanighen	
Daughters Courageous	*Corn Pickin'*..Harry Warren	
	Jeepers Creepers...Harry Warren	
Each Dawn I Die	*Wings Over The Navy*...Harry Warren	
Everybody's Hobby	*Jeepers Creepers*...Harry Warren	
Fagin's Freshman, *Cartoon*	*We're Working Our Way Through College* ....Richard A. Whiting	
For Your Convenience	*You Must Have Been A Beautiful Baby* ....Harry Warren	
Fresh Fish, *Cartoon*	*You Must Have Been A Beautiful Baby* ....Harry Warren	
Jeepers Creepers	*Jeepers Creepers*...Harry Warren	
Kristopher Kolumbus, Jr., *Cartoon*	*Let That Be A Lesson To You* ....Richard A. Whiting	
Lying Lips	*You Must Have Been A Beautiful Baby* ....Harry Warren	
Naughty But Nice	*Corn Pickin'*..Harry Warren	
	Hooray For Spinach ....Harry Warren	
	I Don't Believe In Signs...Harry Warren	
	I'm Happy About The Whole Thing..Harry Warren	
	In A Moment Of Weakness ....Harry Warren	
Pied Piper Porky, *Cartoon*	*Munity In The Nursery*...Harry Warren	
Porky's Tire Trouble, *Cartoon*	*Munity In The Nursery*...Harry Warren	
Seeing Red	*Corn Pickin'*..Harry Warren	
	Jeepers Creepers...Harry Warren	
Smashing The Money Ring	*You Must Have Been A Beautiful Baby* ....Harry Warren	
Sniffles And The Bookworm, *Cartoon*	*Munity In The Nursery*...Harry Warren	
Symphony Of Swing, *Musical Short*	*Jeepers Creepers*...Harry Warren	
They Made Me A Criminal	*Cowboy From Brooklyn* ....Harry Warren	
Vicent Lopez & His Orchestra, *Musical Short*	*Ride, Tenderfoot Ride*...Richard A. Whiting	
Wings Of The Navy	*Wings Over The Navy*...Harry Warren	
Women In The Wind	*You Must Have Been A Beautiful Baby* ....Harry Warren	
Yes, My Darling Daughter	*Girl Friend Of The Whirling Dervish, The (JM & Al Dubin)*................Harry Warren	

1940

Movie	Song	Composer
A Gander At Mother Goose, *Cartoon*	*Munity In The Nursery*...Harry Warren	
Ali-Baba Bound, *Cartoon*	*Girl Friend Of The Whirling Dervish, The (JM & Al Dubin)*................Harry Warren	
Buck Benny Rides Again	*I'm An Old Cowhand (From the Rio Grande)*...................................Johnny Mercer	
Castle On The Hudson	*You Must Have Been A Beautiful Baby* ....Harry Warren	
City Of Conquest	*Corn Pickin'*..Harry Warren	
	Garden Of The Moon (Johnny Mercer & Al Dubin) ....Harry Warren	
Frances Carroll & The Coquettes, *Musical Short*	*Girl Friend Of The Whirling Dervish, The (JM & Al Dubin)*................Harry Warren	
Gambling On The High Seas	*In A Moment Of Weakness (uncredited)*..Harry Warren	
Let's Make Music	*Central Park*...Matt Malneck	
Patient Porky, *Cartoon*	*We're Working Our Way Through College* ....Richard A. Whiting	
Ride Tenderfoot, Ride	*Ride Tenderfoot, Ride*..Richard A. Whiting	
Second Chorus	*Dig It (I Ain't Hep To That Step But I'll)*.......................................Hal Borne	
	Dig You Most ....Hal Borne	
	Love Of My Life, The...Artie Shaw	
	Me And The Ghost Upstairs..Bernie Hanighen	
	Poor Mr. Chisholm (Hoe Down The Bayou).................................Bernie Hanighen	
Slap Happy Pappy, *Cartoon*	*You Must Have Been A Beautiful Baby* ....Harry Warren	
The Hardship Of Miles Standish, *Cartoon*	*You Must Have Been A Beautiful Baby* ....Harry Warren	

1940 (continued)

Movie	Song	Composer
You'll Find Out	*Don't Think It Ain't Been Charming*	Jimmy McHugh
	I'd Know You Anywhere	Jimmy McHugh
	I've Got a One Track Mind	Jimmy McHugh
	Like the Fella Once Said	Jimmy McHugh
	Ting A Ling (The Bad Humor Man)	Jimmy McHugh
	You'll Find Out	Jimmy McHugh
	You've Got Me This Way	Jimmy McHugh

1941

Movie	Song	Composer
A Coy Decoy, *Cartoon*	*Ride, Tenderfoot Ride*	Richard A. Whiting
Birth Of The Blues	*Waiter And The Porter And The Upstairs Maid, The*	Johnny Mercer
Blues In The Night	*Blues In The Night*	Harold Arlen
	Hang On To Your Lids, Kids	Harold Arlen
	In Waikiki	Arthur Schwartz
	Says Who? Says You, Says I	Harold Arlen
	This Time The Dreams On Me	Harold Arlen
	Wait'll It Happens To You	Harold Arlen
Farm Frolics, *Cartoon*	*I'm Happy About The Whole Thing*	Harry Warren
Navy Blues	*In Waikiki*	Arthur Schwartz
	Navy Blues	Arthur Schwartz
	When Are We Going To Land A Broad?	Arthur Schwartz
	You're A Natural	Arthur Schwartz
Notes To You, *Cartoon*	*Jeepers Creepers*	Harry Warren
The Wacky Worm, *Cartoon*	*Daydreaming (All Night Long)*	Harry Warren
Three Sons of O'Guns	*Jeepers Creepers*	Harry Warren
You're The One	*Gee, I Wish I'd Listened To My Mother*	Jimmy McHugh
	Honor Bright	Jimmy McHugh
	I Could Kiss You For That	Jimmy McHugh
	Strawberry Lane	Jimmy McHugh
	Yogi (Who Lost His Will Power), The	Jimmy McHugh
	You're The One (For Me)	Jimmy McHugh

1942

Movie	Song	Composer
All Through The Night	*All Through The Night*	Arthur Schwartz
	Loca Illusion	Xavier Cugat
Bugs Bunny Gets The Boid, *Cartoon*	Blues In The Night	Harold Arlen
Captain Of The Clouds	*Captains Of The Clouds*	Harold Arlen
Casablanca	*You Must Have Been A Beautiful Baby*	Harry Warren
Foney Fables, *Cartoon*	*Munity In The Nursery*	Harry Warren
I Married A Witch	*I Remember You*	Victor Schertzinger
Lady Gangster	*Blues In The Night*	Harold Arlen
My Favorite Duck, *Cartoon*	*Blues In The Night*	Harold Arlen
Star Spangled Rhythm	*He Loved Me Till The All Clear Came*	Harold Arlen
	Hit The Road To Dreamland	Harold Arlen
	I'm Doin' It For Defense	Harold Arlen
	Let's Go Sailor	Harold Arlen
	Old Glory	Harold Arlen
	On The Swing Shift	Harold Arlen
	Sharp As A Tack	Harold Arlen
	Sweater, A Sarong And A Peek, A	Harold Arlen
	That Old Black Magic	Harold Arlen
The Fleet's In	*Arthur Murray Taught Me Dancing In A Hurry*	Victor Schertzinger

1942 (continued)

Movie	Song	Composer
You'll Find Out	*Don't Think It Ain't Been Charming*	Jimmy McHugh
	Fleet's In, The	Victor Schertzinger
	I Remember You	Victor Schertzinger
	If You Build A Better Mousetrap	Victor Schertzinger
	Not Mine	Victor Schertzinger
	Tangerine	Victor Schertzinger
	Tomorrow You Belong To Uncle Sam	Victor Schertzinger
	When You Hear The Time Signal	Victor Schertzinger
The Glass Key	*I Remember You*	Victor Schertzinger
The Hard Way	*Jeepers Creepers*	Harry Warren
	You Must Have Been A Beautiful Baby	Harry Warren
The Major And The Minor	*Blues In The Night*	Harold Arlen
Yankee Doodle Dandy	*Jeepers Creepers*	Harry Warren
You Were Never Lovelier	*Audition Dance*	Jerome Kern
	Barrelhouse Beguine	Jerome Kern
	Dearly Beloved	Jerome Kern
	I'm Old Fashioned	Jerome Kern
	On the Beam	Jerome Kern
	Shorty George, The	Jerome Kern
	These Orchids	Jerome Kern
	Wedding In The Spring	Jerome Kern
	You Were Never Lovelier	Jerome Kern

1943

Movie	Song	Composer
Baby Puss, *Cartoon*	*You Must Have Been A Beautiful Baby*	Harry Warren
Cavalcade Of Dance	*Jeepers Creepers*	Harry Warren
Coming!! Snafu, *Cartoon*	*Strip Polka (Take It Off, Take It Off)*	Johnny Mercer
Cry Havoc	*Blues In The Night*	Harold Arlen
King Of The Cowboys	*I'm An Old Cowhand (From the Rio Grande)*	Johnny Mercer
Riding High	*He Loved Me Till The All Clear Came*	Harold Arlen
	Willie, The Wolf Of The West	Joseph Lilley
The Fifth-Column Mouse, *Cartoon*	*Blues In The Night*	Harold Arlen
The Home Front, *Cartoon*	*Strip Polka (Take It Off, Take It Off)*	Johnny Mercer
The Sky's The Limit	*Hangin On To You*	Harold Arlen
	Harvey, The Victory Garden Man	Harold Arlen
	I've Got A Lot In Common With You	Harold Arlen
	My Shining Hour	Harold Arlen
	One For My Baby (And One More for the Road)	Harold Arlen
They Got Me Covered	*Palsy Walsy*	Harold Arlen
True To Life	*Mister Pollyanna*	Hoagy Carmichael
	Old Music Master, The	Hoagy Carmichael
	Sudsy Suds	Hoagy Carmichael
	There She Was	Hoagy Carmichael
	When Love Walks By	Hoagy Carmichael
Youth Runs Wild	*My Shining Hour*	Harold Arlen
	One For My Baby (And One More For The Road)	Harold Arlen

1944

Movie	Song	Composer
Brother Brat, *Cartoon*	*Munity In The Nursery*	Harry Warren
Bugs Bunny And The Three Bears, *Cartoon*	*Munity In The Nursery*	Harry Warren
Government Girl	*Lazybones* (uncredited)	Hoagy Carmichael
	My Shining Hour (uncredited)	Harold Arlen

1944 (continued)

Movie	Song	Composer
You'll Find Out	*Don't Think It Ain't Been Charming*	Jimmy McHugh
Here Come The Waves	*Ac-cen-tchu-ate The Positive*	Harold Arlen
	Got To Wear You Off My Weary Mind	Harold Arlen
	Here Come The Waves	Harold Arlen
	I Owe It All To You	Harold Arlen
	I Promise You	Harold Arlen
	Let's Take The Long Way Home	Harold Arlen
	My Mamma Thinks I'm a Star	Harold Arlen
	Navy Song, The	Harold Arlen
	That Old Black Magic	Harold Arlen
	There's A Fellow Waiting In Poughkeepsie	Harold Arlen
	Woman's Work Is Never Done, A	Harold Arlen
Janie	*Wings Over The Navy*	Harry Warren
Laura	*Laura*	David Raskin
Make Your Own Bed	*Blues In The Night*	Harold Arlen
Musical Movieland, *Musical Short*	*Hooray For Hollywood*	Richard A. Whiting
Swooner Crooner, *Cartoon*	*You Must Have Been A Beautiful Baby*	Harry Warren
The Doughgirls	*Jeepers Creepers*	Harry Warren

1945

Movie	Song	Composer
Her Highness And The Bellboy	*Dream*	Johnny Mercer
Mildred Pierce	*You Must Have Been A Beautiful Baby*	Harry Warren
My Dream Is Yours	*You Must Have Been A Beautiful Baby*	Harry Warren
Out Of This World	*June Comes Around Every Year*	Harold Arlen
	Out Of This World	Harold Arlen
Radio Stars On Parade	*My Shining Hour*	Harold Arlen
	That Old Black Magic	Harold Arlen
To Have And Have Not	*How Little We Know*	Hoagy Carmichael
	"Rumba Jumps, The "	Hoagy Carmichael

1946

Movie	Song	Composer
Baby Bottleneck, *Cartoon*	*You Must Have Been A Beautiful Baby*	Harry Warren
Centennial Summer	*Two Hearts Are Better Than One*	Jerome Kern
Dirty Gertie From Harlem U.S.A.	*Blues In The Night*	Harold Arlen
Kitty Komered, *Cartoon*	*Blues In The Night*	Harold Arlen
The Blue Dahlia	*Ac-cen-tchu-ate The Positive*	Harold Arlen
The Harvey Girls	*Harvey Girls*	Harry Warren
	Hayride	Harry Warren
	In The Valley	Harry Warren
	It's A Great Big World	Harry Warren
	March Of The Dogies, The	Harry Warren
	My Intuition	Harry Warren
	Oh You Kid	Harry Warren
	On The Atchison, Topeka And The Santa Fe	Harry Warren
	Swing Your Partner Round And Round	Harry Warren
	Train Must Be Fed, The	Harry Warren
	Wait and See	Harry Warren
	Wild Wild West, The	Harry Warren
The Mouse-Merized, *Cartoon*	*You Must Have Been A Beautiful Baby*	Harry Warren

1947

Movie	Song	Composer
Dark Passage	*Too Marvelous For Words*	Richard A. Whiting
Dear Ruth	*Fine Thing!*	Robert E. Dolan
Forever Amber	*Forever Amber*	David Raskin
So You Want To Be In Pictures	*Hooray For Hollywood*	Richard A. Whiting
The Cat Concerto, *Cartoon*	*On The Atchison, Topeka And The Santa Fe*	Harry Warren
The Mild West	*I'm An Old Cowhand (From the Rio Grande)*	Johnny Mercer

1948

Movie	Song	Composer
Mr. Peabody And The Mermaid	*Caribees, The*	Robert E. Dolan
Night Song	*One For My Baby (And One More For The Road)*	Harold Arlen
Charlie Barnet – Redskin Rhumba, *Musical Short*	*Jeepers Creepers*	Harry Warren
Road House	*One For My Baby (And One More For The Road)*	Harold Arlen

1949

Movie	Song	Composer
Always Leave Them Laughing	*Clink Your Glasses*	Sammy Cahn
	You Must Have Been A Beautiful Baby	Harry Warren
Dear Wife	*Fine Thing!*	Robert E. Dolan
Make Believe Ballroom	*Your Make Believe Ballroom (JM, Al Jarvie, Leon Rene)*	JM, Al Jarvis, Leon Rene
My Dream Is Yours	*Jeepers Creepers*	Harry Warren
	You Must Have Been A Beautiful Baby	Harry Warren
Take Me Out To The Ballgame	*Baby Doll*	Harry Warren
	Hayride	Harry Warren
The Inspector General	*Happy Times*	Sylvia Fine

1950

Movie	Song	Composer
All About Eve	*That Old Black Magic*	Harold Arlen
Dark City	*That Old Black Magic*	Harold Arlen
The Petty Girl	*Ah Love Ya*	Harold Arlen
	Calypso Song	Harold Arlen
	Fancy Free	Harold Arlen
	Petty Girl, The	Harold Arlen
What's Up Doc, *Cartoon*	*Hooray For Hollywood*	Richard A. Whiting
	You Must Have Been A Beautiful Baby	Harry Warren
Young Man With A Horn	*Too Marvelous For Words*	Richard A. Whiting

1951

Movie	Song	Composer
Hare We Go, *Cartoon*	*Let That Be A Lesson To You*	Richard A. Whiting
Here Comes The Groom	*In The Cool, Cool, Cool Of The Evening*	Hoagy Carmichael
Meet Danny Wilson	*That Old Black Magic*	Harold Arlen
My Favorite Spy	*I Wind Up Taking a Fall (JM & R E Dolan)*	Johnny Mercer & Robert Emmett Dolan
Texas Carnival	*I'm An Old Cowhand (From the Rio Grande)*	Johnny Mercer

1952

Movie	Song	Composer
Everything I Have Is Yours	*Derry Down Dilly*	Johnny Green
Hare Lift, *Cartoon*	*Captains Of The Clouds*	Harold Arlen
Love Is Better Than Ever	*On The Atchison, Topeka And The Santa Fe*	Harry Warren

1952 (continued)

Movie	Song	Composer
You'll Find Out	Don't Think It Ain't Been Charming	Jimmy McHugh
She's Working Her Way Though College	We're Working Our Way Through College	Richard A. Whiting
The Belle Of New York	Baby Doll	Harry Warren
	Bachelor Dinner Song	Harry Warren
	Bride's Wedding Day Song, A	Harry Warren
	I Love To Beat The Big Bass Drum	Harry Warren
	I Wanna Be A Dancing Man	Harry Warren
	Naughty But Nice	Harry Warren
	Oops!	Harry Warren
	Seeing's Believing	Harry Warren
	When I'm Out With The Belle of New York	Harry Warren
The Devil Makes Three	On The Atchison, Topeka And The Santa Fe	Harry Warren

1953

Movie	Song	Composer
Dangerous When Wet	Ain't Nature Grand	Arthur Schwartz
	C'est La Guerre	Arthur Schwartz
	Fifi	Arthur Schwartz
	I Got Out Of The Bed On The Right Side	Arthur Schwartz
	I Like Men	Arthur Schwartz
	In My Wildest Dreams	Arthur Schwartz
	Liquapep	Arthur Schwartz
Jerry And Jumbo	On the Atchison, Topeka And The Santa Fe	Harry Warren
Macao	One For My Baby (And One More For The Road)	Harold Arlen
Remains To Be Seen	Too Marvelous For Words	Richard A. Whiting
The Eddie Cantor Story	You Must Have Been A Beautiful Baby	Harry Warren
Those Redheads From Seattle	I Guess It Was You All the Time	Hoagy Carmichael

1954

Movie	Song	Composer
Apache	Apache Love Song	David Raskin
Baby Butch, Cartoon	I Got Out Of The Bed On The Right Side	Arthur Schwartz
MGM Jubilee Overture, Musical Short	On The Atchison, Topeka And The Santa Fe	Harry Warren
Seven Brides For Seven Brothers	Bless Your Beautiful Hide	Gene De Paul
	Drat 'Em	Gene De Paul
	Goin' Co'tin	Gene De Paul
	House-Raising Dance	Gene De Paul
	June Bride	Gene De Paul
	Lament	Gene De Paul
	Lonesome Polecat	Gene De Paul
	Queen Of The May	Gene De Paul
	Selections From Seven Brides For Seven Brothers	Gene De Paul
	Shotgun Wedding	Gene De Paul
	Sobbin' Women	Gene De Paul
	Some Place Of My Own	Gene De Paul
	Spring, Spring, Spring	Gene De Paul
	When You're In Love	Gene De Paul
	Wonderful, Wonderful Day	Gene De Paul
Timberjack	He's Dead But He Won't Lie Down	Hoagy Carmichael
Top Banana	Be My Guest	Johnny Mercer
	Bi-Focal Fred	Johnny Mercer
	Dog Is Man's Best Friend, A	Johnny Mercer
	Elevator Song	Johnny Mercer

1954 (continued)

Movie	Song	Composer
	Everybody Is Your Partner In New York	Johnny Mercer
	Girl Of All Nations	Johnny Mercer
	Hail To MacCrackens	Johnny Mercer
	Havin' A Ball	Johnny Mercer
	I Fought Every Step Of The Way	Johnny Mercer
	I Know Your Kiss By Heart	Johnny Mercer
	Man Of The Year This Week	Johnny Mercer
	Meet Miss Blendo	Johnny Mercer
	My Home Is In My Shoes	Johnny Mercer
	Nobody Understands Me	Johnny Mercer
	O.K. For T.V.	Johnny Mercer
	Only If Your In Love	Johnny Mercer
	Overture From Top Banana	Johnny Mercer
	Sans Sousi	Johnny Mercer
	Senorita Diaz	Johnny Mercer
	Slogan Song	Johnny Mercer
	Soap Commercial	Johnny Mercer
	Step To The Rear Of The Car, Please	Johnny Mercer
	That's For Sure	Johnny Mercer
	Top Banana	Johnny Mercer
	Were Those The Days?	Johnny Mercer
	What A Revoltin' Development This Is	Johnny Mercer
	Word A Day, A (Ambiguous Means I Love You)	Johnny Mercer
	You Gotta Have A Slogan	Johnny Mercer
	You're So Beautiful	Johnny Mercer
Young At Heart	*One For My Baby (And One More For The Road)*	Harold Arlen

1955

Movie	Song	Composer
Daddy Long Legs	*Blues Theme, Instrumental*	Johnny Mercer
	Carnival In Rio, Ballet	Johnny Mercer
	C-A-T Spells Cat	Johnny Mercer
	Celestial Caliope, Instrumental	Johnny Mercer
	Daddy Long Legs	Johnny Mercer
	Dancing Through Life	Johnny Mercer
	Dream	Johnny Mercer
	First Auto Theme, Instrumental	Johnny Mercer
	First Chinese Theme, Instrumental	Johnny Mercer
	Guardian Angel	Johnny Mercer
	Hare Piece, Instrumental	Johnny Mercer
	History Of The Beat (That'll Get It)	Johnny Mercer
	Hong Kong Café, Instrumental	Johnny Mercer
	International Playboy, Instrumental	Johnny Mercer
	Julie's Dream, Instrumental	Johnny Mercer
	Mambo, Instrumental	Johnny Mercer
	Minor Nursery, Instrumental	Johnny Mercer
	Montage Theme, Instrumental	Johnny Mercer
	Second Auto Theme, Instrumental	Johnny Mercer
	Sluefoot (Zanhnweh)	Johnny Mercer
	Something's Gotta Give	Johnny Mercer
	Tango, Instrumental	Johnny Mercer
	Texas March, Instrumental	Johnny Mercer
	Texas Millionaire, Instrumental	Johnny Mercer
	Texas Romp And Square Dance	Johnny Mercer
	Texas Waltz, Instrumental	Johnny Mercer
	Third Day Rag, Instrumental	Johnny Mercer

1955 (continued)

Movie	Song	Composer
	Thunderbird	Johnny Mercer
	Welcome Egghead (Freshman Song, The)	Johnny Mercer
I'll Cry Tomorrow	*I'll Cry Tomorrow*	Alex North
That's Life	*Art Of Conservation Has Declined, The*	Alan Bergman
	Dancing Through Life	Johnny Mercer
The Benny Goodman Story	*And The Angels Sing*	Ziggy Elman

1956

Movie	Song	Composer
Autumn Leaves	*Autumn Leaves*	Joseph Kosma
Bus Stop	That Old Black Magic	Harold Arlen
Hilda Crane	*Rainbows In The Night*	David Raskin
That Certain Feeling	*Hit The Road To Dreamland*	Harold Arlen
The Eddie Duchin Story	*You Must Have Been A Beautiful Baby*	Harry Warren
You Can't Run Away From It	*Howdy, Friends And Neighbors*	Gene De Paul
	It Happened One Night	Gene De Paul
	Old Reporters Never Die	Gene De Paul
	Scarecrow Ballet	Gene De Paul
	Temporarily	Gene De Paul
	Thumbin' A Ride	Gene De Paul
	Whatcha-ma-call It	Gene De Paul
	You Can't Run Away From It	Gene De Paul

1957

Movie	Song	Composer
Bernardine	*Bernardine*	Johnny Mercer
	Technique	Johnny Mercer
Deep Adventure	*You Must Have Been A Beautiful Baby*	Harry Warren
Kronos	*Something's Gotta Give*	Johnny Mercer
Love In The Afternoon	*Ariane*	Matt Malneck
	Love In The Afternoon	Matt Malneck
Spring Reunion	*Spring Reunion*	Harry Warren
The Missouri Traveler	*Piney Woods, The (Biarn's Song)*	Jack Marshal
The Unholy Wife	*One For My Baby (And One More For The Road)*	Harold Arlen

1958

Movie	Song	Composer
Merry Andrew	*Buona Fortuna (Here's Cheers/Salud)*	Saul Chaplin
	Charmed Existence, A	Saul Chaplin
	Chin Up, Stout Fellow	Saul Chaplin
	Everything Is Tickety-Boo	Saul Chaplin
	Pipes Of Pan, The	Saul Chaplin
	Square Of The Hypotenuse, The	Saul Chaplin
	You Can't Always Have What You Want	Saul Chaplin
Senior Prom	*That Old Black Magic*	Harold Arlen

1959

Movie	Song	Composer
Li'l Abner, *Play (1956)*	*Country's In The Very Best of Hands, The*	Gene De Paul
	Don't That Take The Rag Off'n The Bush	Gene De Paul
	Finale From Li'l Abner	Gene De Paul
	General Bullmoose (What's Good For)	Gene De Paul
	High Society	Gene De Paul

1959 (continued)

Movie	Song	Composer
	I Wish It Could Be Otherwise	Gene De Paul
	If I Had My Druthers	Gene De Paul
	I'm Too Durn Bashful	Gene De Paul
	In Society	Gene De Paul
	It's A Nuisance Having You Around	Gene De Paul
	It's A Typical Day	Gene De Paul
	Jubilation T. Cornpone	Gene De Paul
	Love In A Home	Gene De Paul
	Matrimonial Stomp	Gene De Paul
	Namely You	Gene De Paul
	Oh, Happy Day	Gene De Paul
	Past My Prime (I'm Way Past My Prime)	Gene De Paul
	Progress Is The Root Of All Evil	Gene De Paul
	Put Them Back The Way They Wuz	Gene De Paul
	There's Room Enough For Us	Gene De Paul
	There's Something Mighty Peculiar Goin' On	Gene De Paul
	Unnecessary Town	Gene De Paul
	Way To A Man's Heart, The	Gene De Paul
	Wedding Song	Gene De Paul
The FBI Story	Jeepers Creepers	Harry Warren

1960

Movie	Song	Composer
The Facts Of Life	Facts Of Life, The	Johnny Mercer
Pepe	Hooray For Hollywood	Richard A. Whiting

1961

Movie	Song	Composer
Breakfast At Tiffany's	Moon River	Henry Mancini
Hatari	Just For Tonight	Hoagy Carmichael

1962

Movie	Song	Composer
Days Of Wine And Roses	Days Of Wine And Roses	Henry Mancini
How the West Was Won	Raise A Ruckus Tonight	Robert E. Dolan
	Wait For The Wagon (Wait For The Hoedown)	Robert E. Dolan
	What Was Your Name In The States?	Robert E. Dolan
Mr. Hobbs Takes A Vacation	Cream Puff	Henry Mancini
Something's Got To Give	Something's Gotta Give	Johnny Mercer

1963

Movie	Song	Composer
Charade	Charade	Henry Mancini
Cleopatra	Nile, The	Alex North
Love With The Proper Stranger	Love With The Proper Stranger	Elmer Bernstein
The Nutty Professor	That Old Black Magic	Harold Arlen
Who's Been Sleeping In My Bed	Tangerine	Victor Schertzinger

1964

Movie	Song	Composer
Man's Favorite Sport	Man's Favorite Sport	Henry Mancini
Scorpio Rising	Fools Rush In	Rube Bloom

1964 (continued)

Movie	Song	Composer
The Americanization Of Emily	*Emily*	Johnny Mandel
The Pink Panther	*It Had Better Be Tonight*	Henry Mancini
	Pink Panther Theme	Henry Mancini

1965

Movie	Song	Composer
Johnny Tiger	*World Of The Heart, The*	Johnny Green
The Cabinet Of Caligari	*Sounds Of The Night, The*	Gerald Fried
The Great Race	*Get A Horse*	Henry Mancini
	He Shouldn't-a, Hadn't-a, Oughtn't-a Swang On Me!	Henry Mancini
	Sweetheart Tree, The	Henry Mancini

1966

Movie	Song	Composer
Alvarez Kelly	*Ballad Of Alvarez Kelly, The*	John Green
Big Hand For The Little Lady	*Mirror, Mirror, Mirror*	David Raskin
Cimarron Strip	*Tomorrow Never Comes*	Morton Stevens
Moment to Moment	*Moment To Moment*	Henry Mancini
Not With My Wife You Don't	*Big Beautiful Ball, A*	John Williams
	My Inamorata	John Williams
	Not With My Wife You Don't	John Williams
The Swinger	*That Old Black Magic*	Harold Arlen

1967

Movie	Song	Composer
Barefoot In The Park	*Barefoot In The Park*	Neal Hefti
Rosie	*Rosie*	Harry Warren
The Swinger	*That Old Black Magic*	Harold Arlen

1968

Movie	Song	Composer
Faces	*Strip Polka (Take It Off, Take It Off)*	Johnny Mercer
The Brotherhood	*Moon River*	Henry Mancini

1970

Movie	Song	Composer
Darling Lili	*Darling Lili*	Henry Mancini
	Girl In No Man's Land, The	Henry Mancini
	I'll Give You Three Guesses	Henry Mancini
	Little Birds, The	Henry Mancini
	Skal (Let's Have Another One On Me)	Henry Mancini
	Smile Away Each Rainy Day	Henry Mancini
	Whistling Away The Dark	Henry Mancini
	Your Good Will Ambassador	Henry Mancini

1971

Movie	Song	Composer
Kotch	*Life is What You Make It*	Marvin Hamlisch
What's The Matter With Helen	*Goody Goody (Johnny Mercer & Matt Malneck)*	Johnny Mercer & Matt Malneck

1972

Movie	Song	Composer
Those Days Before The Way	*October Twilight*	Joseph Myrow

1973

Movie	Song	Composer
Class of '44	*Blues In The Night*	Harold Arlen
Robin Hood	*Phony King Of England, The*	Traditional
The Long Goodbye	*Long Goodbye, The*	Johnny Williams

1974

Movie	Song	Composer
That's Entertainment	*On The Atchison, Topeka And The Santa Fe*	Harry Warren
The Conservation	*I Remember You*	Victor Schertzinger
The Parallax View	*Moon River*	Henry Mancini

1975

Movie	Song	Composer
The Day Of The Locust	*Jeepers Creepers*	Harry Warren

1976

Movie	Song	Composer
That's Entertainment, Part II	*I Wanna Be A Dancin' Man*	Harry Warren

1978

Movie	Song	Composer
Sexette	*Hooray For Hollywood*	Richard A. Whiting
The Cheap Detective	*Jeepers Creepers*	Harry Warren

1979

Movie	Song	Composer
Head Over Heels	*Skylark*	Hoagy Carmichael
Real Life	*Something's Gotta Give*	Johnny Mercer

1980

Movie	Song	Composer
Caboblanco	*Tangerine*	Victor Schertzinger

1982

Movie	Song	Composer
An Officer And A Gentleman	*Moon River*	Henry Mancini
Best Friends	*Jeepers Creepers*	Harry Warren
Frances	*Jeepers Creepers*	Harry Warren
Some Kind of Hero	*Moon River*	Henry Mancini

1983

Movie	Song	Composer
Star 80	*Hit The Road To Dreamland*	Harold Arlen
	That Old Black Magic	Harold Arlen
The King of Comedy	*Come Rain Or Come Shine*	Harold Arlen

1984

Movie	Song	Composer
Best Defense	*Moon River*	Henry Mancini
Friday The 13th: The Final Chapter	*Tangerine*	Victor Schertzinger
Pope Of Greenwich Village	*Summer Wind*	Henry Mayer
Star Trek III	*I Remember You*	Victor Schertzinger
	Tangerine	Victor Schertzinger
	That Old Black Magic	Harold Arlen

1985

Movie	Song	Composer
Fletch	*Moon River*	Henry Mancini
Summer Rental	*Tangerine*	Victor Schertzinger
Target	*That Old Black Magic*	Harold Arlen
That's Dancing	*On The Atchison, Topeka And The Santa Fe*	Harry Warren

1986

Movie	Song	Composer
Hannah And Her Sisters	*I'm Old Fashioned*	Jerome Kern
Off Beat	*Moon River*	Henry Mancini

1987

Movie	Song	Composer
In The Mood	*Dream*	Johnny Mercer
Innerspace	*I'm An Old Cowhand (From The Rio Grande)*	Johnny Mercer
Ishtar	*One For My Baby (And One More For The Road)*	Harold Arlen
Poor Little Rich Girl, *TV Movie*	*You Must Have Been A Beautiful Baby*	Harry Warren

1988

Movie	Song	Composer
Bull Durham	*When A Man Loves A Woman*	Bernie Hanighen, Gordon Jenkins
Rocket Gibraltar	*I'm Old Fashioned*	Jerome Kern
	Shorty George, The	Jerome Kern
The Presido	*Moon River*	Henry Mancini
	Tangerine	Victor Schertzinger
	That Old Black Magic	Harold Arlen

1989

Movie	Song	Composer
Cousins	*Tangerine*	Victor Schertzinger
Loverboy	*I Wanna Be Around (JM & Sadie Vimmerstedt)*	Johnny Mercer & Sadie Vimmerstedt
Man Against The Mob: Chinatown Murders,*TV Movie*	*Come Rain Or Come Shine*	Harold Arlen
New York Stories	*That Old Black Magic*	Harold Arlen

1990

Movie	Song	Composer
Alice	*I Remember You*	Victor Schertzinger
Alligator Eyes	*Lazybones*	Hoagy Carmichael
Arachnophobia	*Summer Wind*	Henry Mayer
Days Of Thunder	*Moon River*	Henry Mancini
Funny About Love	*I Remember You*	Victor Schertzinger
	You Must Have Been A Beautiful Baby	Harry Warren

1990 (continued)

Movie	Song	Composer
Mr. And Mrs. Bridge	*Jeepers Creepers*	Harry Warren
	Rumba Jumps, The	Hoagy Carmichael
The Freshman	*I Wanna Be Around (JM & Sadie Vimmerstedt)*	Johnny Mercer & Sadie Vimmerstedt
White Hunter Black Heart	*Satin Doll*	Duke Ellington, Billy Strayhorn

1991

Movie	Song	Composer
Born To Ride	*Too Marvelous For Words*	Richard A. Whiting
Bugsy	*Ac-cen-tchu-ate The Positive*	Harold Arlen
	Come Rain Or Come Shine	Harold Arlen
	Fools Rush In	Rube Bloom
Dead Again	*Tangerine*	Victor Schertzinger
For The Boys	*Girl Friend Of The Whirling Dervish, The (JM & Al Dubin)*	Harry Warren
Guilt By Suspicion	*Jeepers Creepers*	Harry Warren
My Girl	*One For My Baby (And One More For The Road)*	Harold Arlen
The Naked Gun: 2½	*Satin Doll*	Duke Ellington, Billy Strayhorn"
	Tangerine	Victor Schertzinger

1992

Movie	Song	Composer
Blue Ice	*This Time The Dream's On Me*	Harold Arlen
Class Act	*Jeepers Creepers*	Harry Warren
Cool World	*That Old Black Magic*	Harold Arlen
Innocent Blood	*That Old Black Magic*	Harold Arlen
Ruby	*Blues In The Night*	Harold Arlen
	Day In, Day Out	Rube Bloom
School Ties	*That Old Black Magic*	Harold Arlen
The Mighty Ducks	*Ac-cen-tchu-ate The Positive*	Harold Arlen

1993

Movie	Song	Composer
Boiling Point	*Dream*	Johnny Mercer
Mad Dog and Glory	*That Old Black Magic*	Harold Arlen
Rich In Love	*Skylark*	Hoagy Carmichael
Sleepless In Seattle	*Jeepers Creepers*	Harry Warren
The Man Without A Face	*Moon River*	Henry Mancini
Wilder Napalm	*Moon River*	Henry Mancini

1994

Movie	Song	Composer
Backbeat	*I Remember You*	Victor Schertzinger
Bad Girls	*You Must Have Been A Beautiful Baby*	Harry Warren
Cobb	*That Old Black Magic*	Harold Arlen
Cops and Robbersons	*One For My Baby (And One More For The Road)*	Harold Arlen
Radioland Murders	*And The Angels Sing*	Ziggy Elman
	Love Is On The Air Tonight	Richard A. Whiting
	That Old Black Magic	Harold Arlen
The Little Rascals	*You Must Have Been A Beautiful Baby*	Harry Warren
The Scout	*I Wanna Be Around (Johnny Mercer & Sadie Vimmerstedt)*	Johnny Mercer & Sadie Vimmerstedt

1995

Movie	Song	Composer
Destiny Turns On The Radio	*That Old Black Magic*	Harold Arlen
Forget Paris	*Blues In The Night*	Harold Arlen
Leaving Las Vegas	*Come Rain Or Come Shine*	Harold Arlen
Outbreak	*Days Of Wine And Roses*	Henry Mancini
Sabrina	*I Remember You*	Victor Schertzinger
The Net	*Moon River*	Henry Mancini
Things to Do In Denver When You're Dead	*Ac-cen-tchu-ate The Positive*	Harold Arlen

1996

Movie	Song	Composer
Michael	*Dream*	Johnny Mercer
	I Thought About You	Jimmy Van Heusen
Mrs. Winterbourne	*Ac-cen-tchu-ate The Positive*	Harold Arlen
The Long Kiss Goodbye	*Long Goodbye, The*	John Williams

1997

Movie	Song	Composer
Addicted To Love	*Autumn Leaves*	Joseph Kosma
Breaking Up	*Come Rain Or Come Shine*	Harold Arlen
Déjà Vu	*Dearly Beloved*	Jerome Kern
L.A. Confidential	*Ac-cen-tchu-ate The Positive*	Harold Arlen
	Hit The Road To Dreamland	Harold Arlen
Midnight In The Garden Of Good And Evil	*And The Angels Sing*	Ziggy Elman
	Autumn Leaves	Joseph Kosma
	Come Rain Or Come Shine	Harold Arlen
	Days Of Wine And Roses	Henry Mancini
	Dream	Johnny Mercer
	Early Autumn	"Ralph Burns, Woody Herman"
	Fools Rush In	Rube Bloom
	I Wanna Be Around (JM & Sadie Vimmerstedt)	Johnny Mercer & Sadie Vimmerstedt
	I'm An Old Cowhand (From The Rio Grande)	Johnny Mercer
	In The Cool, Cool, Cool Of The Evening	Hoagy Carmichael
	Jeepers Creepers	Harry Warren
	Laura	David Raskin
	P. S. I Love You	Gordon Jenkins
	Skylark	Hoagy Carmichael
	Tangerine	Victor Schertzinger
	That Old Black Magic	Harold Arlen
	This Time The Dreams On Me	Harold Arlen
	Too Marvelous For Words	Richard A. Whiting
The Devil's Advocate	*Days Of Wine And Roses*	Henry Mancini
	Moment To Moment	Henry Mancini

1998

Movie	Song	Composer
Buffalo '66	*Fools Rush In*	Rube Bloom
Celebrity	*Tangerine*	Victor Schertzinger
City Of Angels	*That Old Black Magic*	Harold Arlen
Why Do Fools Fall In Love	*Goody Goody (Johnny Mercer & Matt Malneck)*	Johnny Mercer & Matt Malneck
You've Got Mail	*Dream*	Johnny Mercer

1999

Movie	Song	Composer
Analyze This	*You Must Have Been A Beautiful Baby*	Harry Warren
Best Laid Plans	*Glow Worm*	Paul Lincke
Blast From the Past	*Ac-cen-tchu-ate The Positive*	Harold Arlen
	That Old Black Magic	Harold Arlen
Final Rinse	*Moon River Cha Cha*	Henry Mancini
Girl Interrupted	*Moon River*	Henry Mancini
Mad Cows	*Lazybones*	Hoagy Carmichael
Paperback Hero	*I Remember You*	Victor Schertzinger
Simply Irresistible	*That Old Black Magic*	Harold Arlen
Summer of Sam	*Come Rain Or Come Shine*	Harold Arlen
The Big Kahuna	*Charade*	Henry Mancini
The Other Sister	*Come Rain Or Come Shine*	Harold Arlen
The Out Of Towners	*That Old Black Magic*	Harold Arlen

2000

Movie	Song	Composer
The Adventures of Rocky and Bullwinkle	*Hooray For Hollywood*	Richard A. Whiting
The Whole Nine Yards	*Autumn Leaves*	Joseph Kosma
What Women Want	*Something's Got To Give*	Johnny Mercer
	Too Marvelous For Words	Richard A. Whiting

2001

Movie	Song	Composer
Jeepers Creepers	*Peekaboo (Johnny Mercer, Carl Sigman, Joseph Meyer)*	Harry Warren
Jeepers Creepers	*Jeepers Creepers*	Harry Warren
Kate And Leopold	*Moon River*	Henry Mancini
Marilyn Monroe, The Final Days, *Documentary*	*Something's Got To Give*	Johnny Mercer
Ocean's Eleven	*Blues In The Night*	Harold Arlen
	Moon River	Henry Mancini
Pearl Harbor	*Blues In The Night*	Harold Arlen
	Jeepers Creepers	Harry Warren
Sidewalks Of New York	Autumn Leaves	Joseph Kosma
Something's Got To Give	*Something's Got To Give*	Johnny Mercer
The Anniversary Party	*Charade*	Henry Mancini
The Majestic	*I Remember You*	Victor Schertzinger
The Score	*Autumn Leaves*	Joseph Kosma

2002

Movie	Song	Composer
High Crimes	*Autumn Leaves*	Joseph Kosma
Hollywood Ending	*Hooray For Hollywood*	Richard A. Whiting
Minority Report	*Moon River*	Henry Mancini
The Truth About Charlie	*Charade*	Henry Mancini

2003

Movie	Song	Composer
Charlie's Angels: Full Throttle	*Hooray For Hollywood*	Richard A. Whiting
House of 1,000 Corpses	*I Remember You*	Victor Schertzinger
How To Lose A Guy In 10 Days	*Moon River*	Henry Mancini
	That Old Black Magic	Harold Arlen
Jeepers Creepers II	*Jeepers Creepers*	Harry Warren

2003 (continued)

Movie	Song	Composer
Matchstick Men	*Summer Wind*	Henry Mayer
Mona Lisa Smile	*The Glow Worm*	Paul Lincke
My House In Umbria *TV Movie*	*Too Marvelous For Words*	Richard A. Whiting
Paycheck	*I Remember You*	Victor Schertzinger
Seabiscuit	*If I Had A Million Dollars*	Matt Malneck
Stuck on You	*Moon River*	Henry Mancini

2004

Movie	Song	Composer
Alfie	*In The Cool, Cool, Cool Of The Evening*	Hoagy Carmichael
Beyond the Sea	*Charade*	Henry Mancini
Shall We Dance	*Moon River*	Henry Mancini
The Last Shot	*Ac-cen-tchu-ate The Positive*	Harold Arlen

2005

Movie	Song	Composer
Elizabethtown	*Moon River*	Henry Mancini
Good Night, and Good Luck	*One For My Baby (And One More For The Road)*	Harold Arlen
Mrs. Henderson Presents	*Goody Goody (Johnny Mercer & Matt Malneck)*	Matt Malneck
No Direction Home: Bob Dylan, Documentary	*Ac-cen-tchu-ate The Positive*	Harold Arlen
The Notorious Bettie Page	*Goody Goody (Johnny Mercer & Matt Malneck)*	Matt Malneck

2006

Movie	Song	Composer
For Your Consideration	*Hooray For Hollywood*	Richard A. Whiting
Invincible	*One For My Baby (And One More For The Road)*	Harold Arlen
Marie Antoinette	*Fools Rush In*	Rube Bloom
Take the Lead	*Moon River*	Henry Mancini
The Good Shepherd	*Come Rain Or Come Shine*	Harold Arlen
	Fools Rush In	Rube Bloom

2007

Movie	Song	Composer
Mama's Boy	*Too Marvelous for Words*	Richard A. Whiting
Midnight Son	*Midnight Son*	Sonny Burke & Lionel Hampton
P. S. I Love You	*P. S. I Love You*	Gordon Jenkins
Reign Over Me	*I'm Old Fashioned*	Jerome Kern
The Savages	*Two of a Kind (Johnny Mercer & Bobby Darin)*	Johnny Mercer & Bobby Darin
The Water Horse	*Goody, Goody (Johnny Mercer & Matt Malneck)*	Matt Malneck
What Love Is	*One For My Baby (And One More For The Road)*	Harold Arlen

2008

Movie	Song	Composer
Before the Rains	*I'm An Old Cowhand (From The Rio Grande)*	Johnny Mercer
Miss Pettigrew Lives For A Day	*Dream*	Johnny Mercer

Johnny Mercer's Songs
in Theatrical Productions

Year
Theatrical Productions/Shows
Song ....Composer

1930
Garrick Gaieties
Out Of Breath...Everett Miller
   (And Scared To Death Of You)

Tattle Tales
   Another Case of Blues ....Richard Myers

The Pajama Lady
Down Through The Ages.....Phil Charig and Richard Myers
One, Two, Three ....Phil Charig and Richard Myers
Three Guesses....................Phil Charig and Richard Myers

1931
Paris In The Spring (Show)
 Don't Ask Too Much Of Love..............Emmerich Kalman
Moon Shines Down, The ....Emmerich Kalman
Until We Kiss......................................Emmerich Kalman
What Have I Done? ....Emmerich Kalman

1932
Americana
Satan's Li'l Lamb (Johnny Mercer & E. Y. Harburg) ....
.... Harold Arlen
Whistling For A Kiss (Johnny Mercer & E. Y. Harburg)......
.... Richard Myers
Wouldja For A Big Red Apple (JM & Everest Miller) ....
.... Henry Sovaine

Ballyhoo of '32
Falling Off The Wagon (Johnny Mercer
   & E. Y. Harburg) .... Lewis Gensler

1936
Blackbirds of 1936 (England)
Dixie Isn't Dixie Anymore ....Rube Bloom
I Knew ....Rube Bloom
Jo-Jo The Cannibal Kid.................................Rube Bloom
Keep A Twinkle In Your Eye ....Rube Bloom
Swing Is The Thing, The ....Rube Bloom
Your Heart and Mine....................................Rube Bloom

Year
Theatrical Productions/Shows
Song ....Composer

1939
Lew Leslie's Blackbirds of 1939
Dixie Isn't Dixie Anymore ....Rube Bloom
I Knew ....Rube Bloom
Jo-Jo The Cannibal Kid.................................Rube Bloom
Keep A Twinkle In Your Eye ....Rube Bloom
Your Heart and Mine....................................Rube Bloom

Swingin' The Dream
Jeepers Creepers ....Harry Warren

1940
Walk With Music (Three After Three)
Break It Up, Cinderella ....Hoagy Carmichael
Darn Clever These Chinee...................Hoagy Carmichael
Even If I Say It Myself ....Hoagy Carmichael
Everything Happens To Me...................Hoagy Carmichael
Friend Of The Family ....Hoagy Carmichael
Greetings Gate...................................Hoagy Carmichael
How Nice For Me (Reprise) ....Hoagy Carmichael
I Walk With Music ....Hoagy Carmichael
I Walk With Music (Reprise)..................Hoagy Carmichael
Ooh, What You Said ....Hoagy Carmichael
Smile For The Press ....Hoagy Carmichael
The Rhumba Jumps ....Hoagy Carmichael
Today I Am A Glamour Girl ....Hoagy Carmichael
Today I Am A Glamour Girl (Reprise)....Hoagy Carmichael
Wait 'Till You See Me In The Morning ... Hoagy Carmichael
Way Back In 1939 A.D. ....Hoagy Carmichael
What'll They Think Of Next.................Hoagy Carmichael

1946
St. Louis Woman
Any Place I Hang My Hat Is Home ....Harold Arlen
Cakewalk Walk Your Lady ....Harold Arlen
Chinquapin Bush ....Harold Arlen
Come On, Li'l Augie ....Harold Arlen
Come Rain, Come Shine ....Harold Arlen
Come Rain, Come Shine (Reprise) ....Harold Arlen
Funeral Scene - A Prelude.........................Harold Arlen
I Feel My Luck Comin' Down ....Harold Arlen
I Had Myself A True Love ....Harold Arlen

1946 (continued)

It's A Woman's Prerogative ....Harold Arlen
Least That's My Opinion ....Harold Arlen
Leavin' Time ....Harold Arlen
Legalize My Name......................................Harold Arlen
Li'l Augie Is A Natural Man (Sweeten' Water) ...Harold Arlen
Lullaby ....Harold Arlen
Racin' Form..Harold Arlen
Ridin' On The Moon ....Harold Arlen
Sleep Peaceful (Mr. Used-To-Be) ....Harold Arlen
We Shall Meet To Part, No Never ....Harold Arlen

1949

Messr. **Marco Polo** (Show–Never Produced)

Best Love Of All ....Robert Emmett Dolan
Come Up and See Me Sometime ....Robert Emmett Dolan
Venice In Spring ....Robert Emmett Dolan
Very Important Man ....Robert Emmett Dolan

Texas, Li'l Darlin'

Big Movie Show In The Sky, The ....Robert Emmett Dolan
Big Movie Show In The Sky, The ....Robert Emmett Dolan
   (Reprise)
Month Of Sundays, A ....Robert Emmett Dolan
Month Of Sundays, A (Reprise) ....Robert Emmett Dolan
Affable, Balding Me........................Robert Emmett Dolan
Down In The Valley......................Robert Emmett Dolan
Hootin' Owl Trail ....Robert Emmett Dolan
Horseshoes Are Lucky....................Robert Emmett Dolan
It's Good To Be Alive ....Robert Emmett Dolan
Love Me, Love My Dog (Reprise).....Robert Emmett Dolan
Politics ....Robert Emmett Dolan
Ride 'em Cowboy..........................Robert Emmett Dolan
Take A Crank Letter......................Robert Emmett Dolan
Take A Crank Letter (Reprise) ....Robert Emmett Dolan
Texas Li'l Darlin' ....Robert Emmett Dolan
They Talk A Different Language......Robert Emmett Dolan
They Talk A Different Language .....Robert Emmett Dolan
   (Reprise)
Whichaway'd They Go ....Robert Emmett Dolan
Whoop'in And Hollerin' ....Robert Emmett Dolan

1951

Top Banana

Be My Guest.................................Johnny Mercer
   (replaced "That's For Sure" during run)
Dog Is A Man's Best Friends, A ....Johnny Mercer
Elevator Song ....Johnny Mercer
Finale (Top Banana) ....Johnny Mercer
Hail To MacCracken's..............................Johnny Mercer
I Fought Every Step Of The Way ....Johnny Mercer
Man Of The Year This Week, The............Johnny Mercer
Meet Miss Blendo......................................Johnny Mercer

1951 (continued)

My Home Is In My Shoes..........................Johnny Mercer
O.K. for TV ....Johnny Mercer
Only If You're In Love..............................Johnny Mercer
Sans Souci ....Johnny Mercer
Slogan Song ....Johnny Mercer
That's For Sure ....Johnny Mercer
Top Banana (Finale) ....Johnny Mercer
Top Banana (Ballet).................................Johnny Mercer
Word Is Day, A ....Johnny Mercer
You're So Beautiful That ....Johnny Mercer

1956

Li'l Abner

Country's In The Very Best Of Hands, The..... Gene De Paul
Finale (Li'l Abner)....................................Gene De Paul
If I Had My Druthers................................Gene De Paul
If I Had My Druthers (Reprise) ....Gene De Paul
I'm Past My Prime ....Gene De Paul
Jubilation T. Compone ....Gene De Paul
Love In A Home ....Gene De Paul
Matrimonial Stomp, The............................Gene De Paul
Namely You..Gene De Paul
Namely You (Reprise)...............................Gene De Paul
Oh Happy Day...Gene De Paul
Progress Is The Root Of All Evil ....Gene De Paul
Progress Is The Root Of All Evil (Reprise).....Gene De Paul
Put 'Em Back (The Way They Wuz) ....Gene De Paul
Rag Offen The Bush..................................Gene De Paul
Sadie Hawkins Day (Ballet) ....Gene De Paul
Typical Day, A ....Gene De Paul
Unnecessary Town...................................Gene De Paul
What's Good For General Bullmoose..........Gene De Paul

Mr. **Wonderful**

That Old Black Magic ....Harold Arlen

You Can't Run Away From It (Never Produced)

You Can't Run Away From It ....Gene De Paul

1959

Blues Opera (Free And Easy) (Show)

Ac-cen-tchu-ate The Positive ....Harold Arlen
Baby-O ....Johnny Rotella
Baby's Born, A ....Harold Arlen
Bees n' Flowers.......................................Harold Arlen
Blind Man..Harold Arlen
Blues In The Night ....Harold Arlen
Cake Song...Harold Arlen
Cakewalk Your Lady ....Harold Arlen
Champagne Fo' De Lady ....Harold Arlen
Come Rain or Come Shine ....Harold Arlen
Conjur Man ....Harold Arlen

1959 *(continued)*

Curse	Harold Arlen
Della's Entrance	Harold Arlen
Dis Little While	Harold Arlen
Easy Street	Harold Arlen
Finale From Blues Opera	Harold Arlen
Free And Easy	Harold Arlen
High, Low, Jack And The Game	Harold Arlen
Higher Than The Moon	Harold Arlen
Howdy Do To You	Harold Arlen
I Ain't Heard	Harold Arlen
I Had Myself A True Love/I Wonder What Became Of	Harold Arlen
I Wonder What Became Of Me?	Harold Arlen
Killing Sequence	Harold Arlen
Leaglize My Name	Harold Arlen
Least That's My Opinion	Harold Arlen
Like Clouds Up In The Sky	Harold Arlen
Li'l Augie Is A Natural Man	Harold Arlen
Lullaby	Harold Arlen
Racin' Form	Harold Arlen
Rainbow	Harold Arlen
Second Wind	Harold Arlen
Sleep Peaceful, Mr. Used-To-Be	Harold Arlen
Sow The Seed And Reap The Harvest	Harold Arlen
Sweetnin' Water	Harold Arlen
That Old Black Magic	Harold Arlen
Toastin' Sequence	Harold Arlen
Whatcha Saying, Bigelow	Harold Arlen
Wheel 'Em 'N Deal 'Em	Harold Arlen
Woman's Prerogative, A	Harold Arlen
Work Hard, Love Hard	Harold Arlen
Ya' Pushin' Ya Luck, Gal	Harold Arlen

Saratoga

Courtin' Our Chickens	Harold Arlen
Cure, The	Harold Arlen
Dog Eat Dog	Harold Arlen
Game Of Poker	Harold Arlen
Game Of Poker (Reprise)	Harold Arlen
Getting' A Man	Harold Arlen
Goose Never Be A Peacock	Harold Arlen
I'll Be Respectable	Harold Arlen
Love Held Lightly	Harold Arlen
Love Held Lightly (Reprise)	Harold Arlen
Man In My Life, The	Harold Arlen
Men Who Runs The Country, The	Harold Arlen
One Step-Two Step	Harold Arlen
Petticoat High	Harold Arlen
Petticoat High (Reprise)	Harold Arlen
Poker, The	Harold Arlen
Railroad Fight, The	Harold Arlen
Saratoga	Harold Arlen
Saratoga (Peprise)	Harold Arlen
The Gamblers	Harold Arlen

1959 *(continued)*

The Gossip Song	Harold Arlen
Why Fight This?	Harold Arlen
You Or No One	Harold Arlen

1964

Foxy

Bon Vivant	Robert Emmett Dolan
Case Of Rape, A	Robert Emmett Dolan
Ebenezer McAfee III	Robert Emmett Dolan
Finale (Foxy)	Robert Emmett Dolan
Finale Act One	Robert Emmett Dolan
I'm Way Ahead Of The Game	Robert Emmett Dolan
In Loving Memory	Robert Emmett Dolan
It's Easy When You Know How	Robert Emmett Dolan
Larceny and Love	Robert Emmett Dolan
Many Ways To Skin A Cat	Robert Emmett Dolan
Money Isn't Everything	Robert Emmett Dolan
My Weight In Gold	Robert Emmett Dolan
Prologue	Robert Emmett Dolan
Rollin' In Gold	Robert Emmett Dolan
Run, Run, Run Cinderella	Robert Emmett Dolan
Talk To Me, Baby	Robert Emmett Dolan
Talk To Me, Baby (Reprise)	Robert Emmett Dolan
This Is My Night To Howl	Robert Emmett Dolan

1967

Mike (Show–Never Produced)

Any Way The Wind Blows	Johnny Mercer
Ballad Of A Private Eye	Johnny Mercer
Betsy And Me	Johnny Mercer
Bully Boys, The	Johnny Mercer
Cat With Nine Lives, A	Johnny Mercer
Equivalent of A Haa-vud Education	Johnny Mercer
Gerfunkt	Johnny Mercer
He Never Knew What Hit Him	Johnny Mercer
I Wanna Be In Love Again	Johnny Mercer
Kiss and Tell	Johnny Mercer
Mama Torpedo	Johnny Mercer
Medium (Couldn't Get Through), The	Johnny Mercer
My Crazy Old Subconscious Won't Leave You Alone	Johnny Mercer
No Wonder It's Banned In Boston	Johnny Mercer
Our Man In Paradise	Johnny Mercer
Thanks But No Thanks	Johnny Mercer
Why Didn't I Tell Him?	Johnny Mercer
Why Didn't She Tell Me ?	Johnny Mercer
You Can't Lose	Johnny Mercer

1971

Pig War, The

Without Benefit of Clergy	n/a

1974

The Good Companions
And Points Beyond ....Andre Previn
Camaraderie...Andre Previn
Dance Of Life ....Andre Previn
Darkest Before The Dawn.............................Andre Previn
Footloose ....Andre Previn
Good Companions......................................Andre Previn
Goodbye ....Andre Previn
I'll Tell The World.......................................Andre Previn
Little Travelling Music, A..............................Andre Previn
Pleasure Of Your Company...........................Andre Previn
Pools, The..Andre Previn
Slippin' Around The Corner...........................Andre Previn
Stage Door Johnny ....Andre Previn
Stage Struck ....Andre Previn
Susie For Everybody....................................Andre Previn
Ta, Luv ....Andre Previn

1975

Bette Midler's Clams On The Half Shell
Drinking Again ....Doris Tauber

1978

The American Dance Machine
Satin Doll .... Billy Strayhorn and Duke Ellington

Dancin'
I Wanna Be A Dancin' Man.......................Harry Warren

1980

42nd Street
Sunny Side To Every Situation ....Harry Warren

A Day In Hollywood/A Night In The Ukraine
Too Marvelous For Words ....Richard A. Whiting

1981

Sophisticated Ladies
Satin Doll .... Billy Strayhorn and Duke Ellington

1982

Blues In The Night
Blues In The Night ....Harold Arlen
When A Woman Loves A Man ....Bernie Hanighen and
....Gordon Jenkins

Seven Brides For Seven Brothers
Bless Your Beautiful Hide ....Gene De Paul
Goin' Courting...Gene De Paul
Sobbin' Women ....Gene De Paul

Wonderful, Wonderful Day.........................Gene De Paul

1983

Peg
Goody, Goody .... Matt Malneck

Singin' In The Rain (England)
Too Marvelous For Words ....Richard A. Whiting

1986

Jerome Kern Goes To Hollywood
I'm Old Fashioned ....Jerome Kern

1987

Barbara Cook: A Concert For The Theatre
Come Rain or Come Shine ....Harold Arlen

1997

Dream
Ac-cen-tchu-ate The Positive ....Harold Arlen
And The Angels Sing ....Ziggy Elman
Blues In The Night ....Harold Arlen
Come Rain, Come Shine ....Harold Arlen
Day In - Day Out...Rube Bloom
Days Of Wine and Roses, The................. Henry Mancini
Dearly Beloved...Jerome Kern
Dixieland Band, The ....Bernie Hanighen
Dream..Johnny Mercer
Fleet's In, The ....Victor Schertzinger
Fools Rush In ....Rube Bloom
G. I. Jive ....Johnny Mercer
Goody, Goody .... Matt Malneck
Have You Got Any Castles, Baby? ....Richard A. Whiting
Hooray For Hollywood ....Richard A. Whiting
I Had Myself A True Love ....Harold Arlen
    I Wonder What Became Of
I Remember You ....Victor Schertzinger
I Thought About You ....James Van Heusen
I'm Doin' It For Defense ....Harold Arlen
I'm Old Fashioned ....Jerome Kern
In The Cool, Cool, Cool ....Hoagy Carmichael
    Of The Evening
Jamboree Jones Jive ....Johnny Mercer
Jeepers Creepers ....Harry Warren
Laura...David Raksin
Lazybones...Hoagy Carmichael
Moon River...Henry Mancini
My Shining Hour ....Harold Arlen
On Behalf Of The Traveling Salesmen ...Walter Donaldson
On The Atchison, Topeka And The Santa Fe ....
....Harry Warren
One For My Baby.......................................Harold Arlen

Year

Out Of This World......................................Harold Arlen
Pardon My Southern Accent ....Matt Malneck

1997 *(continued)*

Satin Doll ....Billy Strayhorn and
.... Duke Ellington
Skylark...Hoagy Carmichael
Something's Gotta Give ....Johnny Mercer
Tangerine ....Victor Schertzinger
That Old Black Magic ....Harold Arlen
This Time The Dream's On Me ....Harold Arlen
Too Marvelous For Words ....Richard A. Whiting
You Go Your Way ....Johnny Mercer
You Must Have Been A Beautiful Baby ....Harry Warren
You Were Never Lovelier ....Jerome Kern

1999

Fosse
Hooray For Hollywood ....Richard A. Whiting
I Wanna Be A Dancin' Man........................Harry Warren

Swing!
Blues In The Night ....Harold Arlen
G. I. Jive...Johnny Mercer

2001

42nd Street
Sunny Side To Every Situation ....Harry Warren

2002

Elaine Stritch At Liberty
Hooray For Hollywood ....Richard A. Whiting

2003

Never Gonna Dance
Dearly Beloved...Jerome Kern
I'm Old Fashioned ....Jerome Kern

Johnny Mercer's Songs
on Compact Discs

Compiled by Ralph Mitchell III

When Ralph Mitchell III moved to Johnny Mercer's hometown, Savannah, Georgia, in 1993, he began his hobby of collecting the great songwriter's works. It has become a genuine labor of love. Mercer wrote over 1,500 songs and the first objective of this listing is to identify as many of these songs as possible, that are, or have been, commercially available on the CD format. The other objective by Ralph, with help from several other Mercer aficionados, is to find and convert to a CD format other Mercer songs which have been only available on movie film or on other recording formats. A secondary objective is to identify the various vocalists associated with these songs.

If you should have any additions to suggest or if you have an inquiry concerning the original format of a song, you may email Ralph at **rcm3@bellsouth.net**. This project is a continuing effort. You may actually see the most current song listing at the Johnny Mercer Educational Archives site maintained by Steve Taksler at **www.JohnnyMercer.com**.

This collection contains **513 different songs** with lyrics by Johmmy Mercer and **2,196 different performances** of these songs by vocalists, all on compact discs.

There are **109 different composers** of the songs in this collection. The number of songs produced per composer is listed below after their name:

Harold Arlen 61	Walter Schertzinger 8	Duke Ellington 2
Johnny Mercer..............52	Jimmy McHugh...............8	Gordon Jenkins...............2
Harry Warren...............45	Matty Malneck 7	Sammy Nestico 2
Gene DePaul 32	Saul Chaplin 6	Phil Ohman 2
Robert Dolan 30	Walter Donaldson...........6	David Raskin...................2
Richard Whiting 23	Jimmy Rowles................5	Alec Wilder 2
Henry Mancini 19	Jimmy Van Heusen 4	Benny Goodman.............2
Hoagy Carmichael.........17	Lewis Gensler 3	Arthur Kent 2
Bernie Hanighen...........16	Wingy Manone...............3	Peter Tinturin 2
Andre Previn................15	Alfred Newman..............3	
Barry Manilow 13	John Williams 3	
Rube Bloom...................9	Paul Weston...................3	
Jerome Kern...................9	Steve Allen 2	
Arthur Schwartz.............9	Fred Astaire 2	
Johnny Green.................8	Blossom Dearie..............2	

Finally, there are **70 composers of one song each** in this collection, including such famous musicians as Woody Herman, Bobby Troup, Benny Carter, Artie Shaw, Lionel Hampton, Laurindo Almeida, Neal Hefti, Errol Garner, Trummy Young, Ziggy Elman and Marian McPartland. Great Composers, such as Kurt Weill and Eugene Brecht, Johnny Mandel, Alex North, Marvin Hamlisch, Elmer Bernstein, Michel LeGrand and even Rimsky-Korsakov, are also represented in the group with one song each.

Song Title	Composer	Date	Vocalists

A

Accentuate The Positive ....Arlen, Harold................ 1944 ......Bing Crosby/Andrews Sisters, Bing Crosby/Sonny Tufts, Dr. John, Nancy LaMott, Susannah McCorkle, Ella Mae Morse, Maxine Sullivan, Clint Eastwood, Johnny Mercer /The Notables, Sylvia Syms, Johnny Mathis/Margaret Whiting, Barbara Cook, Monica Mancini, Dolly Mitchell, Jim Wann, Harold Arlen, Bobby Belfry/Carolyn Montgomery/Keith Anderson/Matt Helton/Wendy Porter/Paul Bernhardt/ Christine Zino/Diane Schwartz/Tex Arnold, Jenny Ferris, Buddy Rich, Huxsie Scott, Mady Kaye, Ella Fitzgerald, Irene Daye, Mel Torme, Imogene Lynn

Affable, Balding Me...............Dolan, Robert ....1949.......Mary Hatcher/Fredd Wayne

After Twelve O'Clock..............Carmichael, Hoagy .... 1932.......Dick Robertson

Afterbeat...............................Astaire, Fred................1959.......Fred Astaire

Ain't Nature Grand................Schwartz, Arthur...........1953 ......Esther Williams/Fernando Lamas/Denise Darcel/ Jack Carson/Barbara Whiting/Charlotte Greenwood/William Demarest, Johnny Mercer/Rhythmaires

Air Minded Executive ....Hanighen, Bernie..........1940 ......Johnny Mercer, Dorothy Claire/Tex Beneke, Lee Lessack

All Through The Night...........Schwartz, Arthur...........1940 ......Johnny Desmond, Barbara Lea

And Points Beyond ....Previn, Andre ....1974.......John Mills/Company, Bing Crosby/Johnny Mercer

And So To Bed ....Dolan, Robert ....1946 ......Michael Feinstein, Mel Torme, Dinah Shore, Bing Crosby

And The Angels Sing..............Elman, Ziggy ....1939.......Chris Chandler, Della Reese, Martha Tilton, Ray Eberle, Johnny Mercer, Jacintha, Rosemary Clooney, Bing Crosby, Jim Wann, Louise Tobin, Ralph Brewster Singers, Etta Jones, Banu Gibson, Virginia Maxey, Elena Bennett, Bon Bon, Helen Humes

Angels Cried, The ....Mercer, Johnny.............1948 ......Martha Tilton

Any Place I Hang My Hat Is Home ....Arlen, Harold................1946 ......Richard Rodney Bennett, Rosemary Clooney, Chris Connor, Judy Garland, Ruby Hill, Johnny Mercer, Helen Merrill, Susannah McCorkle, Marlene Ver Planck, Margaret Whiting, Vanessa Williams, Robert Clary, Lee Lessack, Richard Rodney Bennett, Lena Horne, Joan Ryan, Jo Stafford, Barbara Streisand, Sammy Davis, Jr., Barbara Lea, Ada Moore, Dinah Shore

Arthur Murray Taught Me Dancing In A Hurry ....Schertzinger, Victor.......1942 ......Susannah McCorkle, Maxine Sullivan, Marilyn Cooper, Betty Hutton, Helen O'Connell, Bing Crosby, King Sisters, Mildred Bailey, June Hutton, Daryl Sherman

As Long As You Live ....Hanighen, Bernie..........1938 ......Louis Armstrong, Mildred Bailey, Edythe Wright

At Last ....Manilow, Barry ....1984 ......Nancy Wilson, Monica Mancini

At The Jazz Band Ball............LaRocca, D. J./ ....1950 ......Susannah McCorkle, Louis Armstrong/Bing Crosby, Shields, Larry   Johnny Mercer, Perry Como, Jimmy Atkins, Bing Crosby

Autumn Leaves.....................Kosma, Joseph ....1950 ......Natalie Cole, Billie Eckstine, Eartha Kitt, Nancy LaMott, Gordon MacRae, Johnny Mercer, Matt Monro, Nana Mouskouri, Kiri Te Kanawa, Paula Cole, Eileen Farrell, Jo Stafford, Helen O'Connell, Robert Clary, Jacintha, Frank Sinatra, Lee Lessack, Eva Cassidy, Bing Crosby, Karrin Allyson, Edith Piaf, Gail Thurmond, Kim Polote, Adam Jones, Huxsie Scott, Barbara Streisand, Kitty White, Herb Jeffries, Barbara Lea, Ozzie Bailey, Four Freshmen, Martha Miyake, Sally Sweetland, Tony Martin

Aw, Come On Now ....Mercer, Johnny.............1944 ......Johnny Mercer

B

Baby ....Allen, Steve ....1953 ......Steve Allen

Baby Doll ....Warren, Harry ....1945 ......Fred Astaire, Doris Day, Ella Fitzgerald, Gordon MacRae

Baby, Don't Quit Now............Rowles, Jimmy.............1967.......Jeri Brown/Jimmy Rowles, Ella Fitzgerald, Tony Bennett, Susannah McCorkle, Carol Sloane

Song Title	Composer	Date	Vocalists
Baby-O	Rotella, John	1962	Dean Martin
Bachelor's Dinner Song	Warren, Harry	1945	Fred Astaire
Bad Humor Man	McHugh, Jimmy	1940	Helen O'Connell, Bob Jenney, Harry Babbitt/Sully Mason/Merwyn Bogue
Ballad of Alvarez Kelly	Green, Johnny	1966	Movie Chorus
Barefoot In The Park	Hefti, Neal	1967	Movie Chorus
Bathtub Ran Over Again, The	Cleary, Michael	1934	Johnny Mercer, Lee Lessack, Cliff Weston
Be My Guest	Mercer, Johnny	1950	Gordon MacRae
Bernardine	Mercer, Johnny	1957	Pat Boone
Big Movie Show in the Sky	Dolan, Robert	1949	Modernaires, Bing Crosby, Danny Scholl/Chorus
Big, Beautiful Ball, A	Williams, John	1966	Jackie and Roy, Johnny Mercer
Bilbao Song	Brecht, Eugene /Weill, Kurt	1961	Andy Williams, Julie Wilson, Clay Johnson/ Adam Jones/Trae Gurley
Birmingham Bertha	Mercer, Johnny	1944	Johnny Mercer
Bless Yore Beautiful Hide	DePaul, Gene	1953	Howard Keel, Steve Devereaux
Blue Rain	Van Heusen, Jimmy	1939	Ray Eberle, Bea Wain, Mildred Bailey, Harry Babbitt, Milli Vernon, Jack Leonard, Tommy Traynor

Blues in the Night ....Arlen, Harold................1941.......Louis Armstrong, Chris Chandler, Susannah McCorkle, Johnny Mercer, Van Morrison, Frank Sinatra, Margaret Whiting, Sylvia Syms, Peggy Lee/Lou McGarity, Jennifer Holliday, Dinah Shore, Lee Lessack, Eva Cassidy, Bing Crosby, Jim Wann, Johnny Mercer/Jo Stafford, Harold Arlen, Carolyn Montgomery/Farah Alvin, Catte Adams, Leslie Anderson, Mel Torme, Rosemary Clooney, Kim Polote, Ella Fitzgerald, Dinah Washington, Dr. John, Phyllis Miles, Buddy Rich, Billy Eckstine, Lurlean Hunter, Jo Stafford, Tony Bennett, Jimmie Lunceford, Jo Stafford, Hot Lips Page, Eileen Farrell, Cab Calloway, Woody Herman, Doris Day, Marion Hutton, Jesse Belvin

Bob White ....Hanighen, Bernie..........1937.......Johnny Mercer, Johnny Mercer/Bobby Darin, Maxine Sullivan, Martha Tilton, Mildred Bailey, Banu Gibson, Lisa Hindmarsh, Matthew Helton/David Michael Roth, Barbara Lea, Bing Crosby/Connie Boswell, Carmen McRae, Dick Robertson

Bon Vivant ....Dolan, Robert..............1962.......Johnny Mercer, Bing Crosby, Jim Wann, Rudy Roberson/Ensemble

| Boys Will Be Boys | Gensler, Lewis | 1935 | Betty Grable |
| Break It Up, Cinderella | Carmichael, Hoagy | 1940 | Barbara Lea |

C

Cakewalk Your Lady	Arlen, Harold	1946	Robert Pope/Milton Williams, Joseph Webster/ 1998 Company
Calypso Song	Arlen, Harold	1950	The Ravens
Camaraderie	Previn, Andre	1974	Company
Camptown Races	Foster, Stephen	1944	Johnny Mercer/Pied Pipers
Can't Teach My Old Heart New Tricks	Whiting, Richard	1937	Margaret Whiting, Frances Langford, Richard Rodney Bennett, Martha Tilton, Anita Bradley
Captains of the Clouds	Arlen, Harold	1942	Dick Powell
Casanova's Lament	Dexter	1938	Jack Teagarden
C'est La Guerre	Schwartz, Arthur	1953	Johnny Mercer/Rhythmaires

Charade ....Mancini, Henry.............1963.......Blossom Dearie, Marlene Ver Planck, Andy Williams, Sarah Vaughn, Monica Mancini, Lee Lessack, Mancini Chorus, Johnny Hartman, Bobby Darin

Song Title	Composer	Date	Vocalists
Chin Up, Stout Fellow	Chaplin, Saul	1957	Danny Kaye/Merry Andrew Movie Cast
Cindy	Weston, Paul	1946	Jo Stafford
Come On, Li'l Augie	Arlen, Harold	1946	1998 Company
Come Rain or Come Shine	Arlen, Harold	1946	Johnny Adams, Richard Rodney Bennett, Chris Connor, Judy Garland, Ruby Hill/Harold Nicholas, Billie Holiday, Peggy Lee, Johnny Mercer, Della Reese, Frank Sinatra, Frank Sinatra/Gloria Estafan, Alison Eastwood, Four Freshmen, June Christy, Sylvia Syms, Bette Midler, Vanessa Williams/Stanley Mathis, Robert Clary, Melissa Manchester, Barbara Cook, Dick Haymes, Lee Lessack, Bobby Troup, Bing Crosby, Stuart Foster, Helen Forrest, Richard Rodney Bennett, Connie Haines, Banu Gibson, Anne Runolfsson, Jo Stafford, Kim Polote, Joe Williams, Jenny Ferris, Dr. John, Cathy Carter, Ray Charles, Trae Gurley/Kim Polote, Huxsie Scott, Barbara Streisand, Mady Kaye, Sarah Vaughan, Brenda Lee, Ray Charles, Liza Minnelli, Lorez Alexandria, Trae Gurley, Ella Fitzgerald, Barbara Lea, Anita O'Day, Georgia Gibbs, Rosemary Clooney, Anita Ellis, Sy Oliver, Monica Zetterland, Eileen Farrell, Carmen McRae
Comes the Revolution, Baby	Whiting, Richard	1935	Johnny Mercer/Evelyn Poe
Comet in the Sky	Bright, Ronnell	1967	Lorez Alexandria
Confidentially	Warren, Harry	1938	John Payne
Conversation While Dancing	Weston, Paul	1945	Johnny Mercer/Jo Stafford
Corn Pickin'	Warren, Harry	1939	Maxine Sullivan, Bea Wain
Could Be	Donaldson, Walter	1938	Martha Tilton/Johnny Mercer/Benny Goodman, Bing Crosby/Johnny Mercer, Johnny Mercer/Bing Crosby/Ken Carpenter/Marie Wilson, Beverly
Countin' Our Chickens	Arlen, Harold	1959	Carol Lawrence/Howard Keel
Country's in the Very Best of Hands, The	DePaul, Gene	1956	Peter Palmer/Stubby Kaye
Cowboy From Brooklyn	Warren, Harry	1938	Tex Beneke/Glenn Miller, Skeets Herfert
Cream Puff	Mancini, Henry	1962	Movie Cast
Cuckoo in the Clock	Donaldson, Walter	1938	Johnny Mercer, Bobby Troup, Marion Hutton, Lena Horne, Sully Mason, Steve Jordan, Mildred Bailey, Martha Tilton, Modernaires
Cure, The	Arlen, Harold	1959	Saratoga Ensemble

D

Song Title	Composer	Date	Vocalists
Daddy Long Legs	Mercer, Johnny	1955	Movie Chorus
Dance of Life	Previn, Andre	1974	Judi Dench, Johnny Mercer
Darkest Before Dawn	Previn, Andre	1974	Judi Dench
Darling Lili	Mancini, Henry	1969	Johnny Mathis, Mancini Chorus
Day In-Day Out	Bloom, Rube	1939	Tony Bennett, Nat King Cole, Chris Connor, Ella Fitzgerald, Billie Holiday, Dinah Shore, Frank Sinatra, Mel Torme, Helen Ward, Margaret Whiting, Marlene Ver Planck, Helen Forrest, Eileen Farrell, Ella Mae Morse, Robert Clary, Lee Lessack, Bobby Troup, Petula Clark, Leslie Anderson, Jenny Ferris, Buddy Greco, Buddy Rich, Diana Krall, Joni James, Kenny Sargent, Sarah Vaughan, Harry Babitt
Daydreaming	Warren, Harry	1938	Mildred Bailey
Days of Wine and Roses	Mancini, Henry	1962	Tony Bennett, Chris Chandler, Nancy LaMott, Mancini Chorus, Johnny Mercer, Matt Monro, Frank Sinatra, Nancy Wilson, Cassandra Wilson, Patti Page, Sarah Vaughn, Jacintha, Monica Mancini, Julie London, Lee Lessack, Joe Mooney, Jim Wann, Billy Eckstine, Kim Polote, Adam Jones, Huxsie Scott, Mady Kaye, Lorez Alexandria, Kate Smith, Sue Raney, Peggy Lee
Dearly Beloved	Kern, Jerome	1942	June Christy, Chris Connor, Dinah Shore, Sylvia Syms, Fred Astaire, Skip Nelson, Fred Astaire/Nan Wynn, Peggy King, Bing Crosby, Barry Wood, Banu Gibson, Nancy Wilson, Dorothy Kirsten, Lorez Alexandria, Buzz Alston, David Allyn, Bill Schallen, Maxine Sullivan

Song Title	Composer	Date	Vocalists
Derry Down Dilly	Green, Johnny	1952	Marge Champion
Dig It	Borne, Hal	1940	Fred Astaire, Doris Day
Dixie Isn't Dixie Anymore	Bloom, Rube	1936	Lavaida Carter
Dixieland Band, The	Bloom, Rube	1935	Helen Ward, Kay Starr, Pee Wee Hunt, Alvin Stoller, Johnny Mercer, Bob Crosby, Rebecca Kilgore
Dog Eat Dog	Arlen, Harold	1959	Saratoga Male Ensemble
Dog is a Man's Best Friend, A	Mercer, Johnny	1951	Phil Silvers/Sport Morgan
Down a Long, Long Road	Millham, Margot	1933	Allan Breeze
Down T'Uncle Bill's	Carmichael, Hoagy	1934	Nat Gonella/Bruts Gonella, Skinnay Ennis, Dick Robertson
Dr. Watson and Mr. Holmes	Hanighen, Bernie	1934	Spirits of Rhythm
Dream	Mercer, Johnny	1945	Ella Fitzgerald, Susannah McCorkle, Pied Pipers, Jimmy Scott, Frank Sinatra, Jo Stafford, Sarah Vaughan, Four Freshmen, Robert Clary, Lee Lessack, Hadda Brooks, Joan Edwards, Johnny Peterson, Petula Clark/Rod McKuen/Margaret Whiting, Rosemary Clooney, Mancini Chorus, Doris Day, Dr. John, Jackie DeShannon, June Hutton, Michael Buble, Rebecca Kilgore, Vera Lynn, Martha Miyake
Dream Awhile	Ohman, Phil	1936	Mel Torme/Mel-Tones, Kitty Kallen, Daryl Sherman
Dream Peddler's Serenade	Sharpe, John Rufus	1950	Margaret Whiting
Drinking Again	Tauber, Doris	1961	Frank Sinatra, Cynthia Crane, Steve Jordan, Chris Connor, Banu Gibson, Paul Bernhardt, Aretha Franklin, Elkie Brooks, Laila Dalseth
Duration Blues	Mercer, Johnny	1944	Johnny Mercer, Butch Stone

E

Song Title	Composer	Date	Vocalists
Early Autumn	Burns, Ralph/ Herman, Woody	1952	Billie Eckstine, Ella Fitzgerald, Mel Torme, Marlene Ver Planck, Sylvia Syms, Eileen Farrell, Anita O'Day, King Sisters, Jodi Stevens, Jo Stafford, Lorez Alexandria, Woody Herman, Frances Wayne, Carol Sloane
Eeny, Meeny, Miney, Mo	Hanighen, Bernie	1935	Billie Holiday, Johnny Mercer/Ginger Rogers, Helen Ward, Hildegarde, Bob Crosby, Nappy Lamare, Terry Blaine
Elevator Song	Mercer, Johnny	1951	Top Banana Cast
Emily	Mandel, Johnny	1964	Frank Sinatra, Sherri Roberts, Joe Mooney, Barbara Streisand, Singers Unlimited, Jenny Ferris, Andy Williams, Laila Dalseth, Sue Raney
Empty Tables	Van Heusen, Jimmy	1974	Frank Sinatra, Banu Gibson
Every So Often	Warren, Harry	1947	Ray Eberle, Martha Tilton
Everything Is Ticketty-Boo	Chaplin, Saul	1957	Fred Penner, Danny Kaye

F

Song Title	Composer	Date	Vocalists
Facts of Life	Mercer, Johnny	1960	Eydie Gorme/Steve Lawrence
Fancy Free	Arlen, Harold	1950	Chris Connor, Judy Kaye
Far Across The Sea	Wayne, Bernie	1960	Alfred Apaka
Fare Thee Well to Harlem	Hanighen, Bernie	1933	Johnny Mercer/Jack Teagarden, Jerry Blake, Jack Teagarden/Nappy Lamare
Fine Thing	Dolan, Robert	1947	Ray Kellogg
Fleet's In, The	Schertzinger, Victor	1942	Betty Jane Rhodes

Fleur de Lys............................Carmichael, Hoagy .... 1971.......Tracy Thomas

Fool That I Am ....Malneck, Matty .... 1934 ......Ravens

Fools Rush In............................Bloom, Rube................. 1940 ......Mildred Bailey, Bob Eberle, Billy Eckstine, Four Freshmen, Johnny Hartman, Susannah McCorkle, Frank Sinatra, Keely Smith, Marlene Ver Planck, Rosemary Clooney, Sylvia Syms, Marion Mann, Ray Eberle, Robert Clary, Ginny Simms, Bing Crosby, Bob Eberle, Mario Lanza, Elvis Presley, Jo Stafford, Tony Bennett, Robert Schumann Chorale, Hi-Los, Buddy Rich, Perry Como, Martha Miyake, Lorez Alexandria, Dean Martin, Matt Monro, Rosemary Clooney, Rick Nelson, Brook Benton, Louis Armstrong, Dick Haymes, Tony Martin, Vic Damone, Al Martino, Teddi King, Etta Jones, Bob Stewart, Stacey Kent

Footloose ....Previn, Andre .... 1974.......John Mills/Judi Dench/Christopher Gable

Forever Amber......................Raskin, David .... 1947.......Marion Morgan

Frazier ....Rowles, Jimmy.............. 1972.......Jeri Brown, Carol Sloane, Barbara Lea

Fun Loving Ickies..................Mercer, Johnny............. 1948 ......Johnny Mercer/Eddie Miller/Nappy Lamare

G

G. I. Jive ....Mercer, Johnny............. 1943 ......Rosemary Clooney, Johnny Mercer, Farah Alvin, Louis Jordan, Ray McKinley

Game of Poker, A..................Arlen, Harold................ 1959.......Howard Keel/Carol Lawrence, Howard Keel/Odette Myrtil

Garden of the Moon ....Chaplin, Saul .... 1938 ......Mildred Bailey, Bing Crosby

Gee! I Wish I'd Listened to My Mother ....McHugh, Jimmy .... 1940 ......Bonnie Baker

Get a Horse............................Mancini, Henry............. 1965 ......Movie Chorus

Getting' a Man......................Arlen, Harold................ 1959.......Odette Myrtil/Carol Brice

Girl Friend of the Whirling Dervish ....Warren, Harry .... 1938 ......Chorus, Connie Stevens, Butch Stone, Susannah McCorkle, Trudi Mann

Girl in No Man's Land, The .....Mancini, Henry............. 1969 ......Julie Andrews/Mancini Chorus

Glow Worm ....Lincke, Paul.................. 1952.......Johnny Mercer, Mills Brothers, Robert Clary, Johnny Mathis/Melissa Manchester, Lee Lessack, Jim Wann, Betty Garrett/John Dixon/Greg Thorneycroft/David Werthe, Johnny Mercer/Bing Crosby, Spike Jones, Dean Martin

Goin' Co'tin' ....DePaul, Gene .... 1953 ......Jane Powell, Stanley Donen, Roni Page/Seven Brothers, 1984 London Cast

Good Companions ....Previn, Andre .... 1974.......Christopher Gable/Malcolm Rennie, Rod McKuen, Bing Crosby/Johnny Mercer

Goody Goody ....Malneck, Matty .... 1936 ......Diahann Carroll, Rosemary Clooney, Benny Goodman, Julie London, Johnny Mercer, Frank Sinatra, Maxine Sullivan, Helen Ward, Sylvia Syms, Robert Clary, Harry Roy, Lynn Roberts, Richard Rodney Bennett, Mel Torme, Carolyn Montgomery/Wendy Porter, Kevin Chamberlin, Leslie Anderson, Buddy Rich, Peggy Lee, Modernaires, Buddy Rich, Mady KayeWingy Manone, Ella Fitzgerald

Goose Never Be a Peacock ....Arlen, Harold................ 1959.......Richard Rodney Bennett, Judy Kaye, Carol Brice, Sylvia McNair

Got to Wear You Off My Weary Mind..................Arlen, Harold................ 1947.......Peggy Lee

Gotta Get Some Shuteye ....Donaldson, Walter......... 1939.......Marion Hutton, Harry Babbitt, Martha Tilton, Jean Farney, Rebecca Kilgore

Great Guns............................Warren, Harry .... 1949.......Margaret Whiting

Guitar Country ....Robison, Willard........... 1963 ......Chorus

H

Song Title	Composer	Date	Vocalists
Hangin' Loose	Nestico, Sammy	1972	Bing Crosby
Happy Times	Fine, Sylvia	1949	Jo Stafford, Bob Crosby, Bing Crosby
Harlem Butterfly	Mercer, Johnny	1948	Susannah McCorkle, Maxine Sullivan, Rebecca Kilgore, Richard Rodney Bennett, Lorez Alexandria, Bobby Sherwood
Have a Heart	DiNovi, Gene	1965	Nancy Wilson
Have a Nice Day	Nestico, Sammy	1976	Bing Crosby
Have You Got Any Castles, Baby?	Whiting, Richard	1937	Margaret Whiting, Dick Powell, Connie Stevens, Bing Crosby, Banu Gibson, Keith Anderson/Wendy Porter, Bobby Darin, Jack Leonard, Barry McKinley, Alice Faye
Hayride	Warren, Harry	1945	Ray Bolger/Judy Garland
He Didn't Have the Know How – No How	Dolan, Robert	1950	Pearl Bailey
He Loved Me Till the All Clear Came	Arlen, Harold	1942	Cass Daley
He Should-a Flip'd When He Flop'd	Ellington, Duke/ Strayhorn, Billy	1958	Johnny Mercer/Cootie Williams
He Shouldn't A, Hadn't A, Oughtn't A Swang On Me!	Mancini, Henry	1965	Dorothy Provine
Headless Horseman	DePaul, Gene	1949	Bing Crosby
Heart of Mine, Cry On	Manilow, Barry	1988	Nancy Wilson
Hello Out There, Hello	Manone, Wingy	1952	Johnny Mercer
Here Come The British	Hanighen, Bernie	1934	Johnny Mercer/Peggy Healy/John Hauser, Pee Wee Hunt, Dean Martin
Here Come the Waves	Arlen, Harold	1944	Chorus
Here's to My Lady	Bloom, Rube	1951	Mel Torme, Carole Cook, Nat King Cole, Andy Williams, Perry Como, Joe Williams
Hit the Road to Dreamland	Arlen, Harold	1942	Rosemary Clooney, Nancy LaMott, Susannah McCorkle, K.T. Sullivan, Marlene Ver Planck, Margaret Whiting, Dick Powell/Mary Martin, Robert Clary, Jane Monheit, Sarah Vaughn, Harold Arlen, Paul Bernhardt/Chorus, Leslie Anderson. Jenny Ferris, Dr. John, Joe Mooney, Dean Martin, Connie Stevens
Holy Smoke	Marsh, Royal	1939	Don Burke, Frankie Masters/Swing Masters, Gus Ehrman
Honeymoon is Over, The	Dolan, Robert	1963	Jessica Frankel/Natasha Harper
Honolulu	Mercer, Johnny	1970	Four Hits & A Miss, Bellaires
Hooray for Hollywood	Whiting, Richard	1937	Rosemary Clooney, Scat Davis/Frances Langford, Sylvia Syms, Anita O'Day, Doris Day, Carole Cook
Hooray for Spinach	Warren, Harry	1939	Manhattan Rhythm Kings, Butch Stone, Modernaires
Hootin' Owl Trail	Dolan, Robert	1949	Danny Scholl/Chorus
How Do You Say, Auf Wiedersehn?	Scibetta, Tony	1967	Mel Torme, Marlene Ver Planck, Mabel Mercer, Blossom Dearie, Rebecca Martin
How Little We Know	Carmichael, Hoagy	1945	Chris Connor, Mary Cleere Haran, Barbara Lea/ Bob Dorough, Susannah McCorkle, Mark Sendroff, Tommy Mercer, Anita Boyer, Nancy Dussault, Jo Stafford, Marlene Ver Planck, Carmen McRae, Paul Smith/Noteables, Nat King Cole, Lauren Bacall, Dottie Reid, Randy Carmichael, Klea Blackhurst
Howdy Friends and Neighbors	DePaul, Gene	1956	Stubby Kaye/June Allyson/Jack Lemmon/Chorus

Song Title	Composer	Date	Vocalists

I

**I Boogied When I Should
  Have Woogied**....................Hanighen, Bernie..........1941.......Ray McKinley

**I Can't Teach My Old Heart
  New Tricks**........................Manilow, Barry ....1988 ......Nancy Wilson

I Don't Believe in Signs..........Warren, Harry ....1939......Ray Hendricks

I Feel My Luck Comin' Down ..Arlen, Harold................1946 ......Stanley Mathis

I Fought Every Step...............Mercer, Johnny.............1951.......Rose Marie, Margaret Whiting, Laura Kenyon/ Armelia
  of the Way   McQueen/Mary Gordon Murray, Leslie Anderson

**I Got Out of Bed on the
  Right Side**..........................Schwartz, Arthur..........1953 ......Movie Cast

**I Guess It Was You
  All the Time**.......................Carmichael, Hoagy ....1953 ......Marcie Miller, Teresa Brewer

I Had Myself a True Love........Arlen, Harold................1946 ......June Hawkins, Helen Schneider, Helen Goldsby,
                                                                                  Dinah Shore, Barbara Cook, Barbara Streisand,
                                                                                  Tonya Pinkins, Audrey Lavine, Barbara Lea

I Like Men ....Schwartz, Arthur..........1953 ......Barbara Whiting, Judy Garland/Peggy Lee

I Never Knew.......................Mercer, Johnny.............1956 ......Johnny Mercer

I Never Saw a Better Night .....Gensler, Lewis ....1935 ......Bob Howard, Dolly Dawn/Sonny Schuyler

**I Never Wanna Look
  into Those Eyes Again** ....Raskin, Milt ....1955 ......June Christy, Leslie Anderson

I Promise You ....Arlen, Harold................1944 ......Bing Crosby/Betty Hutton, Jo Stafford, Harry
                                                                                  Babbitt, Don Darcy

I Remember You ....Schertzinger, Victor.......1942 ......June Christy, Rosemary Clooney, Nat King Cole,
  Ella Fitzgerald, Mary Cleere Haran, Penny Parker, Jeri Southern, Marlene Ver Planck, Dinah Washington, Margaret
  Whiting, Four Freshmen, Eileen Farrell, Bette Midler, Gene Lees, Eydie Gorme, Sherri Roberts, Robert Clary, Dorothy
  Lamour, Jacintha, Julie London, Lee Lessack, Diana Krall, Christina Machado, Bing Crosby, Richard Rodney Bennett,
  Jo Stafford, Lesli Margherita, Kim Polote, Jenny Ferris, Doris Day, Tony Bennett, Penny Dawson, Gary Stevens/Star-
  dusters, Mady Kaye, Teal Joy, Lorez Alexandria, Frank Ifield, Sue Raney, Gary Williams, Helen Forrest, Donna Byrne,
  Rebecca Kilgore, Helen Merrill

I Thought About You..............Van Heusen, Jimmy ......1939.......Tony Bennett, Four Freshmen, Billie Holiday,
  Susannah McCorkle, Johnny Mercer, Frank Sinatra, Maxine Sullivan, Dinah Washington, Marlene Ver Planck, Sylvia
  Syms, Eileen Farrell, Gene Lees, Mildred Bailey, Robert Clary, John Pizzarelli, Dardanelle, Lee Lessack, Bing Crosby,
  Banu Gibson, Johnny Hartman, Kim Polote, Penny Dawson, Hi-Los, Emma Kelly, Mady Kaye, Lynn Roman, Lorez
  Alexandria, Trae Gurley, Rosemary Clooney, Barbara Lea, Rebecca Kilgore, Teddy Grace, Betty Bennett, Ella
  Fitzgerald, Jo Ann Greer, Johnny Hartman

I Walk with Music ....Carmichael, Hoagy ....1940 ......Barbara Lea, Daryle Ryce, Marlene Ver Planck,
                                                                                  Frankie Masters, Buddy Clark, Dolores O'Neill, Ginny
                                                                                  Simms, Klea Blackhurst

I Wanna Be a Dancin' Man .....Warren, Harry ....1951.......Fred Astaire, Richard Rodney Bennett, Banu Gibson

I Wanna Be Around................Mercer, Johnny.............1959......Tony Bennett, Peggy Lee, Julie London, Lee Lessack,
                                                                                  Mark Murphy, Joe Mooney, Dorothy Loudon, Bobby
                                                                                  Darin, Joyce Breach, Sam Harris, Emma Kelly,
                                                                                  Adam Jones, Trae Gurley, Tony Bennett/Bono

I Wanna Be in Love Again ......Mercer, Johnny.............1965 ......Johnny Mercer, Marlene Ver Planck

**I Wish I Had Someone
  Like You**............................Hansen, Al ....1958 ......Frankie Laine

Song Title	Composer	Date	Vocalists
I Wonder What Became of Me	Arlen, Harold	1946	Richard Rodney Bennett, K. T. Sullivan, Weslia Whitfield, Henrietta Valor, Helen Goldsby, Chris Connor, Cynthia Crane, Joe Mooney, Richard Rodney Bennett, Diahann Carroll, Audrey Morris, Eileen Farrell
I'd Know You Anywhere	McHugh, Jimmy	1940	Bing Crosby, Bonnie King, Ray Eberle, Frank Sinatra, Ginny Simms, Ronnie Chase, Buddy Clark, Irene Daye
I'd Rather Be Me	Arlen, Harold	1945	Paul Allen
If I Had a Million Dollars	Malneck, Matty	1934	Boswell Sisters, Rosemary Clooney, Ozzie Nelson, Joey Nash
If I Had My Druthers	DePaul, Gene	1956	Johnny Mercer/Bobby Darin, Peter Palmer/Marc Breaux/Ralph Linn/Jack Mathew/Robert McClure/George Reader
If Someday Comes Ever Again	Wilder, Alec	1976	Eileen Farrell
If You Build a Better Mousetrap	Schertzinger, Victor	1942	Penny Parker/Jack Lathrop, Betty Hutton, Bob Eberly/Helen O'Connell, Peggy Lee/Benny Goodman
If You Were Mine	Malneck, Matty	1935	Billie Holiday, Tony Bennett, Etta Jones, Frankie Laine, Nancy Harrow
I'll Be Respectable	Arlen, Harold	1959	Carol Lawrence
I'll Cry Tomorrow	North, Alex	1955	Susan Hayward
I'll Dream Tonight	Whiting, Richard	1938	Nan Wynn, Orrin Tucker, Dick Todd, Jack Leonard
I'll Give You Three Guesses	Mancini, Hanry	1970	Julie Andrews/Mancini Chorus, Julie Andrews
I'll Tell the World	Previn, Andre	1974	Marti Webb/Christopher Gable/Ray Davis
I'm a Man	Allen, Steve	1984	Steve Allen
I'm an Old Cowhand	Mercer, Johnny	1936	Johnny Mercer, Bing Crosby, Sylvia Syms, Peggy Lawson, Harry Connick,Jr., Lee Lessack, Jim Wann, Johnny Ray, Dr. John, Mady Kaye, Jack Teagarden, Chick Bullock, Joe Hostetter
I'm Building Up to an Awful Letdown	Astaire, Fred	1934	Fred Astaire, Barbara Lea, Johnny Mercer, Greg Poland, Maxine Gray, Red McKenzie, Helen Ward
I'm Doing It for Defence	Arlen, Harold	1943	Betty Hutton, Sally Martin
I'm Going Back to the Farm	Mercer, Johnny	1931	Johnny Mercer
I'm Happy About the Whole Thing	Warren, Harry	1939	Maxine Sullivan, Doris Day, Bellaires, Phyllis Kenny, Bon Bon
I'm Like a Fish Out of Water	Whiting, Richard	1937	Dick Powell/Rosemary Lane, Dick Powell, Ginny Simms, Martha Tilton
I'm Old Fashioned	Kern, Jerome	1942	Kitty Kallen, Susannah McCorkle, Kitty Margolis, Johnny Mercer, Dinah Shore, Marlene Ver Planck, Margaret Whiting, Fred Astaire, Eileen Farrell, Peggy King, Rosemary Clooney, Skip Nelson, Robert Clary, Fred Astaire/Nan Wynn, Martha Tilton, Christina Machado, Sandy Stewart, Kiri Te Kanawa, Banu Gibson, Bobby Belfry, Ruth Price, Huxsie Scott, Andy Williams, Barbara Lea, Alyce King, Buzz Alston, David Allyn
I'm Shadowing You	Dearie, Blossom	1973	Blossom Dearie, Eileen Farrell, Singers Unlimited, Cleo Laine
I'm Way Ahead of the Game	Dolan, Robert	1963	Carol Sloane, Jessica Frankel/Rob Lorey, Richard Rodney Bennett, Tony Bennett, Johnny Mercer
I'm With You	Troup, Bobby	1955	The Real Group, Bobby Troup, Anita O'Day
In a Moment of Weakness	Warren, Harry	1939	Dick Powell, Ray Hendricks, Bon Bon
In Loving Memory	Dolan, Robert	1963	Rob Lorey/Jay Brian Winnick/Andrew Gitzy/David Sabella
In My Wildest Dreams	Schwartz, Arthur	1953	Fernando Lamas

Song Title	Composer	Date	Vocalists
In the Cool, Cool, Cool of the Evening	Carmichael, Hoagy	1951	Barbara Lea/Bob Dorough, Dean Martin, The Satisfiers, Frank Sinatra, Bing Crosby/Jane Wyman, Margaret Whiting/John Pizzarelli, Bing Crosby/Fred Astaire, Jim Wann, Mavis Rivers, Bobby Belfry/Keith Anderson/David Michael Roth/Paul Bernhardt/Carolyn Montgomery/Wendy Porter/Matt Helton/Christine Zino/Suzanne Dressler/Jeffrey Pattit/Tex Arnold, Leslie Anderson, Tracy Thomas, Rosemary Clooney, Huxsie Scott, Lucy Ann Polk, Frankie Laine/Jo Stafford, Klea Blackhurst/Billy Stritch
In the Valley	Warren, Harry	1945	Judy Garland, Kenny Baker/Judy Garland, Judy Garland/Kay Thompson, Bonnie Lou Williams
In Waikiki	Schwartz, Arthur	1941	Frances Langford, Ann Sheridan/Martha Raye/Movie Cast
It Had Better Be Tonight	Mancini, Hanry	1963	Buddy Greco, Sarah Vaughn, Fran Jeffries, Monica Mancini, Henry Mancini Chorus, Clay Johnson, Michael Buble, Lena Horne
It Might Have Been a Different Story	?	1933	Buddy Clark, Gary Stevens
It's a Great Big World	Warren, Harry	1945	Judy Garland/Virginia O'Brien/Marion Doenges
It's a Nuisance Having You Around	DePaul, Gene	1956	Rosemary Clooney
It's a Typical Day	DePaul, Gene	1956	Li'l Abner Ensemble
It's a Woman's Prerogative	Arlen, Harold	1946	Pearl Bailey, Richard Rodney Bennett, Yvette Cason, Mildred Bailey, Banu Gibson
It's About Time	Tinturin, Peter	1932	Larry Murphy
It's Easy When You Know How	Dolan, Robert	1964	Rob Lorey
It's Great To Be Alive	Dolan, Robert	1949	Johnny Mercer, Johnny Mercer/Jo Stafford, Kenny Delmar/Mary Hatcher/Chorus
I've Got a Lot in Common with You	Arlen, Harold	1943	Fred Astaire/Joan Leslie, Barbara Lea
I've Got a One-Track Mind	McHugh, Jimmy	1940	Bob Crosby, Jane Essex, Sonny Schuyler
I've Hitched My Wagon to a Star	Whiting, Richard	1937	Dick Powell, Martha Tilton, Sonny Schuyler, Bob Crosby, Woody Herman

J

Song Title	Composer	Date	Vocalists
Jamboree Jones	Mercer, Johnny	1936	Dave Frishberg, Johnny Mercer, Bobby Troup, Bing Crosby, Bobby Belfry/Wendy Porter, Spike Jones, Modernaires, Johnny Mercer/JoStafford/Pied Pipers
Jeepers Creepers	Warren, Harry	1938	Louis Armstrong, Chris Chandler, Doc Cheatham, June Christy, Chris Connor, Frank Sinatra, Maxine Sullivan, Marlene Ver Planck, Mills Brothers, John Pizzarelli, Lee Lessack, Manhattan Rhythm Kings, Bobby Troup, Dick Haymes, Johnny Mercer, Ethel Waters, Banu Gibson, Jack Teagarden/Modernaires, Cleo Laine, Hi-Los, Tony Bennett, Leo Watson, Johnny Mercer/Jack Teagarden, Tony Pastor, Bing Crosby, Ford Leary, Tony Pastor, Nat Gonella
Jezebel	Warren, Harry	1938	Leroy Harris, Jack Leonard, Bob Crosby
Jo-Jo The Cannibal Kid	Bloom, Rube	1936	Lavaida Carter
Jubilation T. Cornpone	DePaul, Gene	1956	Stubby Kaye
June Bride	DePaul, Gene	1953	Jane Powell
June Comes Around Every Year	Arlen, Harold	1945	Woody Herman, Bing Crosby, Nancy Dussault, Larry Stewart, Bill Usher
Just a Quiet Evening	Whiting, Richard	1937	Orlando Roberson, Ross Alexander, Jerry Cooper
Just Across the Mountain	Kent, Arthur	1968	Eddy Arnold
Just Remember	Manilow, Barry	1988	Nancy Wilson, Monica Mancini

K

Keep a Twinkle in Your Eye ....Bloom, Rube.................. 1936 ......Nicholas Brothers, Henry Hall

Kiss From You, A....................Carter, Benny .... 1964 ......Billy Eckstine

L

L'il Augie is a Natural Man ......Arlen, Harold................ 1946 ......Robert Pope, Chuck Cooper, Johnny Mercer

Lady on the Two-Cent Stamp..Warren, Harry .... 1938 ......Bing Crosby, John Payne/Jerry Colonna

Larceny and Love....................Dolan, Robert .... 1963 ......Jessica Frankel/Rob Lorey, Johnny Mercer

Last Dream Home, The ....Manilow, Barry .... 1988 ......Nancy Wilson

Laura ....Raskin, David .... 1945 ......Chris Chandler, Rosemary Clooney, Vic Damone, Billy Eckstine, Ella Fitzgerald, Four Freshmen, Woody Herman, Julie London, Jeanne Lee, Matt Monro, Nana Mouskouri, Kevin Mahogony, Eileen Farrell, Chris Connor, Johnny Mathis, Frank Sinatra, Dick Haymes, Lee Lessack, Bobby Troup, Sandra Lawrence, Richard Rodney Bennett, King Sisters, Patricia Barber, Hi-Lo's, Jenny Ferris, Robert Goulet, Paul Smith/Noteables, Emma Kelly, Singers Unlimited, Mady Kaye Carly Simon, Michael Feinstein, Helen Merrill, Nancy LaMott

Lazy Bones............................Carmichael, Hoagy .... 1933 ......Bob Dorough, Carrie Smith, Kay Starr, Mildred Bailey, Mills Brothers, Fred Norman, Harry Connick,Jr., Joe Crossman, Lee Lessack, Alan Breeze/Ellis Jackson, Johnny Mercer, Hoagy Carmichael, Pee Wee Hunt, Henry Hall, Dr. John, Bing Crosby/Louis Armstrong, Harlan Lattimore, Jeri Southern

Lazy Mood ....Miller, Eddie................. 1947.......June Christy, Barbara Lea, Susannah McCorkle, Marlene Ver Planck, Bobby Troup, Johnny Mercer, Lorez Alexandria

Least That's My Opinion.........Arlen, Harold................ 1946 ......Chuck Cooper/Stanley Mathis

Leavin' Time..........................Arlen, Harold................ 1946 ......Chorus, 1998 Company

Legalize My Name.................Arlen, Harold................ 1946 ......Pearl Bailey, Maxine Sullivan, Yvette Cason/Victor Trent Cook, Rebecca Kilgore, Leslie Anderson

Legend of Old California, The.Warren, Harry .... 1940 ......Dick Harding, Bing Crosby

Let That Be a Lesson to You...Whiting, Richard........... 1937.......Martha Tilton, Louis Armstrong, Frances Langford, Johnny "Scat" Davis/Dick Powell/Rosemary Lane/Mable Todd/Ted Healy/Chorus, Barry McKinley

Let's Take the Long Way Home .Arlen, Harold................ 1944 ......Rosemary Clooney, Bing Crosby, Marlene Ver Planck, Weslia Whitfield, Chris Connor, Richard Rodney Bennett, Cab Calloway, Imogene Lynn

Letter of the Law, The............Dolan, Robert .... 1962 ......Michael Mendiola/Ensemble

Life is What You Make It.........Hamlisch, Marvin........... 1971.......Johnny Mathis, Mancini Chorus

Life's So Complete ....Himber, Richard............ 1933 ......Joey Nash

Lights of Home ....Quadling, Lew .... 1952.......June Hutton

Like Monday Follows Sunday ..Green, Johnny .... 1952.......Marge Champion/Gower Champion

Like the Fella Once Said........McHugh, Jimmy .... 1940 ......Clint Holmes, Ginny Simms/Harry Babbitt/Merwyn Bogue, Irene Daye

Little Acorns..........................Kent, Arthur .... 1970.......Hank Locklin

Little Birds, The.....................Mancini, Henry............. 1967.......Le Lycee Francais de Los Angeles Children's Choir

Little Ingenue ....Rowles, Jimmy.............. 1974.......Johnny Mercer

Little Man with the Hammer ...Hanighen, Bernie.......... 1935 ......Pee Wee Hunt

Little Ol' Tune ....Mercer, Johnny .... 1957.......Johnny Mercer, Bing Crosby, Paul Bernhardt/Chorus

Little Travelling Music, A ....Previn, Andre .... 1974.......Cast

Lock The Barn Door ....Mercer, Johnny .... 1951.......Eileen Barton

Song Title	Composer	Date	Vocalists
Lonesome Polecat	DePaul, Gene	1953	Johnny Mercer/Bobby Darin, Matt Mattox
Long Goodbye, The	Williams, John	1973	Sandra Lawrence, Diane Hubka
Look at You	Manilow, Barry	1988	Nancy Wilson
Lord, I Give You My Children	Hanighen, Bernie	1934	Johnny Mercer
Lorna	Lindsey, Mort	1964	Judy Garland
Lost	Ohman, Phil/ Teetor, Macy	1936	Ruth Etting, Bob Allen, Henry Hall, Willie Lewis, Red Allen, Helen Ward
Love Held Lightly	Arlen, Harold	1959	Peggy Lee, Odette Myrtil
Love in a Home	DePaul, Gene	1956	Mario Lanza, Doris Day, Peter Palmer/Edith Adams, Bing Crosby
Love in the Afternoon	Malneck, Matty	1957	Jerry Vale
Love is a Merry-Go-Round	Bloom, Rube	1937	Sue Mitchell, Janet Blair, Kathleen Lane
Love is on the Air Tonight	Whiting, Richard	1937	Dick Powell, Barry McKinley
Love is Where You Find It	Warren, Harry	1938	Andrews Sisters, Mildred Bailey, Harry Babbitt, Eddy Howard
Love is Where You Find It	Manilow, Barry	1988	Nancy Wilson, Monica Mancini
Love of My Life	Shaw, Artie	1940	Fred Astaire, Dick Harding, Anita Boyer, Woody Herman
Love with the Proper Stranger	Bernstein, Elmer	1963	Jack Jones, Nancy Marano
Lullaby	Arlen, Harold	1946	Ruby Hill, A. J. Baptiste-Cassel/Tavia Rivee' Jefferson

M

Song Title	Composer	Date	Vocalists
Make Believe Ballroom	Jarvis, Al/Rene, Leon	1949	Movie Chorus
Make with the Kisses	Van Heusen, Jimmy	1939	Mildred Bailey, Bea Wain, Rebecca Kilgore, Walter Link, Carlotta Dale
Man in My Life, The	Arlen, Harold	1959	Judy Kaye, Carol Lawrence
Man of the Year This Week, The	Mercer, Johnny	1951	Top Banana Cast
Mandy is Two	McGrath, Fulton	1942	Billie Holiday, Carrie Smith, Penny Parker, Dick Harding, Bing Crosby, Lorez Alexandria, Frank D'Rone
Man's Favorite Sport	Mancini, Hanry	1963	Mancini Chorus
Many Ways to Skin a Cat	Dolan, Robert	1963	Rudy Roberson/Rob Lorey, Johnny Mercer
March of the Dogies	Warren, Harry	1945	Harvey Girls Cast, Judy Garland
Matrimonial Stomp, The	DePaul, Gene	1956	Stubby Kaye/Ensemble
Me and the Ghost Upstairs	Hanighen, Bernie	1940	Fred Astaire
Meet Miss America	Malneck, Matty	1935	Movie Cast
Meet Miss Blendo	Mercer, Johnny	1951	Top Banana Cast
Men Who Run the Country, The	Arlen, Harold	1959	Saratoga Male Ensemble
Merry-Go-Round in the Rain	Green, Johnny	1965	Jackie DeShannon
Midnight Sun	Burke, Sonny/ Hampton, Lionel	1947	June Christy, Ella Fitzgerald, Kitty Margolis, Carmen McRae, Johnny Mercer, Marlene Ver Planck, Nancy Wilson, Diane Krall, Sara Riva Krieger, Jacintha, Mel Torme, Bobby Troup, Christina Machado, Abbey Lincoln, Linda Purl, Huxsie Scott, Jo Stafford, Cleo Laine, Rebecca Martin

Song Title	Composer	Date	Vocalists
Misguided Faith	Minard, Brian	1970	Johnny Mercer
Mister Meadowlark	Donaldson, Walter	1940	Bing Crosby/Johnny Mercer, Jack Lathrop, Jack Pearce, Perry Como, Carmen McRae, Helen Forrest, Dick Haymes
Moment to Moment	Mancini, Hanry	1965	Carmen Lundy, Johnny Mathis, Monica Mancini, Diane Hubka, Frank Sinatra
Money Isn't Everything	Dolan, Robert	1963	Rudy Roberson/Rob Lorey, Johnny Mercer
Month of Sundays, A	Dolan, Robert	1949	Danny Scholl/Mary Hatcher, Johnny Amorosa
Moon Country	Carmichael, Hoagy	1934	Barbara Lea/Bob Dorough, Carrie Smith, Kenny Sargent, Hoagy Carmichael, Nat Gonella, Pee Wee Hunt, Tracy Thomas, Tony Travis, Mary Ann McCall, Al Bowlly
Moon Dreams	MacGregor, Chummy	1943	Johnny Desmond/Crew Chiefs, Martha Tilton/Mellownaires, Meredith D'Ambrosio
Moon River	Mancini, Hanry	1961	Lena Horne, Mancini Chorus, Johnny Mercer, Frank Sinatra, Gail Thurmond, Andy Williams, Eileen Farrell, Nancy LaMott, Four Freshmen, Sarah Vaughn, Helen O'Connell, Jacintha, Johnny Mathis, Monica Mancini, Lee Lessack, Jim Wann, Cate Caplan/Murray Phillips, Audrey Hepburn, Kim Polote, Jenny Ferris, Dr. John, Bobby Darin, Huxsie Scott, Billy Eckstine, Barbara Streisand, Mady Kaye, Lee Wiley, Steve Lawrence
Moonlight on the Campus	Whiting, Richard	1937	Dick Powell, Noteables
Morning Star	Rowles, Jimmy	1969	Jeri Brown, Carol Sloane
Mouthful O' Jam	Bleyer, Archie	1932	Dick Robertson
Mr. Crosby And Mr. Mercer	Gallegher/Shean	1940	Bing Crosby/Johnny Mercer
Mrs. Wiggs of the Cabbage Patch	Weston, Paul	1944	Johnny Mercer
Murder of J. B. Markham, The	Mercer, Johnny	1937	Johnny Mercer
Mutiny in the Nursery	Mercer, Johnny	1938	Nat King Cole, JohnnyMercer/Bing Crosby/Joan Bennett/George Burns/Ken Carpenter/John Scott Trotter, Louis Armstrong/Maxine Sullivan/Movie Cast, Modernaires/Joan Edwards/Jack Teagarden
My Home is in My Shoes	Mercer, Johnny	1951	Bob Scheerer
My Inamorata	Williams, John	1966	Johnny Williams Chorus, Tony Bennett
My Intuition	Warren, Harry	1943	Judy Garland/John Hodiak
My Mama Thinks I'm a Star	Arlen, Harold	1944	Kaye Ballard, Tyne Daly
My Mother's Love	Rowles, Jimmy	1972	Jeri Brown
My New Celebrity is You	Dearie, Blossom	1977	Blossom Dearie, Susannah McCorkle
My Night to Howl	Dolan, Robert	1963	Foxy Ensemble, Johnny Mercer
My Old Man	Hanighen, Bernie	1933	Spirits of Rhythm, Chick Bullock
My Shining Hour	Arlen, Harold	1943	June Christy, Rosemary Clooney, Chris Connor, Richard Rodney Bennett, Mary Cleere Haran, Peggy Lee, Joan Leslie, Daryle Ryce, Frank Sinatra, Margaret Whiting, Marlene Ver Planck, Weslia Whitfield, Sylvia Syms, Mimi Hines, Lee Lessack, Jane Froman, Harold Arlen, Franc D'Ambrosio, Jenny Ferris, Lorez Alexandria, David Allyn

N

Song Title	Composer	Date	Vocalists
Namely You	DePaul, Gene	1956	Marlene Ver Planck, Margaret Whiting, Joanie Sommers, Edith Adams/Peter Palmer, Carmen McRae
Naughty But Nice	Warren, Harry	1951	Anita Ellis, Alice Pearce

Song Title	Composer	Date	Vocalists
Navy Blues	Schwartz, Arthur	1941	Ann Sheridan/Martha Raye/Movie Cast
Night Over Shanghai	Warren, Harry	1937	Helen Forrest
Nine Thorny Thickets	Humphries, Rolfe	1955	Peggy Lee
Not for Sale	Mercer, Johnny	1948	Johnny Mercer
Not Mine	Schertzinger, Victor	1942	Maxine Sullivan, Peggy Lee, Helen O'Connell, Dorothy Lamour/Betty Hutton, Rebecca Kilgore, Bing Crosby, Bobby Darin, Leslie Anderson, Helen Carr, Bob Eberly/ Helen O'Connell, Eddy Howard, Georgia Gibbs

O

Song Title	Composer	Date	Vocalists
Oh, Happy Day	DePaul, Gene	1956	Stanley Simmonds/George Reader/Ralph Linn/ Marc Breaux
Oh, What a Horse Was Charlie	Warren, Harry	1938	Allen Jenkins/Dick Powell/Movie Cast
Oh, What a Memory We Made	Samuels, Eddie	1956	Peggy King
Oh, You Kid	Warren, Harry	1945	Virginia Reece
Old Glory	Arlen, Harold	1942	Bing Crosby
Old Guitaron	Almeida, Laurendo	1964	Joanie Sommers, Dardanelle
Old Jokes Parody	Goodman, Benny	1939	Johnny Mercer/Benny Goodman
Old King Cole	Whiting, Richard	1937	Bill Darnell, Johnny Davis
Old Man Rhythm	Gensler, Lewis	1935	Movie Cast
Old Music Master, The	Carmichael, Hoagy	1943	Nat King Cole, Maxine Sullivan, Hoagy Carmichael, Johnny Mercer/Jack Teagarden, Tracy Thomas, Mady Kaye, Dinning Sisters, Billy Stritch
Old Rob Roy	Dolan, Robert	1944	Ella Mae Morse
On Behalf of the Visiting Firemen	Donaldson, Walter	1940	Bing Crosby/Johnny Mercer
On the Atchison, Topeka and the Santa Fe	Arlen, Harold	1945	Mary Cleere Haran, Nancy LaMott, Johnny Mercer, Sylvia Syms, Harvey Girls Cast, Harry Connick,Jr., Judy Garland, Monica Mancini, Tony Feola, Lee Lessack, Bing Crosby, King Sisters, Sally Martin, Leslie Anderson, Rosemary Clooney, Mady Kaye, Louis Jordan
On the Beam	Kern, Jerome	1942	Fred Astaire
On the Nodaway Road	Bates, Charles	1935	Johnny Mercer/Pied Pipers
On the Swing Shift	Arlen, Harold	1942	Mel Torme, Paramount Girls
On with the Dance	Whiting, Richard	1937	Dick Powell/Rosemary Lane
Once Upon a Summertime	Barclay, Eddie/ LeGrand, Michel	1962	Jeri Brown, June Christy, Blossom Dearie, Gene Lees, Rod McKuen, Vanessa Rubin, Tony Bennett, Dinah Shore, Robert Clary, Joe Mooney, Astrud Gilberto, Barbara Streisand, Dale Kristien, Leslie Anderson, Robert Goulet, Martha Miyake, Sue Raney
One For My Baby	Arlen, Harold	1943	Harold Arlen, Fred Astaire, Tony Bennett, Rosemary Clooney, Billy Eckstine, Billie Holiday, Susannah McCorkle, Johnny Mercer, Frank Sinatra, Margaret Whiting, Weslia Whitfield, Jacintha, Johnny Mathis, Lena Horne, Bobby Troup, Linda Eder, Richard Rodney Bennett, Banu Gibson, Joyce Breach, Ranee Lee, Gail Thurmond, Carla Helmbrecht, Kim Polote, Jenny Ferris, Buddy Rich, Bette Midler, Mady Kaye, Frankie Laine, Mel Torme, Lynn Roberts, Joe Williams
One Step, Two Step	Arlen, Harold	1959	Carol Lawrence/Saratoga Ensemble
Only If You're in Love	Mercer, Johnny	1951	Lindy Doherty/Judy Lynn

Song Title	Composer	Date	Vocalists
Ooh, What You Said	Carmichael, Hoagy	1939	Barbara Lea, Marion Hutton, Marion Mann, Perry Como, The Smoothies
Oops!	Warren, Harry	1945	Fred Astaire, Ella Fitzgerald/Louis Armstrong, Doris Day
Out of Breath and Scared to Death	Miller, Everett	1930	Johnny Mercer, Frank Luther, Sterling Holloway/ Johnny Mercer
Out of this World	Arlen, Harold	1945	Tony Bennett, June Christy, Rosemary Clooney, Chris Connor, Mary Cleere Haran, Johnny Mercer, K. T. Sullivan, Marlene Ver Planck, Weslia Whitfield, Frances Wayne, Jim Bailey, Mel Torme, Marion Carroll, Lee Lessack, Frances Faye, Bing Crosby, David Gaines, Audrey Lavine, Buddy Rich, Eileen Farrell, Lucy Reed, Sarah Vaughan

P

Song Title	Composer	Date	Vocalists
P. S. I Love You	Jenkins, Gordon	1934	Rosemary Clooney, Billie Holiday, Nancy LaMott, Susannah McCorkle, Kay Starr, Mel Torme, Marlene Ver Planck, Bette Midler, Frank Sinatra, Steve Jordan, Bing Crosby, Ralph Brewster Singers, Emma Kelly, Kenny Sargent, Lorez Alexandria, Bob Manning, Mary Ann McCall, Jack Fulton
Pardon My Southern Accent	Malneck, Matty	1934	Chris Chandler, Johnny Mercer/Peggy Healy, Toni Tennille, Pee Wee Hunt, Jim Wann, Banu Gibson, Holly Shelton, Brian Beacock, Red Allen
Past My Prime	DePaul, Gene	1956	Emily Skinner/Alice Ripley, Edith Adams/Stubby Kaye
Peekaboo to You	Sigman, Carl/ Meyer, Joseph	1941	Paula Kelly/Modernaires, Bea Wain
Peter Piper	Whiting, Richard	1936	Helen Ward, Milderd Bailey, Bob Crosby
Petticoat High	Arlen, Harold	1959	Saratoga Ensemble
Phone Call to the Past	Mancini, Hanry	1969	Susannah McCorkle
Pineapple Pete	Aloma, Harold/ Jacobs, Al	1963	Johnny Mercer, Lee Lessack
Piney Woods	Marshall, Jack	1957	
Pipes of Pan	Chaplin, Saul	1957	Danny Kaye
Pleasure of Your Company, The	Previn, Andre	1974	Malcolm Rennie/Christopher Gable, Bing Crosby/ Johnny Mercer, Bing Crosby
Politics	Dolan, Robert	1949	Bob Crosby/Bob-O-Links, Kenny Delmar/Loring Smith
Pools, The	Previn, Andre	1974	John Mills
Poor Mr. Chisholm	Hanighen, Bernie	1940	Fred Astaire
Progress is the Root of All Evil	DePaul, Gene	1956	Howard St. John
Put 'em Back	DePaul, Gene	1956	Carmen Alvarez/Pat Creighton/Lillian D'Honeau/ Bonnie Evans/Hope Holiday/Deedee Wood

Q

Song Title	Composer	Date	Vocalists
Queen of the May	DePaul, Gene	1954	Stanley Donen
Quiereme y Veras	Mendez, Jose Antonio	1954	Chris Chandler

R

Song Title	Composer	Date	Vocalists
Rag Offen the Bush	DePaul, Gene	1956	Li'l Abner Ensemble. Rosemary Clooney/Mellomen
Raise a Ruckus Tonight	Newman, Alfred	1962	Debbie Reynolds

Song Title	Composer	Date	Vocalists
Respectability	Dolan, Robert	1963	Rudy Roberson/Jay Brian Winnick/Andrew Gitzy/David Sabella, Johnny Mercer
Rhumba Jumps, The	Carmichael, Hoagy	1939	Andrews Sisters, Marion Hutton/Tex Beneke, Mel Torme, Tracy Thomas, Woody Herman, Irene Daye, Barbara Lea
Ride 'em Cowboy	Dolan, Robert	1949	Sons of the Pioneers
Ride, Tenderfoot, Ride	Whiting, Richard	1938	Gene Autry, Eddy Howard, Dick Todd
Ridin' on the Moon	Arlen, Harold	1946	Harold Nicholas, Sylvia Syms, Peggy King, Stanley Mathis, Robert Clary, The Skylarks, Lena Horne, Jerri Winters
Riffin' The Scotch	Goodman, Benny/McDonough, Dick	1937	Billie Holiday, Ranee Lee
Rocky Mountain Moon	Mercer, Johnny	1951	Louis Armstrong/Bing Crosby
Rollin' in Gold	Dolan, Robert	1963	Foxy Company, Johnny Mercer
Rosie	Warren, Harry	1967	Movie Chorus
Royce Hall Blues	Mercer, Johnny	1965	Johnny Mercer
Run, Run, Run Cinderella	Dolan, Robert	1963	Liz Callaway, Natasha Harper

S

Song Title	Composer	Date	Vocalists
S. S. Commodore Ebenezer McAfee III	Dolan, Robert	1963	Foxy Ensemble, Johnny Mercer
Salud (Buona Fortuna)	Chaplin, Saul	1957	Danny Kaye/Merry Andrew Movie Cast
Sans Souci	Mercer, Johnny	1951	Rose Marie
Santa Claus Came in the Spring	Mercer, Johnny	1935	Joe Harris
Saratoga	Arlen, Harold	1959	Carol Lawrence/Howard Keel
Satan's Li'l Lamb	Arlen, Harold	1932	Ethel Merman, Natalie Douglas
Satin Doll	Ellington, Duke/Strayhorn, Billy	1958	Chris Chandler, Blossom Dearie, Johnny Mercer, Bobby Short, Sylvia Syms, Nancy Wilson, Four Freshmen, Ella Fitzgerald, Dr. John, Todd Hunter/Jane Lanier, Lorez Alexandria, James Darren, Carmen McRae, Buddy Greco, Jenny Ferris, Huxsie Scott, Anita O'Day, Johnny Hartman, Billy Eckstine
Say It With a Kiss	Warren, Harry	1938	Maxine Sullivan, Benny Morton, Billie Holiday, Helen Forrest, Hadda Brooks, Banu Gibson, Irene Daye
Says Who? Says You, Says I!	Arlen, Harold	1941	Marion Hutton/Tex Beneke/Modernaires, Cab Calloway
Seeing's Believing	Warren, Harry	1945	Fred Astaire
Sentimental and Melancholy	Whiting, Richard	1937	Billie Holiday, Bing Crosby, Mary Ann McCall
Shake It But Don't Break It	Garner, Erroll	1967	Johnny Mercer, Banu Gibson
Sharp as a Tack	Arlen, Harold	1942	Eddie "Rochester" Anderson
Shooby Doin'	Gray, Jerry	1966	Johnny Mercer
Shorty George, The	Kern, Jerome	1942	Fred Astaire, Fred Astaire/Nan Wynn
Show Your Linen, Miss Richardson	Hanighen, Bernie	1939	Johnny Mercer, The Smoothies
Silhouetted in the Moonlight	Whiting, Richard	1937	Frances Langford/Jerry Cooper, Frances Langford, Dick Powell/Rosemary Lane, Bob Crosby, Pug Horton, Joanne Horton, Kathleen Lane, Martha Tilton

Song Title	Composer	Date	Vocalists
Sing You Son of a Gun	Whiting, Richard	1937	Dick Powell
Single O	Kahn, Donald	1964	Ella Fitzgerald
Skal	Mancini, Hanry	1970	Mancini Chorus
Skylark	Carmichael, Hoagy	1942	Hoagy Carmichael, Rosemary Clooney, Bob Eberle, Ella Fitzgerald, Nnenna Freelon, Nancy LaMott, Barbara Lea, Nancy Marano, Susannah McCorkle, Carrie Smith, Maxine Sullivan, Bobby Troup, Marlene Ver Planck, k. d. lang, Billy Eckstine, Sylvia Syms, Eileen Farrell, Ray Eberle, Carmen McRae, Jacintha, Melissa Manchester, Dinah Shore, Monica Mancini, Lee Lessack, Bing Crosby, Jim Wann, Richard Rodney Bennett, Linda Ronstadt, Keith Anderson, Tami Tappan, Leslie Anderson, Tracy Thomas, Kim Polote, Jenny Ferris, Linda Ronstadt, Hi-Los, Buddy Rich, Bobby Darin, Clay Johnson, Singers Unlimited, Tony Bennett, Lorez Alexandria, L. A. Voices, Helen Forrest, Kitty White, Anita O'Day, Helen Forrest, Mel Torme, Teddi King, Woody Herman, Matt Monro, Klea Blackhurst
Sleep Peaceful, Mr. Used-to-Be	Arlen, Harold	1946	June Hawkins, Helen Goldsby, Barbara Lea
Slippin' Around the Corner	Previn, Andre	1974	Ray Davis
Sluefoot	Mercer, Johnny	1955	Bob Crosby/Modernaires, Fred Astaire, Movie Chorus, Johnny Mercer/Bing Crosby
Smarty Pants	Donaldson, Walter	1939	Dolly Dawn, Connie Kay
Smile Away Each Rainy Day	Mancini, Hanry	1969	Julie Andrews/Mancini Chorus
Sobbin' Women	DePaul, Gene	1953	Howard Keel/Seven Brides Cast, Johnny Mercer/Gene DePaul, Steve Devereaux/Seven Brothers
Something Tells Me	Warren, Harry	1938	Louis Armstrong, Maxine Sullivan, Fats Waller
Something Tells Me I'm Falling In Love	Manilow, Barry	1988	Nancy Wilson, Monica Mancini
Something's Gotta Give	Mercer, Johnny	1955	Rosemary Clooney, Sammy Davis, Chris Chandler, Ella Fitzgerald, Johnny Mercer, Marlene Ver Planck, Margaret Whiting, Fred Astaire, Robert Clary, Jacintha, Frank Sinatra, Lynn Roberts, McGuire Sisters, Maxine Sullivan, Mel Torme, Robert Goulet, Mady Kaye, Alan Copeland/Joanie O'Brien, Julius LaRosa
Song of India	Rimsky-Korsakov, Nickolai	1953	Mario Lanza
Song of the Marines (Mercer Co-lyricist with Al Dubin)	Warren, Harry	1937	Dick Powell
Sorry	DePaul, Gene	1956	Doris Day
Sounds Around the House	Wilder, Alec	1976	Dick Haymes, Helen Merrill
Sounds of the Night	Fried, Gerald	1962	Joe Williams, Pat Bowie
Southwind	Manilow, Barry	1976	Diane Schuur
Spring Reunion	Warren, Harry	1957	Mary Kaye Trio
Spring, Spring, Spring	DePaul, Gene	1953	Fred Astaire/Bing Crosby, Johnny Mercer, Movie Cast, 1984 London Cast, Michael Feinstein, Jason Graae
Square of the Hypotenuse	Chaplin, Saul	1957	Danny Kaye/Merry Andrew Movie Cast
Stage Door John	Previn, Andre	1974	Marti Webb
Stage Struck	Previn, Andre	1974	Marti Webb
Star Sounds	Mercer, Johnny	1965	Lou Lanza, Mark Murphy
Strawberry Lane	McHugh, Jimmy	1940	Bonnie Baker
Strip Polka	Mercer, Johnny	1942	Johnny Mercer, Andrews Sisters, Jack Martin/The Glee Club, King Sisters
Summer Wind	Mayer, Henry	1965	Johnny Mercer, Frank Sinatra, Frank Sinatra/Julio Iglesis, Marlene Ver Planck, Bing Crosby, Wayne Newton, Lou Rawls, Dale Kristien, Kim Polote, Buddy Greco, Jane Morgan, Emma Kelly, Trae Gurley, Eddy Arnold, Michael Buble, Johnny Hartman

Song Title	Composer	Date	Vocalists
Susie For Everybody	Previn, Andre	1974	Marti Webb/Christopher Gable
Sweater, A Sarong and A Peek-A-Boo Bang, A	Arlen, Harold	1942	Paulette Goddard/Dorothy Lamour/Veronica Lake (dubbed by Martha Mears)
Sweeten' Water	Arlen, Harold	1946	Victor Trent Cook/Chuck Cooper/Wendell Pierce/ Vanessa Williams
Sweetheart Tree, The	Mancini, Henry	1965	Mancini Chorus, Johnny Mathis, Johnny Mercer, Huxsie Scott
Swing Into Spring	Swanson, Robert	1959	Peegy Lee/Ella Fitzgerald/Hi-Lo's/ Chorus
Swing is the Thing	Bloom, Rube	1936	Mills Brothers, Valaida Snow
Swing Your Partner Round and Round	Warren, Harry	1945	Judy Garland/Marjorie Main

T

Song Title	Composer	Date	Vocalists
Ta Luv	Previn, Andre	1974	John Mills
Tailgate Ramble	Manone, Wingy	1944	Wingy Manone/Johnny Mercer
Talk To Me, Baby	Dolan, Robert	1963	Rosemary Clooney, Nancy LaMott, Susannah McCorkle, Johnny Mercer, Mark Murphy, George Pellegrino/Natasha Harper, Peggy Lee, Frank Sinatra
Tangerine	Schertzinger, Victor	1942	Chris Chandler, Carl Denny, Tony Bennett, Johnny Mercer, Helen O'Connell/Bob Eberle, Bobby Troup, Four Freshmen, Helen O'Connell, Harry Connick,Jr., Steve Jordan, Leslie Anderson, Dr. John, Clay Johnson, Singers Unlimited, Art Lund, Johnny McAfee
Technique	Mercer, Johnny	1957	Pat Boone
Temporarily	DePaul, Gene	1956	June Allyson/Jack Lemmon
Texas Millionaire	Mercer, Johnny	1955	Movie Chorus
Texas, Li'l Darlin'	Dolan, Robert	1949	Kenny Delmar/Chorus
Thank You, Mr. Currier, Thank You Mr. Ives	Warren, Harry	1945	Anita Ellis
Thanksgivin'	Carmichael, Hoagy	1932	Pee Wee Hunt, Dick Robertson
That Old Black Magic	Arlen, Harold	1942	Bing Crosby, Sammy Davis, Ella Fitzgerald, Mary Cleere Haran, Johnny Hartman, Shirley Horn, Nancy LaMott, Johnny Mercer, Louis Prima, Marlene Ver Planck, Margaret Whiting, Kevin Spacey, Johnny Johnston, Toni Tennille, Sylvia Syms, Skip Nelson/Modernaires, Ray Eberle, Billy Barty, Frank Sinatra, Lee Lessack, Bobby Troup, Rosemary Clooney, Henri Smith, Billy Daniels, Loretta Devine, Leslie Anderson, Kim Polote, Tony Martin, Dr. John, Adam Jones, Clay Johnson, Billy Eckstine, Larry Cotton, Mady Kaye, Tony Bennett, Rose Carlino, Carol Sloane, Frances Wayne, Spike Jones, Emer McParland, Herb Jeffries, Mel Torme, Bobby Rydell
That's For Sure	Mercer, Johnny	1951	Lindy Doherty/Judy Lynn, Lee Wiley
There's A Fellow Waiting in Poughkeepsie	Arlen, Harold	1944	Bing Crosby/Andrews Sisters, June Hutton/Pied Pipers
There's a Ring Around the Moon	Green, Johnny	1933	Al Bowlly
There's a Sunny Side to Every Situation	Warren, Harry	1938	Dick Powell
There's Nothing Like a College Education	Whiting, Richard	1935	Movie Cast

Song Title	Composer	Date	Vocalists
There's Room Enough For Us	DePaul, Gene	1956	The Li'l Abner Chorus
These Orchids	Kern, Jerome	1942	Bell Boys Quartet
They Talk a Different Language	Dolan, Robert	1949	Johnny Mercer/Jo Stafford
Thirteenth Street Rag	Manone, Wingy	1949	Wingy Manone/Johnny Mercer
This Time the Dream's on Me	Arlen, Harold	1941	Chris Chandler, June Christy, Ella Fitzgerald, Susannah McCorkle, Rod McKuen, K. T. Sullivan, Jeri Southern, Alison Krauss, Weslia Whitfield, Ray Eberle, Harry Connick, Jr., Robert Clary, Judy Kaye, Johnny Desmond, Buddy Rich, Banu Gibson, Mel Torme, Johnny Peterson, Pat Marshall, Jenny Ferris, Phyllis Lynn, Ingrid Lucia, Lorez Alexandria, Bonnie Lake, Anthony Newley, Helen Ward, Nancy Wilson
Three Guesses	Charig, Philip/ Myers, Richard	1930	Anson Weeks
Thumbin' a Ride	DePaul, Gene	1956	June Allyson/Jack Lemmon
Time to Smile	Clarkson, Geoffrey	1966	Tony Bennett
Tomorrow You Belong to Uncle Sammy	Schertzinger, Victor	1942	Cass Dailey
Tonight May Have to Last Me All of My Life	Bozage, Donald	1964	Nancy Wilson
Too Marvelous for Words	Whiting, Richard	1937	June Christy, Nat King Cole, Ella Fitzgerald, Billie Holiday, Johnny Mercer, Andy Russell, Frank Sinatra, Kiri Te Kanawa, Margaret Whiting, Joe Williams, Bing Crosby, Sylvia Syms, Eileen Farrell, Doris Day, Robert Clary, Melissa Manchester, Lee Lessack, Michael Feinstein, Helen Forrest, Jo Stafford, Bobby Short, Rosemary Clooney, Jenny Ferris, Ross Alexander/Ruby Keeler, Buddy Rich, Trae Gurley/Kim Polote, Mady Kaye, Lorez Alexandria, Helen Ward, Oscar Peterson, Buddy Moreno, Eydie Gorme, Jeri Southern, Jerry Cooper
Top Banana	Mercer, Johnny	1951	Top Banana Cast, Johnny Mercer/Rose Marie
Trav'lin' Light	Mundy, Jimmy/ Young, Trummy	1943	Ella Fitzgerald, Billie Holiday, Shirley Horn, Carmen McRae, Jacintha, Anita O'Day, Peggy Lee, Marlene Ver Planck, Buddy Rich, Lorez Alexandria, Marcey Lutes, Al Hibbler, Laila Dalseth, Irene Daye
Twilight World	McPartland, Marian	1973	Eden Atwood, Sherri Roberts, Jenny Ferris
Two Hearts are Better than One	Kern, Jerome	1946	Frank Sinatra
Two of a Kind	Darin, Bobby/ Mercer, Johnny	1960	Johnny Mercer/Bobby Darin, Johnny Mercer/Helen O'Connell

U

Song Title	Composer	Date	Vocalists
Unnecessary Town	DePaul, Gene	1956	Edith Adams/Peter Palmer

W

Song Title	Composer	Date	Vocalists
Wait and See	Warren, Harry	1945	Kenny Baker/Marion Doenges, Frances Wayne, Blue Flames
Wait for the Hoedown	Newman, Alfred	1962	Debbie Reynolds, Ken Darby Singers
Wait'll It Happens to You	Arlen, Harold	1941	Peggy Lee
Waiter, The Porter and The Upstairs Maid, The	Mercer, Johnny	1941	Bing Crosby/Mary Martin, Paul Keith/Lesli Margherita/Henry Polic II, Johnny Mercer/Bing Crosby/Betty Ann Rhodes, Jimmy Miller/Sid Colin/George Chisholm, Johnny Mercer/Robert Alda/Constance Moore

Song Title	Composer	Date	Vocalists
Watch a Darkie Dance	Tinturin, Peter	1933	Johnny Mercer
Way Back in 1939 AD	Carmichael, Hoagy	1939	Ginny Simms/Harry Babbitt, Bob Allen
Wedding in the Spring	Kern, Jerome	1942	Fred Astaire, Lina Romay/Movie Chorus
Weekend of a Private Secretary	Hanighen, Bernie	1938	Eileen Farrell, Mildred Bailey, Monica Mancini, Carlotta Dale
Welcome Egghead	Mercer, Johnny	1955	Movie Chorus
We're Working Our Way Through College	Whiting, Richard	1937	Bobby Belfry/Wendy Porter/Matthew Helton, Noteables
What Was Your Name in the States?	Newman, Alfred	1962	Debbie Reynolds
What'll They Think of Next?	Carmichael, Hoagy	1940	Barbara Lea, Helen Forrest
Whatcha-Ma-Call-It, The	DePaul, Gene	1956	Johnny Mercer, Lee Lessack, Sally Struthers/Mic Thompson/Jamie Curry
What's Good for General Bullmoose	DePaul, Gene	1956	Howard St. John/Lanier Davis/Robert McClure/Jack Mathew/George Reader
When a Woman Loves a Man	Hanighen, Bernie	1934	Ella Fitzgerald, Peggy Lee, Kay Starr, Nancy Wilson, Dardanelle, Rebecca Kilgore, Abbey Lincoln, Joey Nash, Leslie Anderson, Billie Holiday, Lorez Alexandria, DeMarco Sisters, Sylvia Syms, Dinah Washington
When Are We Going to Land Abroad?	Schwartz, Arthur	1941	Jack Haley/Jack Oakie/Movie Cast
When I'm Out with the Belle of New York	Warren, Harry	1945	MGM Chorus
When October Goes	Manilow, Barry	1984	Rosemary Clooney, Nancy LaMott, Nancy Wilson, Monica Mancini, Lee Lessack, Kevin Mahogany, Lea Salonga, Wendolina
When the Meadow Was Bloomin'	Manilow, Barry	1988	Nancy Wilson, Monica Mancini
When The World Was Young	Philippe-Gerard	1951	Blossom Dearie, Rod McKuen, Frank Sinatra, Nancy Wilson, June Christy, Dinah Shore, Johnny Mathis/Margaret Whiting/Melissa Manchester/John Pizzarelli, Mabel Mercer, Bing Crosby, Peggy Lee, Anita Kerr Singers, Sheila Jordan, Aretha Franklin, Nat King Cole
When You Hear the Time Signal	Schertzinger, Victor	1942	Dorothy Lamour
When You're in Love	DePaul, Gene	1953	Jane Powell, Howard Keel, Stanley Donen
While We Danced at the Mardi Gras	Opler, Alfred	1931	Vince Vance/The Valiants
Whistling Away the Dark	Mancini, Henry	1969	Trudy Desmond, Nancy LaMott, Johnny Mathis, Julie Andrews, Mancini Chorus, Lee Lessack, Jim Wann, Richard Rodney Bennett, Bill Hutton, Leslie Anderson, Dick Haymes, Monica Mancini
Who's Excited?	Hodges, Johnny	1952	Lucy Ann Polk/The Four Hits
Why Fight This?	Arlen, Harold	1959	Carol Lawrence/Howard Keel
Wild, Wild West, The	Warren, Harry	1945	Virginia O'Brien
Willie the Wolf of the West	Lilley, Joseph	1943	Cass Daley
Windmill Under the Stars	Kern, Jerome	1942	Russ Morgan
Wings Over the Navy	Warren, Harry	1938	Alan Breeze
With My Lover Beside Me	Manilow, Barry	1988	Nancy Wilson, Monica Mancini
With You, With Me	Green, Johnny	1960	Johnny Green
Wonderful, Wonderful Day	DePaul, Gene	1954	Jane Powell, Roni Page/Seven Brides, 1984 London Cast

Song Title	Composer	Date	Vocalists
Word A Day, A	Mercer, Johnny	1951	Phil Silvers/Rose Marie
World is My Apple	Whiting, Richard	1937	Lee Dixon
World of the Heart	Green, Johnny	1965	Movie Chorus

Y

Song Title	Composer	Date	Vocalists
Yodel Blues	Dolan, Robert	1949	Riders In The Sky, Bing Crosby, Modernaires, Kenny Delmar/Mary Hatcher, Jack Duffy
Yogi, The	McHugh, Jimmy	1941	Johnny Mercer, Jerry Colonna
You and Your Love	Green, Johnny	1939	Pied Pipers, Irene Daye, Anita Boyer, Teddy Grace, Helen Humes, Mildred Bailey
You Can't Always Have What You Want	Chaplin, Saul	1957	Danny Kaye/Merry Andrew Movie Cast
You Can't Run Away From It	DePaul, Gene	1956	Four Aces
You Go Your Way	Mercer, Johnny	1973	Margaret Whiting, Polly Podewell, Johnny Mercer
You Gotta Have a Slogan to Sell	Mercer, Johnny	1951	Top Banana Cast
You Grow Sweeter as the Years Go By	Mercer, Johnny	1939	Johnny Mercer, Margaret Whiting, Eileen Farrell, Helen Forrest, Jo Stafford/Pied Pipers, Jack Smith, Connie Boswell, Jack Leonard
You Have Taken My Heart	Jenkins, Gordon	1933	Kenny Sargent, Ralph Brewster Singers, Al Bowlly, Bob Stevens
You Know You Don't Want Me	Dolan, Robert	1963	Connie Francis
You Must Have Been a Beautiful Baby	Warren, Harry	1938	Hi-Lo's, Nancy LaMott, Johnny Mercer, Toni Tennille, Dick Powell, Sylvia Syms, Sam Costa/Dorothy Carless, The Three Ickeys, Bing Crosby, Perry Como, Dick Haymes, Nancy Dussault, George Maharis, Dr. John, Woody Herman, Lee Wiley, Nat Gonella, Edythe Wright
You or No One	Arlen, Harold	1959	Howard Keel
You Were Never Lovelier	Kern, Jerome	1942	Mary Cleere Haran, Fred Astaire, Movie Chorus, Larry Neil
You're a Natural	Schwartz, Arthur	1941	Russ Morgan, Herbert Anderson/Ann Sheridan, Eddie Howard
You're OK for TV	Mercer, Johnny	1951	Top Banana Cast, Nat King Cole, Johnny Mercer
You're So Beautiful That	Mercer, Johnny	1951	Lindy Doherty
You've Got Me This Way	McHugh, Jimmy	1940	Marion Hutton, Helen O'Connell, Harry Babbitt, Pied Pipers
You've Got Me Where You Want Me	Warren, Harry	1944	Judy Garland/Bing Crosby, Johnny Mercer, Penny Piper
You've Got Something There	Whiting, Richard	1937	Dick Powell, Edythe Wright
Your Good Will Ambassador	Mancini, Hanry	1968	Gloria Paul
Your Heart and Mine	Bloom, Rube	1936	Nicholas Brothers, Denny Dennis
You're the One for Me	McHugh, Jimmy	1941	Daryl Sherman, The Bodyguards, Woody Herman, Orrin Tucker, Janet Blair

Index